Armenia

Postcommunist States and Nations

Books in the series

This book is part of a series. The publisher will accept continuation orders which may be cancelled at any time and which provide for automatic billing and shipping of each title in the series upon publication. Please write for details.

Armenia

AT THE CROSSROADS

Joseph R. Masih
Robert O. Krikorian

Routledge
Taylor & Francis Group

LONDON AND NEW YORK

2 Park Square, Milton Park,
Abingdon, Oxon, OX14 4RN

270 Madison Ave,
New York NY 10016

British Library Cataloguing in Publication Data

Masih, Joseph R.
    Armenia: at the crossroads. – (Postcommunist states &
nations; v. 2)
    1. Armenia (Republic) – History – 1991–   2. Armenia (Republic) –
Economic conditions – 1991–   3. Armenia (Republic) –
Economic policy – 1991–   4. Armenia – Foreign relations
    I. Title   II. Krikorian, Robert O.
    947.5'6'086

    ISBN   90-5702-345-8 (softcover)
    ISSN   1028-043X

TABLE OF CONTENTS

CHRONOLOGY

1991

February 20	Thousands gather in Yerevan to declare their solidarity with Nagorno-Karabagh.
March 17	Armenia boycotts the All-Union referendum on preserving the union.
March 18	A poll conducted in Armenia indicates that 80% of Armenians support secession from the USSR.
September 21	In a referendum on independence, 99% of voters (95% participation) support secession.
September 23	Parliament issues a declaration of independence.
October 17	Levon Ter-Petrossyan is elected president with 83% of the vote.

1992

May 9	Armenian forces seize the Azerbaijani town of Shusha, reportedly with little resistance.
May 18	Armenian forces capture the town of Lachin, thus securing a corridor between Armenia and Nagorno-Karabagh.
June 16	Leaders of the Dashnak party and the Association for National Self-Determination call upon the government to resign for its conciliatory stance in Nagorno-Karabagh.
August 9	Ter-Petrossyan, invoking the CIS collective security pact, asks for intervention in the Nagorno-Karabagh region citing Azerbaijani aggression.

1993

January 22	A pipeline explosion in Georgia cuts Armenia's gas supply in half.
February 5	100,000 demonstrate to demand the resignation of Ter-Petrossyan, the dissolution of parliament, and the creation of a new constitution.
February 12	Hrant Bagratyan appointed prime minister.
July 7	15,000 people gather in a demonstration organized by the Association for National Self-Determination to demand the resignation of Ter-Petrossyan.
November 22	The national currency, the *dram*, replaces the ruble as the sole legal currency in the republic.

1994

July 1	20,000 demonstrators organized by the National-Democratic Union gather to denounce the government for political persecution.
December 17	The former mayor of Yerevan, Humbartsum Galstayn, is murdered. Ter-Petrossyan accuses the Dashnaks of complicity.
December 29	Ter-Petrossyan suspends the Dashnaks for six months.

1995

January 26	Three Dashnak leaders are arrested.
March 16	A treaty is signed with Russia establishing a Russian military base in Armenia, thereby granting the Russian troops already stationed in Armenia official legal status.

June	Several opposition parties are banned from running in the July parliamentary elections.
June 15	Opposition parties call for postponing the elections.
June 21	Clashes occur between the opposition and government supporters.
July 5	Armenians go to the polls to cast their ballots in a referendum on a new constitution and to elect a new legislature. The Armenian National Movement wins a majority of seats in the National Assembly.
October 27	The first block of the Metsamor nuclear power plant is reactivated after an eight year hiatus that followed a referendum in 1988 to close it for safety reasons.

1996

February 6	The National Assembly elects five members of the constitutional court established by the new constitution. Gagik Harutiunyan resigns as Vice-President to become the first President of the Constitutional Court.
March	The first international bank in Armenia, British Midland Bank, opens its Yerevan branch.
August–September	Pariur Hairikyan, Aram Sargsyan, and Lenser Aghavolyan withdraw their candidacy for President and support Vazgen Manukyan.
September 22	President Levon Ter-Petrossyan claims victory after receiving just over 50% of the vote.
September 25	After three straight days of demonstrations over election results, violence breaks out as rumors circulate amongst demonstrators that Vazgen Manukyan is arrested and the Armenian National Assembly is stormed. The Army and Interior Ministry take control of Yerevan.
November	Prime Minister Hrant Bagratyan resigns and is replaced by Armen Sarkissyan, Armenia's Ambassador to the United Kingdom.

1997

March	Prime Minister Sarkissyan resigns for health reasons and Robert Kocharyan the President of Nagorno-Karabagh is appointed the new Prime Minister.

PREFACE

A decade ago, few would have imagined that a book series would be dedicated to the republics of the former Soviet Union, because few would have thought it possible that the Soviet Union would cease to exist and be replaced by independent republics. No single volume can hope to describe in all its rich detail the many developments that have taken place in Armenia since 1988. The far-reaching social, political, economic, and geo-strategic changes that the Republic of Armenia has undergone are worthy of far greater attention than can be given in this one volume. The goals of this volume, therefore, remain modest. This book is intended to give an overview of the factors that determine Armenia's foreign and domestic policies and the interaction of these factors. Many of the events described below are still in process. Therefore no definitive political history can be written at the present time. Instead, we have tried to outline the main course of events in the Republic of Armenia since the beginning of the democratic movement in 1988. Although the focus is on the post-Soviet period, politics and history in Armenia, and indeed in all of the Caucasus, are intricately interwoven, so that knowledge of the historical context becomes necessary to grasp current policy choices and dilemmas. In attempting to understand the interplay between past and present in the region known as Transcaucasia (Georgia, Armenia and Azerbaijan), many dimensions of the current conflicts become clearer. This is not to argue, of course, that finding solutions thereby becomes easier, but it can give the analyst an awareness which would otherwise be lacking.

Another modest goal of this volume is to stimulate debate and further research on contemporary Armenia. Thus far, numerous articles have appeared which deal with specific aspects of current political developments in Armenia, but very few monographs have been published which attempt to tie together the developments of the last decade. Many of the books that have appeared employ a regional approach which, although useful in many respects, tend to limit the amount of coverage devoted to developments in Armenia. This short book is intended to outline developments in Armenia up to the present while putting these developments in a historical context. One of the inherent risks of a project such as this is the fast-paced course of events. By the time information finds its way between covers, it could very easily be outdated and irrelevant. We have endeavored as much as possible to provide analysis and interpretation along with the recitation of facts. In this way it is hoped that scholars conducting research subsequently will be able to use this work as a helpful base. If this goal is achieved, then the authors will be satisfied with their labors.

Much of what has occurred in the Republic of Armenia since 1988 is subject to heated and often acrimonious debate. The road to independence for Armenia has been a long and difficult one. Current events are often viewed with the perspective of hindsight and motives are imputed which may or may not have been active in policy making. Armenian politics today is polarized and interested observers run the risk of alienating all parties by their writings and analyses. Despite these risks, the authors have endeavored to maintain their scholarly objectivity throughout. The interpretative and analytical sections have benefited from over three years of fieldwork and participant observation in Armenia, as well as from numerous discussions with leading officials which have taken place off the record. In the Byzantine world of post-Soviet politics, the insights offered by participants and observers have been invaluable in providing context for reading the political landscape in Armenia. The risk of alienating is one that must be taken if the study of political developments in the Republic of Armenia is to be elevated to the level of non-partisan academic discourse. As the Republic of Armenia establishes itself as a member of the community of nations, it is the responsibility of those studying it to provide an accurate portrayal of a country coming to grips with independence. It is with this ultimate goal that the writing of this volume has been undertaken.

One of the most pleasurable aspects of writing a book is the opportunity to thank those who have generously given of their time and energy for the success of the project. The intellectual and emotional debts accrued by the authors in the preparation of this book are substantial. The authors have benefited from the help of many people who have discussed ideas and challenged arguments, reviewed parts of the manuscript, and otherwise given encouragement. Many may not be aware of their contribution, given that books are written with the help of discussions and debates with colleagues which are only later committed to paper. The authors would particularly like to acknowledge the help of Levon Avdoyan, Armenia and Georgia Area Specialist in the Near East Section of the Library of Congress, who not only read parts of the draft with a critical eye, but has also provided unfailing encouragement and support throughout many years of professional collaboration. The Library of Congress Working Group on Armenia, organized by Dr Avdoyan, was a particularly fruitful venue to exchange ideas. In addition, helpful discussions were held with Jonathan Moore, Ara Ghazarians, David Siefkin, Steven Movsessian, Tigran Harutyunyan, Steven Anlian and Victor Vartanian.

In addition to those named above, Joseph Masih would like to thank Dr Rouben Adalian of the Armenian National Institute and Kalli Raptis of the Armenian Assembly of America. Much of his contribution to this book is a result of numerous discussions with Rouben when they worked together. He thanks Kalli for assisting him whenever he had a request for information. Finally, he would like to thank Tamar Terzian, his fiancé, for her encouragement and support in addition to the more detail oriented aspects of indexing and footnoting. Finally, Joseph Masih would like to thank his parents Rusk and Janet Masih, whose constant inquiries about the progress of the book helped to drive it to completion.

Robert Krikorian would like to acknowledge the assistance of his colleagues at the Kennan Institute for Advanced Russian Studies of the Woodrow Wilson Center for International Scholars who provided a stimulating intellectual environment in which to work on portions of the draft. The staff and scholars at the Institute gave much needed encouragement and logistical help at various times, especially Monique Principi, Program Specialist. Special thanks go to his wife, Paola Martino, who provided constant encouragement and support throughout the entire project. Finally, this book could not have been written without the unconditional support of B. Paul and Gladys Krikorian.

Needless to say, despite all the assistance that the authors have received, if errors in fact and judgment remain, they are the responsibility of the authors alone.

Note on transliteration: In addition to the complications arising from writing about Transcaucasian politics and history, differing alphabets and systems of transliteration create added difficulties. Words and names have been transliterated from Russian and Armenian according to the Library of Congress systems, except in cases of familiar usage. Transliteration from Armenian is based on the dialect of Eastern Armenian and presents difficulties when discussing events in Western Armenia. In addition, the Russian language lacks some sounds found in Armenian, which results in certain discrepancies. For example, Karabagh in Armenian becomes Karabakh in Russian. In order to maintain consistency, the authors have used Karabagh and Nagorno-Karabakh when rendering these terms into English.

Since the original manuscript of this book was submitted, some of the key players in Armenian politics have departed the scene. Most importantly Levon Ter-Petrossyan is no longer President. The departure of the longest-lasting leader in the region since the collapse of the Soviet Union necessitated that a short description and analysis of events leading up to and following Ter-Petrossyan's resignation be included.

The controversy surrounding the 1996 Presidential elections posed a challenge to the political legitimacy of Levon Ter-Petrossyan's government. The continuing question of the government's legitimacy coupled with the appointment of Robert Kocharyan as the new Prime Minister in March 1997 set the stage for a new political crisis. The key issues driving this new crisis were the economic situation and the Nagorno-Karabagh conflict.

The Ter-Petrossyan government was seen by many, especially the inhabitants of the capital Yerevan, as being corrupt and unwilling to address the people's economic suffering. One of the primary election issues, if not the most important, was economic policy and government corruption. Vazgen Manukyan's opposition alliance of 1996 promised to deal with the economic situation by reducing government corruption and providing a social safety net.

The other major issue was Nagorno-Karabagh. Many Armenians viewed the liberation of Nagorno-Karabagh and the buffer zone created by force around the enclave as the primary success of the Armenian people following independence. However, the opposition charged that Ter-Petrossyan would "sell out" Nagorno-Karabagh, thereby eliminating Armenia's only post-independence success.

The linkage of the economic situation with the Nagorno-Karabagh conflict created a contradiction which would lead to another political crisis in January/February 1998. The appointment of Robert Kocharyan as the Armenian Prime Minister, following the resignation of Armen Sarkissian, represented the extent to which the Ter-Petrossyan government would go to regain legitimacy and change the public's perception of his administration. Kocharyan possessed impeccable nationalist credentials, earned while leading the Nagorno-Karabagh Armenians in their struggle against Azerbaijan. He was also perceived as being opposed to the rampant corruption within the government.

It is likely Ter-Petrossyan believed that as Prime Minister of Armenia Kocharyan's views would become similar to his own rather than representing Nagorno-Karabagh's more narrow interests. With hindsight it appears the ambitious Kocharyan came to Yerevan with his own ideas. Kocharyan's previous career as the Chairman of Nagorno-Karabagh's State Defense Committee and the elected President of the region, meant that he would not do anything which would harm Nagorno-Karabagh's security.

Within seven months of Kocharyan's tenure the differences in position over the Nagorno-Karabagh issue and the economy came to the forefront. Armenia, feeling increasingly isolated, consolidated its relationship with Russia by signing a friendship treaty in August 1997, which increased its reliance upon Russia. Ter-Petrossyan, seeing the growth of Azeri influence through the use of oil politics, believed that the time was ripe for Armenia to come to an accommodation with Azerbaijan over Nagorno-Karabagh through the Organization for Security and Cooperation in Europe's (OSCE) Minsk Group.

In one of Ter-Petrossyan's rare press conferences he told the Armenian people that they had to choose between prosperity and Nagorno-Karabagh; that they could not have prosperity without peace in Nagorno-Karabagh. This statement provoked resounding criticism from both Ter-Petrossyan's political opposition as well as from elements within his own government, including the Prime Minister.

On the surface the growing conflict between Kocharyan and Ter-Petrossyan was over negotiating methodology. Kocharyan believed that a package solution was needed, where all issues were settled together, along with the most important, the status of Nagorno-Karabagh. Ter-Petrossyan believed that a step-by-step method should be followed in which the final issue of status would be dealt with at the end. Ter-Petrossyan's methodology was based on his perception of Armenia's domestic situation as well as its international position.

Armenia's economy, while showing some signs of growth, was essentially hampered by the continuing blockades and the trepidation of foreign investors confronting the volatility of the Transcaucasus region. Furthermore, Armenia was being sidelined by a Georgia-Azerbaijan-Turkey axis for trans-shipment of oil. This axis threatened to marginalize Armenia within the region. In addition, Armenia was further driven into the arms of Russia. Russia was capable of providing Armenia with valuable military assistance, but Ter-Petrossyan was concerned with the possibility of changing Russian strategic interests. Finally, the western world and in particular the United States was gradually shifting its attentions in line with its developing commercial interests. This was a major concern as the United States, at this time, provided Armenia with the highest per capita amount of foreign aid amongst the Newly Independent States. Commercial interests driven by Caspian oil deposits implied a realignment towards Azerbaijan.

Following the public criticism, Ter-Petrossyan wrote a lengthy article in which he laid out his argument for choosing his current course and criticized the opposition for lacking any alternative plan. The controversy following Ter-Petrossyan's speech and his article led to a rift within the Armenian government. Forces in the National Assembly (dominated by the President's party) and the political opposition began to criticize the President's negotiating strategy and accused him of a "sell out." The public rhetoric became intense and it was no doubt driven in part by concerns over the December Copenhagen summit of the OSCE. Those opposed to Ter-Petrossyan wanted to insure that there would be no repeat of the 1996 Lisbon summit where Azerbaijan's territorial integrity was reaffirmed and Nagorno-Karabagh was granted autonomy.

The opposition, still upset over having been cheated out of power in the 1996 elections, recognized that the fissures within the government could be capitalized upon by persisting in the public criticism of the President. The final crack within the government came during a January 7–8, 1998 Security Council meeting between Armenia and Nagorno-Karabagh officials. The animosity between those for and against Ter-Petrossyan's plan was intense. The key player in this affair was the Defense Minister, Vazgen Sargsyan. Sargsyan's forces had maintained order during the outbursts following the 1996 Presidential elections and he was a staunch advocate of maintaining Nagorno-Karabagh's independence. Along with the Defense Minister was Serge Sargsyan, the Minister of National Security, which controls both the Ministry of the Interior and the Foreign Intelligence Service. Sargsyan was the former Defense Minister of Nagorno-Karabagh. These two men were critical to Kocharyan's rise to power. The final outcome of this power struggle was the collapse of the President's position and his resignation on February 3, 1998.

Immediately upon Ter-Petrossyan's resignation, Kocharyan lifted the ban on the Dashnak Party. This move decisively divided the coalition of opposition forces which had rallied around Vazgen Manukyan in the 1996 elections. Kocharyan stated that free and fair elections would be held within 40 days. These moves were aimed at increasing his popularity, creating a coalition of forces both within what remained of the former government and members of the opposition, and addressing the crisis of legitimacy surrounding government in Armenia which had afflicted Ter-Petrossyan.

The March 16, 1998 Presidential elections and the March 30 run-off election were symbolic of those contradictions which Armenian society has suffered: the need for a healthy economy and maintaining Nagorno-Karabagh's independence. Karen Demirchyan, the last communist leader of the Armenian

Soviet Socialist Republic represented the most significant challenge to Kocharyan. Demirchyan appealed to those who remembered a previous era when the Armenian people lived relatively well. He capitalized on the weariness of the population in relation to both the Nagorno-Karabagh conflict and their economic plight. Regarding Nagorno-Karabagh, Demirchyan would only say that he could work with Aliyev.

Kocharyan ran on a platform of fighting corruption, reconciling differences amongst Armenians and, as a corollary, allowing for the diaspora to aid in guiding Armenia; and he called for a total change in the Armenian position regarding the OSCE negotiating process. Kocharyan's reputation was primarily built on his Nagorno-Karabagh experience and thus the election became a contest between nationalism and the certainty of Armenia's Soviet past. Kocharyan defeated Demirchyan in a run-off election which the OSCE determined to be marred by irregularities. But the OSCE stated that the irregularities did not call into question the results of the election.

With his position as President temporarily consolidated, Kocharyan will face serious obstacles in the future. His most daunting challenge will be revitalizing Armenia's economy. Kocharyan believes that Armenia can have a healthy economy by combating corruption and by actively encouraging the Armenian diaspora to invest heavily in the economy. One of his priorities, which he has already acted upon, is to establish a department within the Foreign Ministry at the deputy-minister level to institutionalize diaspora relations. However, he will not be able to successfully implement this program if he does not vigorously combat corruption.

Despite his commitment to eliminate corruption, Kocharyan is confronted with a serious dilemma. Vazgen Sargsyan, the Defense Minister, and the man who helped insure Kocharyan's rise to power by deserting Ter-Petrossyan, is widely perceived as one of the more corrupt figures in Armenian politics. If Kocharyan follows through with his program he will inevitably clash with his current ally. In order to deal with Sargsyan, Kocharyan will have to create a power base independent of the Defense Minister. In addition to Sargsyan's control of the armed forces, he is also linked to the Yerkrapa, a nationalist, pro-military bloc within the National Assembly. This raises another issue confronting Kocharyan: the President lacks a political party and is currently juggling a diverse coalition whose members, for now, deem it to be in their best interests to support him.

Finally, it is unclear how Kocharyan plans to secure his objectives in the negotiations over Nagorno-Karabagh while also improving the Armenian economy. If he can deliver the latter independent of the former then he will be able to successfully resist the pressure building on Armenia from the

OSCE, the United States, Russia, and the oil pressure of Azerbaijan. If Kocharyan cannot do this, he may become a transitional figure, to be replaced by a more compliant leadership.

INTRODUCTION

HISTORICAL BACKGROUND

With the collapse of the Soviet Union and emergence of fifteen independent states on its territory, the great Eurasian land mass experienced yet another of its periodic realignments of geo-strategic forces. Out of this chaos and confusion Armenia was able to grasp one more chance to reestablish an independent state. The current Republic of Armenia occupies but a fraction of the territories historically known as Armenia for millennia. Contemporary political developments in Armenia and the Transcaucasus can best be understood within the framework of the geography and history of the region. Historical memory in the Caucasus is measured in terms of centuries and it is not uncommon for people to discuss events that took place hundreds if not thousands of years ago with an urgency unparalleled in the West.

GEOGRAPHY: ADVANTAGES AND DISADVANTAGES

For Armenia, geography has been a key to its fortunes throughout most of its recorded history. Armenia has been called the "Armenian Fortress" and the "Armenian Island." Geographically, Armenia is situated on a high mountainous plateau between 37 degrees 30' and 41 degrees 30' north latitude, encompassing approximately 300,000 square kilometers, formed as the east-west Syrian and Pontic chains draw closer together.[1] This area includes the territory of the present Republic of Armenia, much of eastern Turkey, the northwestern corner of Iran, as well as territories in the republics of Georgia and Azerbaijan. "Towering over both the South Caucasian plain in the north and the lowlands of Mesopotamia in the south, it is linked with Asia Minor to the west and Iran to the east, primarily through the valleys of the upper Euphrates and Arax rivers. It is bounded in the north by the Pontic chain and in the south by the Taurus and the mountains of Kurdistan south of Lake Van."[2] The average height of the Armenian plateau is between 1000–2000 meters and contains such geographic landmarks as Mount Ararat (about 5,205 meters) and Mount Aragats (4,180 meters).[3] Numerous other mountains dot the landscape as well as lakes such as Van and Sevan. Rivers such as the Euphrates, the Tigris and the Arax flow through the land providing life-sustaining water to the fertile soil. Armenia was noted for its harsh winters and hot summers as well as the abundance of its soil. Ironically, the present-day Republic of Armenia finds itself situated on the some of the least fertile land of historic Armenia.

The Armenians, who speak an isolated branch of the Indo-European language family, have been both blessed and cursed by their geography. Armenia's geographic position at the crossroads of intersecting and often competing interests has meant that throughout its history Armenia has been fought over either to provide a buffer against neighboring states and tribal confederations or as a means to achieve greater strategic goals. "As a land bridge between East and West, the people both reaped the benefits of and endured the consequences of populating a mountainous terrain."[4] One of the leading authorities on ancient and medieval Armenian history writes:

> The sharply accented and austere character of the highlands has considerably influenced Armenian history. The lofty "Fortress" rising above the Mesopotamian plain has repeatedly provided refuge from attacks, and its strategic position has not escaped the notice of Armenia's powerful neighbors over the centuries. The fragmentation of the country into small, isolated units has continually impeded attempts to create a centralized state. The relative accessibility of the "Armenian Fortress" from the east and the west both increased its vulnerability to invasion and enhanced its cultural variety and its role in international trade. Finally, the close proximity of high mountains and plains within the country fostered the simultaneous development of two nearly irreconcilable socioeconomic systems: sedentary agriculture and nomadic pastoralism.[5]

EARLY HISTORY OF THE ARMENIANS: AT THE CROSSROADS OF EMPIRE

Throughout much of its history, Armenia has rarely been united in a single political entity. More frequently, Armenia was used by one or more regional powers as either a buffer or a battlefield. When surrounding powers were in equilibrium, either equal in strength or in weakness, Armenia flourished, but when this equilibrium was disturbed and became unbalanced, and one side or another grew too strong, the stronger power filled the vacuum and turned Armenia into a battlefield.[6] The mountainous terrain which often protected Armenia from invaders also acted as a barrier to the full integration and development of any unified Armenian state. The isolation of communities and the difficulty of communications led to the development of independent traditions and the society which grew out of this environment fostered several states and regions, which were often at odds with one another.[7] Caution should be used when talking about a single entity called Armenia during the ancient and medieval periods, for in fact there were several entities called Armenia, each either controlled by a foreign power or having some sort of limited local autonomy. In light of the political and geographic realities, local Armenian rulers were forced to seek legitimization externally. For example, in 885/886 the Bagratid Prince Ashot received a crown from both the Caliph in the east and the Byzantine Emperor in the west.[8]

One of the most important events during the ancient period was the evangelization and ultimate christianization of Armenia. The Armenians claim the date 301 A.D. for the official acceptance of Christianity by King Tiridates III, after being converted by Saint Gregory the Illuminator, but the actual date is most likely 314 A.D.[9] An official proclamation by the king effectively made Armenia the first Christian state, although the process of full conversion to the new faith would take centuries. This event marks a watershed in Armenia's history and changed the political, economic and social status of Armenia indelibly. The influence of Persia so evident for centuries in Armenia would eventually be rivalled by the influences of the various Christian powers, such as Rome, Byzantium, and Syria. Another milestone in ancient Armenian history was the creation of a unique Armenian script in the beginning of the fifth century. This alphabet created by Saint Mesrob Mashdots under the patronage of the head of the universal Armenian church, Catholicos Sahak, further reinforced Armenians' sense of separateness. Originally intended to translate the Bible and other religious texts from Greek and Syriac, eventually it became a potent symbol of national identity.[10]

In succeeding centuries, Armenia once again became a battlefield as Arabs, Mongols, Turks and Persians swept over the land and occupied it for long periods. After the fall of the last Armenian kingdom in historic Armenia in the eleventh century, many Armenians joined their compatriots already settled in Cilicia, on the Mediterranean Sea. An Armenian kingdom was eventually established and played a vital role in Near Eastern affairs until it was conquered by the Mamelukes in 1375. This marked the end of the last independent Armenian political entity until the establishment of the Republic of Armenia in 1918, almost 550 years later.

ARMENIA AND THE RIVALRY OF EMPIRES

By the time of the Ottoman Turkish invasion and occupation of Armenia in the fifteenth century, the people and lands of Armenia were exhausted. Armenia became a battlefield yet again as Ottoman Turks and Safavid Persians fought each other, resulting in the partition of Armenia between the two great regional powers, with the bulk of Western Armenia going to the Ottomans and the remaining parts of Eastern Armenia passing into the Persian sphere of influence.[11] This situation would remain relatively static until the arrival of the Russians on the scene in the eighteenth and nineteenth centuries to challenge both Ottoman and Persian hegemony in Armenia and the entire Caucasus. The arrival of the Russians on the horizon drastically altered the geo-political balance of forces in the region. The Armenians who found themselves on the Russian side of the newly-created border took advantage of educational, commercial and civil service opportunities. Many Armenians travelled to Russia and from there went on to Europe where they came into contact with the intellectual trends then current, including rising national self-consciousness.[12]

During the nineteenth century, many of the centers of Armenian cultural and intellectual life were found outside of Armenia proper, in Constantinople and Smyrna in the Ottoman Empire, Tbilisi (Tiflis) in the Russian Empire and Madras in British India. Through these communities, developments in the outside world were brought to the attention of the Armenians of the Anatolian interior. Communications between Russian and Turkish Armenians provided the necessary cross-fertilization for the evolution of new ideas. By the end of the nineteenth century, Armenian intellectuals in the Russian Empire and in such European centers as Geneva had created revolutionary societies through which they hoped to effect reform in the Ottoman Empire to ameliorate the more onerous aspects of Ottoman rule. These revolutionary parties were strongly influenced by socialism as well as nationalism. The leading parties of the day, the Armenian Revolutionary Federation (ARF/Dashnaktsutyun) and the Hunchakian Revolutionary Party were both created outside of historic Armenia, in Tbilisi, Georgia and Geneva respectively, with the goal of reforming the Ottoman government and allowing autonomy for the Armenians.

The diaspora has played a critical role in the formation of Armenian national consciousness throughout the last several centuries. As a crossroads subject to the fortunes of war, Armenia suffered frequent losses of population, through mortality, emigration and forced resettlement. Throughout the centuries Armenians sought more suitable areas for habitation while remaining emotionally attached to their homeland. Armenian colonies appeared throughout Eurasia, the Middle and Far East and came into contact with a wide array of influences. Armenian national consciousness slowly evolved through the centuries as it absorbed foreign influences and assimilated them. As Armenian communities developed in the diaspora, they took with them some spiritual piece of the homeland. Many diaspora Armenians kept in close contact with the communities they left behind and through these diaspora Armenians new concepts and ideas filtered back into Anatolia and the Caucasus. The ideas of the Enlightenment and the French Revolution were transmitted back to the homeland through various channels. The Armenian Catholic brotherhood on the island of San Lazzaro was instrumental in reviving a sense of Armenianness among the masses and Armenians located in such far off places as India and Burma kept the flame of Armenian patriotism alive.[13]

THE DECLINE OF EMPIRES AND THE RISE OF STATES

The continuing decline of the Ottoman Empire and the successful independence movements of the Balkan peoples with European support gave inspiration to many Armenians and created great suspicion among the Sultan and the Ottoman authorities. Previously known as the "loyal millet" (nation), the Armenians now came to be viewed with increasing unease and hostility. Although the overwhelming majority of the Armenians in the Ottoman Empire were illiterate peasants and had very little connection to either their community leaders in the major cities or the revolutionary societies, the entire community became the object of distrust.[14] For the Turkish rulers of the Ottoman Empire, the loss of their territories in the Balkans and North Africa although painful could be reconciled, but the loss of the Anatolian heartland to the Armenians would be intolerable. Turkish Armenia had to remain firmly within the Ottoman Empire. With Russia and the European powers becoming increasingly active in the affairs of the Ottoman Empire, the Armenians became encouraged and thought that European intervention would provide them with the necessary reforms to enable them to lead a more secure existence.[15] This misplaced hope of the Armenians only exacerbated relations between Armenians and Turks and various groups of Kurds. The Ottoman authorities used the tensions already existing between predatory and semi-nomadic groups of Kurds and the sedentary and agricultural Armenians to increase pressure on the Armenians to stop agitating for outside intervention. Special irregular Kurdish cavalry units called *Hamidiye* were created to harass and plunder Armenians as well as rival groups of Kurds.[16] Tensions reached a peak in 1894–1896, as hundreds of thousands of Armenians were massacred under orders of Sultan Abdul Hamid, who ruled from 1876 to 1909. But this was merely a prelude for what was to come.

Meanwhile, on the Russian side of the border, Armenians took advantage of the security of Russian rule to develop their talents in commerce and the arts, as well as in the tsarist civil service. During this period Armenian attitudes towards both the Russians and their neighbors underwent significant transformations. In the beginning, Armenians greeted the Russians as liberators from the Persian yoke and looked forward to better and more prosperous days. Armenians migrated to the largest cities in the Transcaucasus, Tbilisi and Baku, where they soon came to dominate commerce and industry to the detriment of the native Georgians and Azerbaijanis. Tbilisi and Baku became thriving centers of Armenian culture and intellectual activity. From the outset, Russian authorities tried to take advantage of existing tensions by playing one nationality off against another. During the unsuccessful 1905

Russian Revolution, tsarist officials in Baku spread rumors among Azerbaijanis that Armenians were arming themselves in order to massacre peaceful Muslims and among the Armenians that Azerbaijanis would be organizing pogroms against them at any moment. In this charged atmosphere, in February 1905, fighting erupted which left immense property damage and thousands dead.[17] The disturbances soon spread to other parts of the Caucasus, including Elizavetpol, Shushi and Tbilisi. Armed self-defense units were created on both sides, although the Armenians had the advantage because of their recent experiences of partisan warfare against both the Ottomans and the Russians. In each instance, tsarist officials either incited both sides or remained idle while violence was being perpetrated against one or the other community. In many instances, however, Armenian and Azerbaijani community leaders were either able to halt the fighting or prevent it altogether.[18]

On the Ottoman side of the frontier, the situation was also far from stable. The Ottoman Empire in the beginning of the twentieth century was plagued by numerous problems, including the rise of nationalism among both the Turks and their subject peoples as well as the pervasive influence of European notions of egalitarianism and liberty. The Ottoman autocracy found itself in a fight for its very existence. In 1908, a group of young, idealistic Ottoman officers, who called themselves the Committee for Union and Progress, or Young Turks, instigated a revolution which severely diminished the power of the Sultan.[19] In the beginning, all the subject nationalities, including Armenians, welcomed the Young Turk revolution with its slogans borrowed from the French Revolution about equality and fraternity among all peoples of the Ottoman Empire. Unfortunately, Armenians were soon disillusioned in 1909 when an alleged counter-coup engineered by supporters of the Sultan tried to overthrow the Young Turks. In the wake of this coup, tens of thousands of Armenians were massacred in the city of Adana in Cilicia. This event sobered the Armenians despite Young Turk assurances that they had nothing to do with the massacre.[20]

Armenian suspicions grew even further as the extreme national wing of the Committee of Union and Progress (CUP) took over leadership of the organization and began a policy of increased Turkification of the non-Turkish population. The CUP was led by a triumvirate consisting of Talaat, Enver and Jemal. It appeared increasingly likely that Turkey would be entering the war on the side of Germany and against Russia. Having been rebuffed in Europe and North Africa, Turkey's ambitions were turning increasingly to the East, to Caucasia and Central Asia, where millions of Turkic peoples lived. The major geographic and demographic obstacle to Turkish expansion was Armenia. The Armenian population found itself in a very precarious position, straddling the border between two states about to go to war against each other. This classic dilemma, which has recurred throughout Armenian history, would prove disastrous. When the Ottoman Empire initiated a war against Russia in the fall of 1914, the fate of the Ottoman Armenians was all but sealed. Immediately after the declaration of war, Turkish armies, led by Enver Pasha, began to move eastward towards the Russian frontier. They engaged the Russian forces in battle at Sarikamish in December and were almost totally annihilated. Looking for a scapegoat in order to save face, Enver denounced the Armenians as being responsible for the Turkish defeat by their treacherous behavior behind the front lines. This fabrication was the beginning of an organized, premeditated plan to exterminate the Armenian population of Western Armenia and solve the Armenian Question once and for all.[21]

In spring 1915, orders went out to the leading officials of all the Ottoman provinces to prepare for the deportation of the Armenian population. The ostensible reason given was that the Armenians were caught in a war zone and for their own protection needed to be evacuated. Their destination was to be northern Syria, a largely lifeless desert. Deportation was merely a euphemism for the total eradication of the Armenian population from their ancestral homeland. The Armenian men had already been drafted into the Ottoman Army which left the Armenian community without adequate pro-tection. On the night of April 24, 1915, several hundred leading members of the Armenian community were rounded up in Constantinople and sent off into exile and eventual death. This group included members of the Ottoman Parliament, writers, editors, artists, political activists and members of the clergy. Thus denied their leadership, the remaining Armenians were caught off-guard by the deportation orders. The deportees usually had no more than a few hours to prepare for the long trek and were able to take few of their belongings. In the end it did not matter, because very few of them reached their destination.[22]

En route, the convoys of Armenian deportees were attacked either by groups of Kurdish bandits, many of them former Hamidiye, marched endlessly until they died of exhaustion or murdered outright by Turkish gendarmes or soldiers. Some were able to save themselves by converting to Islam, although this was not considered sufficient in many cases, while many women and children were taken into Turkish and Kurdish homes, either forcibly or out of a sense of charity. Although the exact number of Armenians killed during the Genocide may never be determined, it has been estimated that 1.5 million Armenians were killed between 1915 and 1923.[23]

INDEPENDENCE IMPOSED

By the end of 1916, Russian troops were able to occupy most of Turkish Armenia, but the revolutions of February and October 1917 jeopardized these gains. The war-weary Russian troops were already abandoning the front, thus exposing Eastern Armenians to the fate of their Western Armenian compatriots. Armenian volunteer militias were formed to guard the frontline in the absence of Russian troops. The Bolsheviks, who came to power in Russia following a near bloodless coup in November 1917, signed the Treaty of Brest-Litovsk, which among other things, consigned most of Armenia to the Turks. In April, 1918, the Armenians, Azerbaijanis and Georgians separated from Russia and formed the Transcaucasian Federation in order to negotiate a more equitable treaty with the Ottoman Empire. The interests of the three peoples were sharply at odds with one another and the federation proved unworkable. The Georgians secured German backing and declared independence on May 27, 1918. The Azerbaijanis, hoping to gain the support of the Ottoman Empire, declared independence the next day. This left the Armenians with little choice but to declare independence on May 28, 1918. The declaration came on the heals of Armenian battlefield victories against the Turks at Sardarabad, Karakilise and Bash-Abaran. Through these victories, the remnants of the Armenian nation were able to cling to a small portion of their ancestral homeland and avoid the fate of their kin in the Ottoman Empire.[24]

The tasks facing the Armenian Republic were daunting. It had little prospect for survival without massive outside intervention, hundreds of thousands of refugees, rampant disease and hostile neighbors on all sides, most observers believed that the Republic of Armenia would not be able to maintain its existence for very long without outside intervention. The Armenians hoped that the Allied powers would remain true to their pledges and guarantee the viability of the republic. All the major powers had denounced the massacres and the other excesses of the Ottomans and had promised never to subject the Armenian people to the tyranny of the Turks again. This high-sounding rhetoric came up against some harsh realities on the ground. Western Armenia, which should have made up the core of any future state, was a near wasteland, with almost no Armenians, the sole inhabitants now being almost exclusively Kurds and Turks. The Republic of Armenia was not considered viable, either from a security standpoint nor from an economic one without having significant portions of Western Armenia attached to it. Armenia was also at odds with the newly created independent republics of Georgia and Azerbaijan over territorial issues.[25]

Although the Republic of Armenia was able to survive the first terrible year leaving some room for optimism for the expansion and ultimate viability of the state, circumstances and the vacillation of the Great Powers combined to extinguish the small struggling republic. Weakened by conflicts with Azerbaijan and Georgia, frustrated by the lack of movement on the issue of Western Armenia, and burdened with both numerous refugees and an almost non-existent economy, the Republic of Armenia found itself in an increasingly hostile geo-political position by 1920. The Turkish Nationalist forces under the leadership of Mustafa Kemal Pasha were engaged in a struggle to expel Western Imperialist forces and create a republic, albeit one cleansed of almost all Armenians, Greeks and other minorities. The Bolsheviks were consolidating power in Russia after having defeated the majority of the counter-revolutionary Russian White forces. Turkey and Bolshevik Russia alike viewed the Republic of Armenia as an ally and outpost of the Imperialist West as well as a physical obstacle between revolutionary Russia and its erstwhile ally, Turkey. After the sovietization of Azerbaijan in spring 1920, only Armenia remained in the path between the Russian Bolshevik forces and the forces of Nationalist Turkey.[26]

THE BOLSHEVIK EMBRACE

The destruction of the first independent Armenian state in over five hundred years occurred at the end of 1920. Turkish forces attacked and occupied important parts of the republic, while the Bolsheviks, claiming to be the liberators of the Armenians from the Turkish yoke, moved in from the north and east. Soviet rule was proclaimed in Armenia in December 1920, but within a very short period of time, the burden of Bolshevik rule became unbearable. The early period of sovietization was accompanied by Bolshevik excesses. In February 1921, exhausted and disgusted with the policies of the Bolsheviks, the country under the leadership of the Dashnaks rose in rebellion and drove the Bolsheviks out of Erevan. Unfortunately, the geo-political situation in the region did not provide circumstances beneficial to the Armenians. With the lack of outside assistance, the rebellion was eventually crushed and by the summer of 1921, Armenia was once again under Soviet rule. The uprising of February, although ending in ultimate defeat for the Dashnaks, provided future generations of their adherents with a potent and inspiring mythology. The short but unsuccessful experience of national independence demonstrated painfully the precarious nature of Armenia's geo-political position. When Armenia's larger and more powerful neighbors were in equilibrium, either in strength or in weakness, Armenia was able to carve out some sort of autonomous existence, whereas when the balance of power tipped one way or the other, disaster for the Armenians was but a short way off.

The first years of Soviet rule in Armenia were traumatic. The Soviets inherited a mostly agricultural, scarcely industrialized, devastated land. The impediments to creating a viable state were daunting indeed. Moscow poured resources into Armenia to rebuild the country almost from the ground up. Shipments of grain and other food supplies allowed the population a measure of security against famine which they had not known in a number of years. Agricultural output was improved and industrialization of the country began in earnest. As Russia itself recovered from the devastation of war and revolution, in the early 1920s, Lenin instituted a relatively liberal economic regime known as the New Economic Policy (NEP). Private commerce was allowed to develop with only limited interference, but these policies were soon to change with the advent of Stalin.[27]

SOVIET NATIONALITIES POLICY: THE MAKING OF NATIONS

It was during this initial period that the foundations for future conflict were laid. Soviet nationality policies were based on the ancient Roman principle of divide and rule. It was Lenin who developed a theoretical framework to deal with the complexities of the nationalities question. Lenin was a pragmatist and this was reflected in his manipulation and co-optation of nationalism in the service of the revolution. Lenin argued for autonomy and the right to self-determination for the numerous minorities of the Russian Empire.[28] But this was purely a tactical move, one designed to further the cause of revolution by weakening the hold of the autocracy. It was once fashionable among many students of Soviet nationality affairs to believe that had it not been for the corruption of Leninist nationality policy by Stalin, then developments would have been much different, but in fact Lenin never intended to honor his pledges about self-determination. One of the major legacies of Soviet nationality policy was the territorialization of ethnicity. During the formative years of the Soviet Union, Stalin, first as Chairman of the Commissariat of Nationalities and later as General Secretary of the Communist Party of the Soviet Union (CPSU), developed the notion that each nationality must have a corresponding territorial unit. This has had profound consequences with the demise of the Soviet Union. A situation was created whereby ethnicity became defined territorially, and those denied a specific territory began to think of the acquisition of territory to legitimate their claims to ethnic uniqueness.

The impact of Soviet nationality policies on Armenia is difficult to overestimate. Geographically the smallest Soviet republic, Armenia lost land and population to almost all of its neighbors. The predominantly Armenian-populated regions of present-day southern Georgia, Akhalkalak and Akhaltsekhe, were given over to Georgian administration, as well as half of the Lori district. The historically Armenian district of Nakhichevan became an autonomous formation within the Azerbaijan Soviet Socialist Republic, while Karabagh, with its overwhelming Armenian majority, was turned into an autonomous region under the jurisdiction of Baku.[29] These territorial losses paled in comparison to the devastating loss of all of Western Armenia and even parts of Eastern Armenia to Kemalist Turkey. The implications of these losses are still being felt today as Armenia and the other former Soviet republics in the Caucasus struggle to recreate themselves and overcome the legacy of seven decades of Soviet misrule.

Although many Armenians looked upon Soviet rule as the lesser of two evils, obviously more preferable to annihilation at the hands of the Turks, Armenians nonetheless paid a heavy price for inclusion in the Soviet Union. Many Armenians were repressed by the Soviet authorities in the initial phase of sovietization through confiscation of property, deportation, and internal exile as well as execution and then again under Stalin. By the 1930s, Armenian Communists were being purged from the ranks of the Party and soon the purges reached every sector of society and by the eve of World War II, Armenia had lost another generation of intellectuals.[30] The country and society had barely begun to rebuild itself after the catastrophes of the First World War and the Genocide, when it was once again decimated. The generation of intellectuals and leaders lost during the Stalin's Great Terror of the 1930s was a devastating loss to the country.

Despite the bitterness and fear engendered by Stalin's capricious reign, Armenians proved their loyalty during the Second World War. It has been estimated that between 300,000 and 500,000 Armenian soldiers served in the Soviet Armed Forces during the war.[31] Their contribution included over fifty generals, as well as Marshals of the Soviet Union, such as Baghramyan, Babajanyan, Khudyakov and even admirals such as Isakov. Over 32,000 Armenian soldiers were decorated during the war and over one hundred received the prestigious "Hero of the Soviet Union" award for extraordinary bravery, while Karabagh produced a number of top military leaders. Losses were extremely heavy among the Armenian soldiers.[32]

Due to the losses suffered during the war, the Armenian population had diminished significantly. The Armenian Communist Party leadership appealed to Stalin who agreed to allow Armenians from abroad to repatriate to Soviet Armenia as a prelude to an ultimately unsuccessful attempt to seize the formerly Armenian inhabited parts of eastern Turkey and repopulate them with Armenians. Hundreds of thousands of Armenians from the Middle East, Eastern Europe as well as from Western Europe and the Americas emigrated to Soviet Armenia. This wave of repatriation in the aftermath of World War II was followed by smaller emigrations in the 1960s from the Middle East and in the 1970s from Lebanon during its civil war and the Islamic Revolution in Iran. Instead of being greeted as returning compatriots, these early repatriates were either exiled to other parts of the Soviet Union, never to set foot in Armenia or segregated from the general Armenian population. Deep social, cultural, political and linguistic divisions developed between the Eastern Armenians of Soviet Armenia and the Western Armenians of the diaspora as a consequence. Discrimination was rampant and shook the confidence of the returnees. According to one of the repatriates:

> In the aftermath of World War II, we, the repatriates, also had in mind in our venture with so many unknowns, to be of service to our fore-fathers' country and people. It didn't work out that way. We were suspected as agents of Western powers, we were paralyzed and our ambitions shattered, some of us punished for being from a different world with no justifiable reason.[33]

By the 1960s, Armenia had recovered sufficiently from the traumas of the last few decades. Industrialization was advanced, agriculture was collectivized and gradually the Armenian Soviet Socialist Republic began to resemble a modern society. Then came 1965, the fiftieth anniversary of the Armenian Genocide. The Soviet authorities were always circumspect about allowing the Armenians to express themselves on the issue of the Genocide, fearing potential damage to Soviet-Turkish relations as well as an incipient fear of Armenian nationalism. No high-profile official commemorations took place and certainly no public demonstrations. In April 1965, an unsanctioned demonstration took place in Erevan to pay homage to the victims of the Genocide. Armenians gathered outside the Erevan Opera House while a low-key official commemoration was taking place inside. Those gathered began to get agitated and loudly called for Turkey to return Western Armenian lands; they then proceeded to throw stones.[34] At this point, security forces were called in to maintain order. Even the highest religious authority of the Armenian Church, the Catholicos, was unable to calm the crowd. As a concession to Armenian national sentiment, a memorial to the victims of the Genocide was eventually built on a hill overlooking Erevan. Among those briefly arrested and detained by authorities were several figures who would later assume prominence in the democratic movement, including Levon Ter-Petrossyan. This first mass outburst of Armenian nationalism in Soviet Armenia caught both the central authorities in Moscow and the local Communist Party officials in Erevan off-guard. In the coming years, several other monuments were erected to honor Armenian national heroes. But Armenian nationalism in this period was kept within certain confines. Some people, however, were determined not to be constrained by official sanctions. These dissidents fought the Soviet government every step of the way and refused to compromise their beliefs in Armenian independence no matter what the circumstances. The most prominent among these individuals was Pariur Hairikian.[35]

As nationalist sentiment was reemerging after a long slumber in the Armenian SSR, the diaspora was also experiencing a significant awakening of its own. In 1973, an elderly survivor of the Genocide, Gourgen Yanikian, lured the Turkish Consul-General and Consul in Los Angeles to a meeting on a pretext and then proceeded to assassinate them. In this premeditated attack, Yanikian hoped to gain attention to the continuing Turkish denial of the Genocide. Although the act of a single elderly man, it is considered the opening salvo in a campaign by Armenian terrorists directed against the Turkish government and its allies. Beginning in 1975, two rival Armenian organizations spearheaded the campaign of terror. The Armenian Secret Army for the Liberation of Armenia (ASALA) was an avowedly Marxist organization that sought to annex Turkish Armenia to the Armenian SSR, while the Justice Commandos of the Armenian Genocide (JCAG) was a more nationalist organization which claimed to be fighting for a free and independent Armenia.[36] The advent of this militancy must be viewed within the context of 1970's Middle Eastern politics, for Armenian terrorism was born in the Beirut of Civil War Lebanon and was heavily influenced by the Palestinian liberation struggle. Throughout the latter half of the seventies and first half of the eighties, Armenian terrorists were considered the most lethal and successful militants in the shadowy underground world of terrorism. By the mid-to late-1980s the threat of Armenian terrorism had significantly decreased. Despite the dissemination of information inside the Soviet Union being controlled, Soviet Armenians tried to follow developments as closely as possible. Anecdotal evidence points to the feeling that such terrorism provided Soviet Armenians with a certain sense of satisfaction that at least one segment of the Armenian people was able to defend their interests in the international arena, even if by unacceptable methods.[37] As an indication that the Soviet authorities were alarmed by the prospect of Armenian terrorism three Armenians were executed in Moscow in 1979, for their alleged role in a 1977 bombing of the Moscow subway. Although it was obvious that the charges were trumped up, the court's pre-determined guilty verdict sent a clear signal to the Armenians that their national reawakening was being viewed by Moscow with extreme misgivings. In 1986, Gorbachev had the three rehabilitated. Among the most celebrated of the Armenian militants was Monte Melkonian, an American-born Armenian who would later be considered a hero of

Karabagh and one of the architects of many of the brilliant military victories of the Karabagh Defense Forces.

Within a few years of the peak of Armenian terrorism in the mid-1980s, Armenians around the world would focus their attention on developments in the Caucasus which would ultimately lead to the end of Communist rule and the establishment of an independent homeland.

1   Nina Garsoian, "Armenia, Geography," in J.R. Strayer, ed., *Dictionary of the Middle Ages* (New York: Charles Scribner's Sons, 1983), p. 470.
2   Ibid.
3   Ibid.
4   Levon Avdoyan, "The Past as Future: Armenian History and Present Politics," (Unpublished lecture, Kennan Institute for Advanced Russian Studies, Washington, DC, March 1997), p. 4–5.
5   Garsoian, "Armenia, Geography," p. 472.
6   Nina Garsoian, "Arsacids/Arsakuni, Armenian," in J.R. Strayer, ed., *Dictionary of the Middle Ages* (New York: Charles Scribner's Sons, 1983), p. 559. See also Cyril Toumanoff, *Studies in Christian Caucasian History* (Washington, DC: Georgetown University Press, 1963).
7   Avdoyan, "Past as Future," p. 5.
8   Ibid, p. 7.
9   The date of the conversion of Armenia to Christianity has been subject to considerable controversy. Sirarpie Der Nersessian, *Armenia and the Byzantine Empire* (Cambridge, MA: Harvard University Press, 1945), p. 29 uses the traditional date 301 A.D., while Nina Garsoian, "Armenia: History of," in J.R. Strayer, ed., *The Dictionary of the Middle Ages* (New York: Charles Scribner's Sons, 1983), p. 475, uses 314 A.D.
10 Krikor Maksoudian, "Armenian Alphabet," in J.R. Strayer, ed., *Dictionary of the Middle Ages* (New York: Charles Scribner's Sons, 1983), pp. 491–492.
11 On the partition of Armenia, see George Bournoutian, *History of the Armenian People, Volume II: 1500 A.D. to the Present* (Costa Mesa, CA: Mazda Publishers, 1994).
12 Ronald Grigor Suny, *Looking Toward Ararat: Armenia in Modern History* (Bloomington, IN: Indiana University Press, 1993), pp. 52–63. See also Louise Nalbandian, *The Armenian Revolutionary Movement: The Development of Armenian Political Parties through the Nineteenth Century* (Berkeley, CA: University of California Press, 1963).
13 Nalbandian, *Armenian Revolutionary Movement*, pp. 34–36.
14 For an extensive discussion of this period of Armeno-Turkish relations, see Vahakn Dadrian, *The History of the Armenian Genocide: Ethnic Conflict from the Balkans to Anatolia to the Caucasus* (Providence, RI: Berghahn Books, 1995).
15 On outside intervention in Ottoman Armenian affairs, see Manoug Somakian, *Empires in Conflict: Armenia and the Great Powers 1895–1920* (London: I.B. Tauris Publishers, 1995).
16 On the formation and role of the Hamidiye, see Selim Deringil, "The Ottoman Twilight Zone of the Middle East," in Henri J. Barkey, ed., *Turkey's Role in the Middle East* (Washington, DC: United States Institute of Peace Press, 1996), pp. 13–23.
17 On Armenian-Azerbaijani relations during the 1905 revolution, see Tadeusz Swietochowski, *Russian Azerbaijan, 1905–1920: The Shaping of National Identity in a Muslim Community* (London: Cambridge University Press, 1985), pp. 37–64.
18 Ibid.
19 On the Young Turk revolution, see Ernest Edmondson Ramsaur, Jr., *The Young Turks: Prelude to the Revolution of 1908* (Princeton, NJ: Princeton University Press, 1957).
20 On events in Adana, see Vahakn Dadrian, "The Circumstances Surrounding the 1909 Adana Holocaust," *Armenian Review*, Vol. 41, No. 1/164 (Winter 1988), pp. 1–16.
21 On the pre-meditated nature of the Armenian Genocide, see Dadrian, *History of the Armenian Genocide*.

22 For a sample of survivors' accounts, see Donald E. Miller and Lorna fouryan Miller, *Survivors: An Oral History of the Armenian Genocide* (Berkeley, CA: University of California Press, 1993).

23 For an analysis of the demographic situation in the Ottoman Empire and Armenian casualties as a result of the Genocide, see Levon Marashlian, *Politics and Demography: Armenians, Turks, and Kurds in the Ottoman Empire* (Cambridge, MA: Zoryan Institute, 1991).

24 The most detailed account of the period is Richard Hovannisian, *Armenia on the Road to Independence, 1918* (Berkeley, CA: University of California Press, 1967) and his four-volume *The Republic of Armenia, 1918–1920* (Berkeley, CA: University of California Press, 1971–1996).

25 Ibid.

26 Ibid.

27 For an account of events in Armenia during the first decades of Soviet rule, see Mary Kilbourne Matossian, *The Impact of Soviet Policies in Armenia* (Leiden: E.J. Brill, 1962).

28 Walker Connor, *The National Question in Marxist-Leninist Theory and Strategy* (Princeton, NJ: Princeton University Press, 1984), pp. 28–42; Robert Conquest, *Soviet Nationality Policy in Practice* (New York: Praeger, 1967), pp. 15–20. For specifics on Armenia, see Vahakn Dadrian, "Nationalism in Soviet Armenia-A Case Study of Ethnocentrism," in George Simmonds, ed., *Nationalism in the USSR and Eastern Europe in the Era of Brezhnev and Kosygin* (Detroit, MI: The University of Detroit Press, 1977), pp. 202–258.

29 For a discussion of the drawing of borders in the Transcaucasus in the early Soviet period, see Levon Chorbajian, Patrick Donabedian and Claude Mutafian, *The Caucasian Knot: The History and Geo-Politics of Nagorno-Karabagh* (London: Zed Books, 1994).

30 Manuel Sarkisyanz, *A Modern History of Transcaucasian Armenia* (Leiden: E.J. Brill, 1975), pp. 282–320.

31 Christopher Walker, *Armenia: Survival of a Nation* (New York: St. Martin's Press, 1990) pp. 355–356.

32 Ibid.

33 Personal correspondence to the author, June 1, 1992. See also, Hagop Touryantz, *Search for a Homeland* (New York: H.J. Touryantz, 1987).

34 Suny, *Looking toward Ararat*, pp. 186–187.

35 For details on the Armenian dissident movement, see Ludmilla Alexeyeva, *Soviet Dissent: Contemporary Movements for National, Religious, and Human Rights* (Middletown, CT: Wesleyan University Press, 1987), pp. 121–132. For details on the career of Hairikian, see Robert Krikorian, "Pariur Hairikian: The Making of a Dissident," (Unpublished paper, 1993).

36 For details on Armenian terrorism, see Monte Melkonian, *Patmutyun ASALA-i* (Lausanne: n.p., 1990); Markar Melkonian, ed., *The Right to Struggle: Selected Writings of Monte Melkonian on the Armenian National Question* (San Francisco, CA: Sardarabad Collective, 1993); and Michael Gunter, *"Pursuing the Just Cause of Their People": A Study of Contemporary Armenian Terrorism* (New York: Greenwood Press, 1986).

37 Personal communications with the author.

Map of Armenia

Chapter 1

THE COLLAPSE OF COMMUNISM IN ARMENIA

With the death of Brezhnev in 1982, a period of political uncertainty in the USSR began and was only dispelled upon the accession to power of Mikhail S. Gorbachev as General Secretary of the Communist Party of the Soviet Union in 1985. After years of stagnation, Soviet society and economy were suffering from a deep malaise. Realizing the importance of reinvigorating the USSR, Gorbachev embarked upon a bold plan to breathe new life into the system. He introduced the processes of glasnost (openness) and perestroika (restructuring), which he hoped would inspire the people to break out of their stagnation and revitalize a sagging Soviet system. Gorbachev was a committed Communist and never intended to destroy the system, only to renovate and improve it within the guidelines of Marxism-Leninism. Glasnost and perestroika looked very different from the periphery than from the center. Gorbachev had envisioned a more open and healthy debate within strictly defined limits regarding what was ailing the USSR. He did not assume that the debate would turn to issues of substance which he was unprepared to handle. Gorbachev was the only General Secretary of the Communist Party of the Soviet Union without any experience with the nationality question. All other heads of the Communist party had served in a non-Russian region and had at least some exposure to the sensitive nature of ethnic relations within the country, even if they paid lip service to platitudes of "friendship among peoples" and the resolution of all "national questions" on the territory of the USSR.[1] Gorbachev underestimated the power of national consciousness and could not foresee how more open discussion could turn to sensitive topics.

In the beginning, the non-Russian peoples of the USSR found relatively safe topics to discuss, such as ancient history. As the discussions turned to the environment and the legacy of Stalin, however, events took an unexpected turn, especially in Armenia. The environment was an issue that all Armenians could relate to. The heavy industrialization of Armenia resulted in severe ecological damage to the country. The effects of pollution in Yerevan could be seen on a daily basis. The presence of a noxious chemical factory, Nairit, within the city limits of Yerevan, was a stark indication that the health concerns of the population were a distant second to the overall production needs of the Soviet Union. Automobile and factory emissions were slowly poisoning the country. Although much of the pollution was not readily evident to the naked eye, the thick black soot that covered every open space in the course of a normal day in Yerevan was a grim reminder that something was seriously wrong. The water level of Lake Sevan, the jewel of Armenia, was dropping precipitously and the famed *ishkhandzuk* species of fish was all but extinct due to the callous misuse of water resources to fuel the industrialization of the country. In addition, the presence of the Medzamor Nuclear Reactor so close to the major populations centers of Armenia and so precariously poised near the convergence of three major fault lines gave the environmental movement in Armenia multiple issues to focus on.[2]

These environmental concerns were to the Armenians yet another attempt at "genocide." The psychological burden of the 1915 Genocide was played out in the environmental movement which claimed that the policies of the center were endangering the existence of the Armenian people. Although the movement was ultimately successful in drawing attention to the ecological situation in Armenia and in forcing the closure of both Nairit and Medzamor, the most important outcome was the galvanization of the population around issues that soon came to be regarded as national. Specifically, the environmental movement became inseparable from the larger national movement, and the national movement was centered around issues which to the Armenians transcended the environment.[3] The status of the Nagorno-Karabagh Autonomous Oblast (Region) (NKAO) was the issue which within a very short period of time was able to capture the imagination and energies of an entire nation. From 1988 to the present, it is impossible to discuss any developments in Armenia without reference to the Nagorno-Karabagh conflict.

KARABAGH AND THE BEGINNING OF THE END OF THE USSR

Karabagh was a defining issue for the Armenian people and its history is important for understanding the current situation in Armenia as well as the underlying causes of the current de facto state of war between Armenia and Azerbaijan. Armenians have inhabited Karabagh since antiquity.[4] This historically Armenian area maintained a quasi-independent status under the leadership of local Armenian rulers, *meliks*, for centuries. The overwhelming majority of the population of the enclave was ethnically Armenian. For Armenians, Karabagh was and still is considered a symbol of their struggle for survival and desire for independence. As the Transcaucasus was gradually absorbed into the Russian Empire during the first three decades of the nineteenth century and as the Russians consolidated their rule, they immediately began to set up the institutions and mechanisms of colonial administration. In order to contain any potential opposition, the Russians intentionally designed administrative units that did not correspond to ethno-territorial settlements. Thus, it was thought that local nationalisms would not be encouraged if administrative units of mixed ethnicities were created. This was the Imperial Russian version of the old Roman method of divide and rule. During these few years of independence, hostility between Armenia and Azerbaijan increased with both Armenia and Azerbaijan claiming the regions of Nakhichevan, Zangezur and Karabagh.[5] Much blood was shed for control of these strategically important areas. Upon Sovietization, the disputed territories were initially ceded to Armenia. In a telegram sent to the Armenian government on December 1, 1920, the Azerbaijani Soviet government declared:

> As of today the borders disputed between Armenia and Azerbaijan are declared resolved. Mountainous Karabagh, Zangezur and Nakhichevan are considered part of the Soviet Republic of Armenia.
>   Chairman of Azerbaijan's Revolutionary Committee N. Narimanov Commissioner of Foreign Affairs Huseinov.[6]

This decision was reversed in July 1921 on the insistence of Stalin who was then Chairman of the Commissariat for Nationalities.[7] Partly with an eye towards better relations with Kemalist Turkey and partly in accord with his conscious decisions to sow discord among the subject nationalities, Stalin applied the tactic of divide and rule. Thus, the Armenians and Azerbaijanis would remain divided and rely that much more on the center. It should be mentioned that there is a distinction between Karabagh and Mountainous Karabagh (Nagorno-Karabagh in Russian, Lernayin Gharabagh in Armenian). As its name implies, Nagorno-Karabagh is only the mountainous highland portion of Karabagh, which was historically known by the old Armenian name of Artsakh. A Kurdish autonomous region was formed in the surrounding lowlands in the 1920s to create an artificial barrier between Armenia proper and Nagorno-Karabagh.[8]

Protest against this situation of a divided people was muted throughout the Stalin years. Armenians in Karabagh were discriminated against by the authorities in Baku. Development in Karabagh lagged behind that of the other regions of Azerbaijan. Karabagh Armenians were denied opportunities for education in the Armenian language and cultural ties to Armenia were limited. Books, radio programs and cultural exchanges were also restricted. Legal justice was also heavily against the Armenian majority of the enclave.[9] Several attempts were made to raise the issue with Moscow during subsequent administrations but nothing ever came of those efforts.[10] With the accession of Mikhail Gorbachev as General Secretary of the Communist Party of the Soviet Union, and his implementation of glasnost and perestroika, the Armenians of

Nagorno-Karabagh once again agitated for a revision of the borders, claiming economic, legal and cultural discrimination by the authorities in Baku. The problems of the Armenians of Nagorno-Karabagh were exacerbated by the policies of Moscow and Baku. One of Gorbachev's first initiatives as General Secretary was an anti-alcohol campaign. Drunkenness in the Soviet Union was a serious problem and was affecting output in almost all spheres of the economy. Karabagh was covered in vineyards as a result of Heidar Aliyev's directive to concentrate on grape-growing to the neglect and detriment of other important crops. In the 1970s and 1980s, Karabagh farmers had to uproot their other crops and plant grape vines, which was both economically harmful as well as logistically difficult. But with no recourse, the Karabagh Armenians begrudgingly complied. With the imposition of the anti-alcohol campaign, new orders were issued to dig up and destroy the vineyards. The economic impact of these short-sighted policies was disastrous for the already economically disadvantaged region and only increased resentment towards the authorities in both Baku and Moscow.

The struggle over Nagorno-Karabagh should be seen within the broader context of All-Union developments. Gorbachev was consolidating his power through various means, including reshuffling Politburo members. Heidar Aliyev, formerly head of the KGB in Azerbaijan and later First Secretary of the Azerbaijani Communist Party, had already been removed from the Polit- buro and disgraced.[11] Meanwhile, Gorbachev was also maneuvering to remove those republican first secretaries who were also seen as closely aligned with Brezhnev, such as Armenian Communist Party First Secretary Karen Demirchyan. The issue of Nagorno-Karabagh coincided with other, larger issues which none of the participants were necessarily aware of at the time. By 1987, the situation of the Armenians of Nagorno-Karabagh had deteriorated to the point where a reaction was seen as inevitable. In the middle of October 1987, a demonstration of about a thousand people took place in Yerevan to protest inter-ethnic clashes that took place in the Karabagh village of Chardakhlou and to demand the reunification of Nagorno-Karabagh to Armenia.[12] This demonstration immediately followed one the previous day which was protesting the disastrous environmental situation in Armenia. Local police forces dispersed the crowd[13] and the situation remained relat- ively calm for the next several months.

In the fall of 1987 a petition-drive had been initiated in Nagorno-Karabagh, hoping that tens of thousands of Armenian signatures requesting a change in the status of the autonomous region would help convince the authorities in Moscow to intervene on their side. These petitions were sent to Moscow in January 1988, where the Karabagh Armenians were optimistic that the central authorities would recognize the justice of their cause, which they naively thought was in line with Gorbachev's policy of new thinking. Mass demonstrations in support of unification with Armenia took place in Karabagh beginning in mid-February. On February 20 1988, the Soviet of People's Deputies of Nagorno-Karabagh officially requested union with Armenia. The legislature voted 110 to 17 in favor of unification, with 13 abstentions.[14] This unprecedented action was justified by the deputies on the grounds that territorial adjustments were within the limits set by the constitution of the USSR. In addition, the precedents of the transfer of the Crimea from the Russian Soviet Federative Socialist Republic (RSFSR) to the Ukrainian SSR in 1954 in honor of the three hundredth anniversary of the "voluntary unification" of Ukraine with Russia as well as numerous changes in the North Caucasus in the 1930s and 1940s were cited by proponents of the transfer of Karabagh to Armenia. This action was denounced as illegal by both Moscow and Baku.[15] Gorbachev promised to review the status of the Karabagh region, but few concrete results seemed to flow from this and many viewed it as a delaying tactic. From the outset, it was clear that Gorbachev was taken by surprise by events and that his lack of experience with the nationalities question severely limited his ability to make informed decisions.

REVERBERATIONS IN YEREVAN

The news of demonstrations in Karabagh was greeted with enthusiasm by many in Armenia. Mass demonstrations took place in Yerevan in solidarity with the Armenians of Karabagh. Opera Square in Yerevan became the venue for these massive displays of national self-consciousness. Located in the center of the capital, Opera Square was at the confluence of two major boulevards and thus ideally situated as a place of gathering. The unique architecture of the opera house itself, which was a mix of classical Armenian motifs and more modern designs, symbolised the Armenian attempt to reconcile their ancient sense of uniqueness with the demands of modern statehood. On February 23, as Soviet troops arrived in Yerevan, Armenian CP First Secretary Karen Demirchyan called for calm, while Communist Party of the Soviet Union Politburo members Pyotr Demichev and Georgi Razumovsky were sent to Stepanakert. The Catholicos Vazgen I went on national television to urge the population to remain calm. On February 26 1988, it was estimated that one million people demonstrated in support of the demands of the Karabagh Armenians.[16] This large number when viewed in the context of a total population of 3.7 million in the republic is all the more remarkable. These were the largest pro-democracy demonstrations in the history of the Soviet Union and were unprecedented. The scale of the demonstrations frightened both the central authorities in Moscow and the local republican authorities in Armenia.

Even more remarkable than the numbers of participants is the disciplined manner in which they took place. In a rare display of people's democracy, those gathered at Opera Square transcended the usual brusqueness of life in the capital and acted with unusual correctness towards each other. There was no pushing and shoving for a more advantageous position as was common in the endless lines which characterized Soviet consumer society. During these February days, it was as if the Armenian people had transcended the numbing monotony of Soviet life and lifted the nation to a higher moral and spiritual plane. It was reported that demonstrators remained silent while passing by hospitals in order not to disturb the sick and many people brought food and water to the marchers as they passed through their neighborhoods. The impact of these mass meetings on the psyche of the Armenian people was tremendous. The mood of those heady days was captured by Mark Malkasian, an analyst and eyewitness to these events. He records:

> The Karabagh movement was made by the people of Armenia. They shared in the mass rallies, celebrated their new-found ability to influence the political process, and agonized over the realization of their own limitations. Just as Americans who lived through the economic depression of the 1930s or the social turbulence of the 1960s were indelibly stamped by the temper of the times, so the Karabagh movement left a deep imprint on the collective consciousness of the people of Armenia. The turmoil of the late 1980s and early 1990s marks a bridge between the Soviet period and a new era in Armenian history. The worldview that gradually coalesced among Soviet Armenians was demolished. The relative security that characterized seven decades of Soviet rule melted away, as did the constraints of the Soviet political system and the central planning of the Soviet economy.[17]

From the outset, it was clear that the demonstrations would need some kind of leadership so that they would not lose momentum. In the early days of the demonstrations, a leadership group emerged, which included: Rafael Ghazaryan, physicist, born 1924; Vazgen Manukyan, mathematician, born 1946; Hambartsum Galstyan, ethnographer, born 1956; Samson Ghazaryan, teacher, born 1953; Samvel Gevorkyan, journalist, born 1949; Alexander Hakobyan, medieval oriental historian, born 1955; Ashot Manucharyan, teacher, born 1954; Vano Siradeghyan, writer, born 1946; David Vardanyan, physicist, born 1950; and Levon Ter-Petrossyan, philologist and ancient historian, born 1945.[18] These men, who would play instrumental roles in the establishment of independence in Armenia:

consisted of an ad hoc organizing committee, soon dubbed the "Karabagh Committee," composed of young intellectuals, mainly non-Party, without direct connections to government. They decided on strategy and tactics, and took primary responsibility for articulating a program and disseminating correct information at "public meetings." An informal, fluctuating group of intellectuals and writers (many with family roots in Karabagh) played an advisory role, generating documents to legitimate Armenian claims to the broader Soviet and Western audience. The composition of the Karabagh Committee gradually changed, as advocates of extreme positions were expelled so as to avoid provocations and maintain a moderate face to the rest of the country.[19]

After meeting with Gorbachev, the protest leaders convinced the demonstrators on February 27 to call a one-month moratorium on further demonstrations. The Armenians were hopeful that in the interim Gorbachev would review the situation and give the Armenians what in their view was simple justice.

AZERBAIJAN ANSWERS WITH SUMGAIT

The Azerbaijani response to the Karabagh Armenians' initiative was swift. On February 22, Azerbaijanis from the city of Aghdam, just outside the boundaries of NKAO, marched towards Karabagh in order to protest the actions of the Armenians. On the way they attacked Armenian villages and destroyed Armenian property.[20] Just inside the borders of Karabagh, local Armenians organized themselves to repel the oncoming Azerbaijani mob. Local Azerbaijani police were also on the scene. In the ensuing clashes, many people were injured and two Azerbaijanis were killed, one by an Azerbaijani policeman.[21]

News of this disturbance was broadcast on national television, with the Deputy Prosecutor of the USSR announcing provocatively the nationality of those killed, despite numerous warnings that to do so would exacerbate already existing tensions. Azerbaijanis in the industrial city of Sumgait began to hold demonstrations denouncing the events in Karabagh. Local youths and unemployed people from other regions were brought into Sumgait, a city of 250,000 of whom about 18,000 were Armenian, which suffered from both high unemployment and severe ecological degradation. Prominent among the outsiders were Azerbaijanis from the region of Kafan in the Armenian SSR. In the public squares of Sumgait, they claimed that Armenians in Kafan had attacked them and driven them out, raping Azerbaijani women and torturing them in the process. This misinformation was used to whip up the crowds present who called for revenge and "Death to the Armenians." Many in the crowd were armed with sharpened rods, knives and stones. With the aid of prepared lists, Azerbaijani mobs attacked Armenian dwellings through-out Sumgait while the authorities did nothing to stop the violence. In fact, according to numerous eyewitnesses, the local Azerbaijani officials incited the mobs to attack Armenians. Men, women and children were subjected to three days of unspeakable horror. Finally, on March 1st, Soviet Army personnel accompanied by armored personnel carriers evacuated the remaining Armenians.22 The official death toll was thirty-one, but most observers believe that the actual toll was much higher.

The impact of Sumgait on Armenian attitudes is difficult to overestimate. For most of the period of Russian and then Soviet rule, Armenians could always justify their dependent status as a necessary evil in order to protect themselves from the Turks. The memory of the 1915 Genocide was foremost in Armenians' thoughts when weighing the pluses and minuses of Soviet rule. After all, the Armenian SSR was the only part of historical Armenia which was still inhabited primarily by Armenians and that Armenian cultural life was allowed to develop, albeit within the guidelines laid down by the Communist Party of the Soviet Union. For most if not all Armenians, the thought of massacres or pogroms inside the USSR, especially in the post-Stalin years, was a near impossibility. For this reason, the shock of the massacre in Sumgait was even more pronounced. Memories of the Genocide were recalled as well as the notion that the Azerbaijanis were little different than their Turkish co-ethnics. Some observers believed that the central authorities in Moscow either instigated the episode or allowed it to continue in order to impress upon the Armenians the vulnerability of their present situation.[23] Others began the slow process of re-examining the entire justification of the inclusion of Armenia within the USSR, namely the securing of the physical existence of the Armenian people. Armenian confidence in the ability of the center to act as an honest broker was shaken but anger was also aroused, both against the Azerbaijanis and against the central authorities.

THE CENTER REACTS

Within a short period the Karabagh movement began to encompass a whole host of grievances which ranged from the environment and the status of the Armenian language within the republic to more broad-based democratic reform issues. The Karabagh Committee was vested with the trust of the majority of the citizenry and soon became the real spokesperson for the nation. This was the birth of civil society in Armenia, a process that was begun during the first republic but which was kept in a state of suspended animation for almost seventy years. What was occurring would have been considered unthinkable a short while before: the people of Armenia were actively engaged in searching for an alternative to Communist rule.

The central authorities were faced with a serious dilemma. To accede to Armenian demands for the reunification of Karabagh to Armenia would have opened up a pandora's box of other ethnic grievances across the Soviet Union. It was believed that the precedent of Karabagh would be used by other groups to push their claims on Moscow and the risk of alienating the Azerbaijanis could have ramifications well beyond the borders of Azerbaijan. Moscow had always been fearful of the millions of Muslims in the USSR and did not want to take the risk of alienating them in the process of resolving the Nagorno-Karabagh dispute. Moscow instead tried to mollify both parties and thus in fact alienated both. In late March, the Supreme Soviet acknow-ledged that there were indeed serious problems in the past and that Azerbai-jan had neglected the development of the Nagorno-Karabagh Autonomous Oblast. Therefore it would be in the interests of the working class of both Armenia and Azerbaijan to institute a wide-ranging package of reforms for the region, including political, economic, social, cultural as well as educa-tional components.[24] Neither side was pleased by this decision and tensions continued to mount.

On March 23, the USSR Supreme Soviet Presidium adopted a measure that urged both local governmental and law enforcement bodies in Armenia and Azerbaijan to prevent further disturbances.[25] Both the Armenian Min-ister of Internal Affairs and Communist Party First Secretary Karen Demirchyan warned that continued demonstrations could lead to unpredictable circum-stances. Meanwhile in Stepanakert, the Armenians had begun a general strike. The following day the Karabagh Committee cancelled a mass meeting intended for Saturday March 26, and instead called for everyone to stay at home in a protest strike, an example of the growing authority of the Karabagh Committee in the public sphere. On March 24, the Soviet news program *Vremya* announced a number of concessions intended to de-escalate tensions in Nagorno-Karabagh. These concessions included a $664 million plan to build schools, hospitals, factories and roads in Karabagh as well as the broadcast of Armenian television into the autonomous region.[26] The Kremlin believed that the problems of Nagorno-Karabagh could be resolved if the economic situation were improved, which was an oversimplification of the situation and one which would eventually prove disastrous for Moscow's attempt to impose a settlement in the region. At the end of March, the well-known Armenian dissident Pariur Hairikyan was arrested in Yerevan for giving information to the Western media regarding the atrocities in Sumgait. He was promptly expel-led to Ethiopia and stripped of his Soviet citizenship.[27]

Relative quiet reigned in April. April 24, however, was commemorated by a huge procession to the Martyrs' Monument overlooking Yerevan. This year, the mourners also grieved over the massacre at Sumgait and laid flowers at a newly installed stone cross (*khatchkar*) near the monument. On May 18, Gorbachev ordered the dismissal of the Communist Party First Secretaries of both Armenia and Azerbaijan, Karen Demirchyan and Kyamran Bagirov, who were replaced by two pro-Gorbachev candidates, Suren Harutyunyan and Abdul-Rahman Vezirov.[28] At the end of May these new appointees met to discuss ways of strengthening economic and cultural ties as well as finding means of defusing tensions in their republics. In Yerevan demonstrations took place marking the 70th anniversary of the first independent Armenian Republic of 1918, a celebration which would have been inconceivable a short time ago. Events in the region were moving at such a fast pace that what was considered radical one day would be timid the next.

ESCALATION AND RECRIMINATION

By June, the atmosphere in Armenia, Azerbaijan and Nagorno-Karabagh had worsened considerably, with strikes crippling both Yerevan and Stepanakert. With the Presidium of the Azerbaijani Supreme Soviet refusing to cede control of Nagorno-Karabagh, Suren Harutyunyan informed the people that the Armenian Supreme Soviet would take up the issue of the status of Karabagh on June 15. He also pledged that the Supreme Soviet of Armenia would take a positive stance towards unification. Gradually, the Communist Party leadership in Armenia were forced to make a decision about the strategy that they must adopt. Appearing to be too subservient to Moscow had already cost them a considerable amount of credibility in the eyes of the people. On the other hand, to appear to give in to the demands of the masses and be associated with the rising nationalism in Armenia and Nagorno-Karabagh would have cost them the support of Moscow which at this point was still crucial. In the end, however, the Communists were driven peacefully from office before they fully resolved the dilemma. Assured by the Armenian Communist Party First Secretary that the Supreme Soviet would support unification, the leaders of the Karabagh Committee called off the general strike which was in progress. As expected, the Armenian Supreme Soviet unanimously called for the unification of Nagorno-Karabagh to Armenia, justifying their stand by referring to Article 70 of the USSR Constitution which states that "The Union of Soviet Socialist Republics is an integral, federal multinational state formed on the principle of socialist federalism as a result of the free self-determination of nations and the voluntary association of equal Soviet

Socialist Republics."[29] In response to the Armenian Supreme Soviet's decision, the Azerbaijani Supreme Soviet unanimously voted against any compromise over the issue of the territorial status of Nagorno-Karabagh.

In order to get Karabagh out from under Azerbaijani control demonstrators in Yerevan demanded, in early July, that the USSR Supreme Soviet establish legal jurisdiction over Karabagh. Soon the conflict escalated to a level of low-intensity warfare between the Armenians of Nagorno-Karabagh and the Azerbaijanis. Moscow appeared unable to cope with this crisis. On July 12 1988, the Supreme Soviet of Nagorno-Karabagh voted unanimously to secede from Azerbaijan as well as changing the name of the region to the old historical Armenian designation, Artsakh.[30] As could be expected, the Presidium of the Supreme Soviet of the Azerbaijani SSR immediately denounced the vote and decreed that Nagorno-Karabagh should remain within the Azerbaijan SSR. This only exacerbated tensions in the region. On July 18, an emergency session of the USSR Supreme Soviet convened in order to examine the situation in Nagorno-Karabagh, at which Gorbachev assailed the Armenians as nationalists and opponents of reform. In an attempt to soften the blow, the USSR Supreme Soviet Presidium promised more aid to the region while categorically rejecting the decision of the Nagorno-Karabagh legislature for secession. As a compromise measure, the USSR Supreme Soviet assigned a task force to oversee the implementation of the reform package and a second commission was promised to study the need for any additional measures. The leaders of the Nagorno-Karabagh party organization warned that the resolution would have negative repercussions within the region.[31]

In response to the continuing strikes in Nagorno-Karabagh, which had been going on for two months, Soviet troops were sent in to intimidate the strikers. The tactic worked and the strike was called off. On August 2, the heads of the Communist Parties of Armenia and Azerbaijan met in Stepanakert and pledged close cooperation in order to solve the problems of the region.[32] In a transparent attempt to regain some of the initiative in Armenia, Suren Harutyunyan announced an anti-corruption campaign which would target certain sectors such as the police, food distribution, transport and health care, and he stated that the Central Committee of the Armenian Communist Party would turn over some of their summer homes which would be converted into rest homes for children and veterans.[33]

REFUGEES AND NATURAL DISASTER

In September, a new wave of unrest swept over Stepanakert. The Armenians claimed that there was a large influx of Azerbaijanis into the region which they feared would alter the delicate demographic balance. They accused the Azerbaijani government of deliberately trying to increase the numbers of Azerbaijanis in Karabagh, which brought back memories of what had happened in Nakhichevan, where the Armenian population had diminished from 15% in 1926 to only 1.5% in 1979.[34] According to estimates, about 20,000 of the 170,000 Azerbaijanis in Armenia, fearing reprisals, had left the country thus far.[35] On September 19, a gun battle took place between Armenians and Azerbaijanis near Stepanakert in which dozens on both sides were wounded. In the aftermath of the escalation of violence, a state of emergency was declared in Karabagh and Soviet Interior Ministry (MVD) troops were deployed around Stepanakert.[36] The state of emergency meant that a strict curfew was in effect and that striking workers could be arrested. In conjunction with the state of emergency in Armenia, MVD troops also moved into Yerevan, where they cordoned off a number of important buildings and large areas of the city. Similar scenes were repeated throughout the rest of the republic.

In a triumph for the environmental movement, Suren Harutyunyan announced that the Armenian nuclear power plant would be closed down. By conceding this issue to the protesters, the Armenian Communist Party leadership was trying to demonstrate that they could still deliver something substantive to the population. In line with this strategy, the Prime Minister of Armenia announced that Moscow's assistance in solving the problems of Nagorno-Karabagh was essential and then went on to detail plans to improve the living situation of the population in the region by constructing a Palace of Culture, a House of Pioneers and a library in Stepanakert.[37] In this instance the Armenian Communist authorities realized that it would take more than economic incentives to improve the situation, but they still fell short of the expectations of the masses.

Meanwhile in the diaspora, the three main political parties, the Armenian Revolutionary Federation, the Ramgavar Liberal Democratic Party and the Hunchakian Social Democratic Party came together to issue a joint declaration. The declaration appeared to be not in support of, but in opposition to, what was happening in Armenia. The three political parties felt that the overriding national interests demanded extreme caution and that precipitous action could lead to disaster. Many inside Armenia felt that these three established parties, having been isolated and detached from developments in Armenia for decades, had lost touch with the reality of life in Soviet Armenia and misunderstood the democratic character of developments there. Their joint declaration, while claiming solidarity with the people of Armenia and Nagorno-Karabagh, in fact put them on the side of the authorities. The declaration called for the people to "forgo such extreme acts as work stoppages, student strikes, and some radical calls and expressions that unsettle law and order in public life in the homeland; that subject to heavy losses the economic, productive, educational, and cultural life; that [harm seriously] the good standing of our nation in its relations with the higher Soviet bodies and other Soviet republics. These zealous attitudes also provide for the ulterior motives of the enemies of our people."[38] This declaration came as a blow to the people of Armenia who were actively engaged in what they saw as a struggle for human rights and democracy and planted the seed of suspicion towards the diaspora which would eventually lead to serious conflict in the years after independence.

By November, the increasing violence of the confrontation over Nagorno-Karabagh unleashed a wave of refugees from both Armenia and Azerbaijan. Azerbaijanis living in Armenia, numbering around 160,000, fearing for their safety, fled back to Azerbaijan. In this early period, many of them were able to exchange apartments with Armenians residing in Azerbaijan who wished to relocate to Armenia. They left Armenia with much of their property, although some left under threat of retaliation for what had happened in Sumgait and elsewhere. At the same time, about 200,000 Armenians living in areas of Azerbaijan other than Nagorno-Karabagh and Baku were forcibly driven out of their settlements thus adding to a multi-directional flow of refugees.[39] As the Armenian Supreme Soviet was discussing proposed constitutional amendments, it received reports that violence against Armenians in Azerbaijan was increasing in intensity. Reports indicated that these assaults were taking place in Baku, as well as in Kirovabad and the few remaining Armenian villages in the Nakhichevan ASSR.[40] Soviet troops were assigned to guard the homes of Armenians in Baku while in Kirovabad a state of emergency was declared. Throughout the violence, officials appealed for calm as armed force was deployed to prevent even further bloodshed. The Armenian Supreme Soviet decided to adjourn early. On November 25, a military commandant took control of Yerevan imposing a curfew and instituting military patrols, roadblocks and, most significantly, a ban on further demonstrations.[41] Gorbachev, alarmed by the increase in violent confrontations in the Caucasus, met with Armenian and Azerbaijani officials on December 1 and accused them of losing control of the situation, urging them to act quickly and decisively in order to halt further inter-ethnic strife. While ordering the officials to work together on a Commission on Refugee Problems, he refused to consider any possible border rectifications.

These discussions became moot within a matter of days, however, as the situation in Armenia took a disastrous turn for the worse. Just before noon on

December 7, a major earthquake struck the northern part of Armenia, totally devastating the second largest city, Leninakan and obliterating scores of villages. The official death toll was put at 25–30,000, although many estimates reached upward to as much as 100,000 victims. According to one informed source:

> This minimum figure of 100,000 deaths seems all the more plausible when we consider that a coordinator for Doctors without Borders, not of Armenian background and well-informed, fixed the number of deaths in Leninakan (population 300,000) at 70,000. If we add to this the victims of the city of Spitak (population 27,000), which was nearly 100% destroyed; Kirovakan (population 170,000); Stepanavan (population 40,000); the large number of victims among the 100,000 Armenians from Azerbaijan who had sought refuge in the region after fleeing pogroms during the preceding several months; and the casualties in the 50 or so villages affected, including Nalband where 1,800 of 2,000 inhabitants perished; the figure of 100,000 seems to be a bottom-line estimate.[42]

Within seconds, the city of Leninakan with a population of approximately 300,000 and one of the largest industrial areas of Armenia was almost completely destroyed. The casualty figures were compounded by the presence of numerous Armenian refugees who had fled the violence in Kirovabad and other areas of Azerbaijan in the previous weeks. Another contributing factor was the shoddy construction of apartment buildings in the area. Much of the cement needed for proper construction was stolen or bartered on the black market and as a result the remaining cement was mixed with sand thus weakening its structural resistance. This fact tragically illustrated the effects of corruption and the Armenians were furious at both the central authorities and their own corrupt leadership.

Local and central authorities proved incapable of dealing with the enormity of the task confronting them. One eyewitness, a seasoned veteran of numerous disaster-relief operations, was "truly shocked by the scale of this disaster and its consequences. In Armenia it was Hell with a capital H."[43] Gorbachev, who had been visiting the United States, cut short his visit and returned home. In line with his policies of glasnost and perestroika, Gorbachev appealed to the international community for assistance in dealing with the aftermath of the earthquake. Within hours of this appeal, international aid was en route to the beleaguered survivors. For the first time since international efforts to combat famine in the Soviet Union in the 1920s, the Soviet Union opened up its doors to the outside world and welcomed in international aid workers. The situation in Armenia was chaotic. Although troops had been deployed to the area, many of them stood idle as people tried frantically to rescue survivors. Confusion reigned. The airport in

Yerevan became the terminus for all aid and it was a major feat just being able to unload the planes and prevent them from crashing into each other. The international community rallied around the Armenian people in their hour of need. Although many Armenians were paralyzed by grief, others quickly stepped in to fill the void left open by the tragedy. The Karabagh Committee swung into action organizing convoys of relief supplies as well as sending hundreds of volunteers to the earthquake zone to help in rescue work.[44]

In the politicized and volatile atmosphere of Armenia, Gorbachev's arrival was heralded in a manner entirely different to what he was expecting. Instead of being greeted sympathetically, he was assailed by angry Armenians who wanted to know why the central authorities had not responded more quickly to the emergency and why he had not given them justice with regard to Nagorno-Karabagh. The General Secretary was shocked and angry denouncing the Armenians as nationalists who even at this tragic moment could not forgo their nationalist demands.[45] Emotions were so aroused and passions so volatile that many Armenians even believed that the Kremlin had actually planned the earthquake as a means to destroy the national movement. The Armenians had so much distrust towards the authorities that nothing seemed beyond the realms of possibility.

THE CENTER STRIKES

With the entire Armenian nation and the world distracted by the events unfolding in the earthquake zone, Gorbachev had the members of the Karabagh Committee arrested in December and January. Fearful that they were taking advantage of the chaos to highlight the ineptitude of the authorities and angry at the response of the Armenian people to his visit, Gorbachev used the ensuing chaos to incarcerate the Committee members first in Yerevan and then have them transferred to Moscow.[46] At the end of December, Andrei Sakharov travelled to the Caucasus at the request of Gorbachev and Yakovlev who had asked him to attempt to negotiate some type of compromise between the Armenian and Azerbaijani leaderships over Nagorno-Karabagh. His mission, unfortunately, was not successful.

In early January 1989, the Central Committees, Supreme Soviets and Councils of Ministers of Armenia and Azerbaijan issued a joint statement which called for an end to inter-ethnic strife as well as appealing to all refugees to return to their homes.[47] These statements, like the numerous pronouncements which had preceded them, fell on deaf ears. Shortly thereafter, the Supreme Soviet of the USSR appointed a special administrative commission to govern Nagorno-Karabagh pending a review of the situation.[48] Thus,

Nagorno-Karabagh, although officially remaining a part of Azerbaijan, was taken out from the jurisdiction of Azerbaijan and ruled directly from Moscow through the Special Administration Committee, headed by senior Gorbachev adviser, Arkadi Volsky. This was the first time that a newly adopted constitutional amendment allowed the USSR Supreme Soviet the authority to create "special forms of administration" to protect the safety of Soviet citizens. Following this, an announcement was made that Nagorno-Karabagh Autonomous Oblast First Secretary Henrikh Poghosyan would retire.[49] Once again, Moscow hoped to come up with a compromise solution which succeeded only in further aggravating tensions on both sides.

On April 24 1989, hundreds of thousands of Armenians marched to the Martyrs' Monument to commemorate the 1915 Genocide as well as to protest the continuing detention of the members of the Karabagh Committee. Continual pressure was also applied for the release of the members of the Committee. This determination finally paid off in late May. The Congress of People's Deputies made an official inquiry requesting clarification of the status of these men who were being held without trial.[50] On May 31 they were released by the central authorities and subsequently flown home to Armenia where they were greeted by adoring crowds.[51] On June 25, the Armenian Supreme Soviet officially registered the Armenian National Movement and listed the Karabagh Committee as its founder.[52] The Karabagh Committee thus institutionalized its role as the nucleus of a national movement intent on challenging the Communist system. The Armenian National Movement (ANM), or *Hayotz Hamazgain Sharzhoum (HHSh)*, was intended to act as an umbrella organization of all organizations and individuals who had been involved in the struggle since February 1988.

Throughout the summer of 1989, tensions continued to mount between Armenians and Azerbaijanis in Nagorno-Karabagh. In August, the newly-formed Azerbaijani Popular Front (APF) called for a strike in Baku to support their demands for legal recognition as well as more Azerbaijani control over Nagorno-Karabagh. By September, the APF was able to force the Communist Party First Secretary Vezirov to sign a "protocol" with them in order to call off the strike and gain the legal recognition which they had sought. In addition, Vezirov agreed to convene a special session of the Supreme Soviet in order to pass a new law on sovereignty. A few days later, the Azerbaijani Supreme Soviet called for the suspension of emergency rule over Karabagh by Moscow. On September 25 Gorbachev, in his speech to the opening session of the USSR Supreme Soviet, declared that he would intervene in forty-eight hours if Azerbaijan did not lift its blockade on trains trying to enter Armenia. Although the Azerbaijani Popular Front had declared an end to the strike it continued.[53]

At the end of November, the USSR Supreme Soviet voted to restore Azerbaijani jurisdiction over Nagorno-Karabagh, with Armenians receiving a proportional share in local government. Despite this revocation of the special status that had governed the region since January, MVD troops, under the supervision of an observer commission of the USSR Supreme Soviet, remained in order to maintain order. This decision was greeted by protests in Stepanakert and Yerevan. In a clear reaction to the decision of the USSR Supreme Soviet to revoke Nagorno-Karabagh's special status, the Armenian Supreme Soviet voted to unite the region with Armenia. This serious move was countered by Azerbaijan through a renewed blockade against Armenia in retaliation for the Armenian Supreme Soviet's resolution on annexation. As the conflict developed, Azerbaijan, which controlled most of the rail links to Armenia, instituted a series of intermittent economic blockades against both Armenia and Nagorno-Karabagh. Due to the peculiar nature of the Soviet, transportation system, Armenia was dependent upon rail lines that ran through Azerbaijan for 85% of its rail traffic and the remaining 15% upon lines running through Georgia.

In October 1989, Azerbaijan passed its "Law on Sovereignty," which in effect declared the sovereignty of the Azerbaijani people over the entire territory of the republic, including Karabagh. It was further declared that no border changes could take place without the express consent of the Azerbaijani nation. By so doing, Azerbaijan attempted to portray the conflict as an internal one, the resolution of which could only lie within the competence of Baku not Moscow. Shortly thereafter, the Volsky commission was withdrawn, having realized that it was incapable of resolving the conflict between the two groups. The Special Administration Commission was disbanded and the administration of Nagorno-Karabagh was handed back over to direct Azerbaijani rule.[54] Once again, the Supreme Soviet of the USSR tried to soften the blow to the Armenians by calling upon Azerbaijan to form an ethnically-mixed administrative body that would guarantee reforms in the region. Accordingly, an "Organizing Committee" was formed which was dominated by Azerbaijanis and headed by the notorious former Second Secretary of the Azerbaijan Communist Party, Viktor Polyanichko. In response, the National Council of the Nagorno-Karabagh Autonomous Region and the Supreme Soviet of Armenia declared on December 3, 1989 that they were forming a "United Republic of Armenia," under a single government in Yerevan.

In December 1989, the situation in Azerbaijan grew more volatile. In the Azerbaijani city of Djalilabad, it was reported that protesters had run local Party leaders, police officials and other authorities out of town after local law security forces had fired on demonstrators who had gathered in front of the local party headquarters demanding limitations on party power. Meanwhile, disturbances broke out in the Azerbaijani enclave of Nakhichevan. Local Azerbaijanis were protesting against the border installations which separated them from their ethnic kin across the Arax River in Iranian Azerbaijan and were demanding that the central authorities allow them greater access to the Iranian Azerbaijanis. Along the length of the Soviet Azerbaijan-Iran border, border posts were torn down and destroyed by Azerbaijani demonstrators. In January 1990, the protests spread to Baku where large demonstrations took place in support of the border protests as well as Azerbaijani control over Nagorno-Karabagh. The First Secretary of the Nakhichevan ASSR was sacked from his position. Armenia and Karabagh were watching these developments with keen interest. The Supreme Soviet of Armenia approved legislation which called for the inclusion of Karabagh in the socio-economic plans of Armenia, thus contributing to the spiraling level of tension which was already reaching the boiling point. In the southern Azerbaijani town of Lenkoran, protesters seized the radio station and blocked access to government offices, while in Baku protesters demanded the resignation of the republican leadership due to their inability to deal with the situation in Nagorno-Karabagh. In fact the Azerbaijani Popular Front was on the verge of achieving the seemingly impossible: the overthrow of the Communist government in Baku.[55]

In the midst of these demonstrations, the Armenian community of Baku became the target of mob violence. Since the beginning of the problem over Nagorno-Karabagh in 1988, the Armenians of Baku had tried desperately to keep a low profile to avoid the same fate as their fellow Armenians in Sumgait and Kirovabad. Although victims of discrimination and random violence during the past two years, they had been able to maintain a precarious existence. In mid-January, Azerbaijanis repeated the scenes of horror witnessed in Sumgait. For several days, the mobs were allowed free reign to terrorize, murder and plunder the Armenians with impunity. Finally, on January 15 1990 a state of emergency was declared in Baku and 11,000 troops were sent into Baku to regain control of the city. With indiscriminate brutality, the Soviet troops killed hundreds of civilians in their attempt to reinstall Soviet power throughout the city. This slaughter was burned into Azerbaijani national consciousness and became known as "Black January." In response to this brutal occupation, which Gorbachev claimed was undertaken in defense of the Armenians, but in fact was nothing more than a frightened reaction to the possibility of having Soviet power overthrown in Baku, the Azerbaijani Supreme Soviet voted to secede if the occupation did not end immediately.[56]

In the aftermath of the January events, the Baltic Council offered to host talks between the Armenian National Movement and the Azerbaijani Popular Front to be held in Riga, Latvia in the beginning of February. In an unusual display of solidarity, the Armenian National Movement condemned the Soviet use of force in Baku and both sides issued a communique in which they called for a cease-fire to be effective February 15 and for the creation of a council to resolve all outstanding disputes. The talks, however, were suspended, as news reached the ANM of APF officials entering the Armenian villages of Azat and Kamo just outside of Nagorno-Karabagh and ordering the villagers to leave.[57] Thus, although an attempt was made by a neutral third party to mediate the conflict, events outpaced such attempts and doomed them to ultimate failure.

In April 1990, Vladimir Movsisyan was elected first secretary of the Armenian Communist Party, replacing Suren Harutyunyan. This rapid turn-over of Communist Party cadres reflected the party leadership's fear that they had lost control of the situation as well as credibility in the eyes of the people. This realization was a shock to the Armenian Communist Party, who had never before been accountable to any constituency. The election of Movsisyan was an attempt to give the party a more human face, but in the end it turned out to be too little, too late. A new parliament was elected in Armenia in May, where supporters of the Armenian National Movement won a majority. In this first application of limited democracy, the people overwhelming supported the democratic movement. The Armenian Supreme Soviet voted to suspend the spring draft of youth into the Soviet Armed Forces and also demanded guarantees that links would be maintained between Armenia and Nagorno-Karabagh.[58] These bold moves could not go unchallenged by Moscow. It was obvious that the central authorities would somehow try to destabilize the situation in Armenia in order to discredit the newly-elected parliament and provide cause for a reimposition of Soviet law and order. In late May, a serious provocation occurred inside the Yerevan train station. A group of Soviet troops were passing through on the train on their way out of the county. According to some sources, an armed volunteer unit had arranged a deal with the departing troops whereby the troops would leave behind some weapons in exchange for money or other unspecified goods. From the scene that evolved, however, it became clear that no such deal was going to take place. When the armed volunteer unit showed up at the train station, an exchange of gun-fire occurred and the Armenian volunteers were gunned down. The Soviet authorities claimed that their soldiers were attacked and forced to fire in self-defense, but eyewitnesses contradicted those statements.[59] Provocative incidents were beginning to occur and many feared that a showdown was only a matter of time.

THE CREATION OF ARMED VOLUNTEER FORMATIONS

On July 25, Gorbachev decreed that all illegal armed formations must be disbanded and should turn in their arms within fifteen days or be subjected to the full force of the law.[60] This order from Gorbachev was rejected by the leadership of the democratic movement who were put in a precarious position due to the popular appeal and importance of these armed formations.

Beginning in early spring 1988, the Armenians of Armenia and Nagorno-Karabagh began to form armed self-defense groups. This initiative came about as a result of the massacre of Armenians in Sumgait in February. As soon as the Armenians overcame their shock at events, they realized the need to protect themselves and prevent future massacres. The central Soviet authorities had proven themselves unwilling or unable to prevent violence against Armenians and many people felt that the dangerous and bold step of arming themselves was a better alternative to facing death at the hands of the Azerbaijanis. Memories of the Armeno-Tatar clashes of 1905 as well as the numerous massacres associated with the Genocide and World War I began to be resurrected. Unwilling to be victims yet again, Armenians organized for self-defense. In the beginning, these spontaneous groups that sprung up throughout Armenia and Nagorno-Karabagh were unorganized, ill-equipped and poorly trained. The nucleus of these units were the numerous veterans of the Soviet Armed Forces and especially veterans of the fighting in Afghanistan. Although not tied together by any central command structure, they followed a similar pattern of development. A local leader would usually organize between ten and twenty of his friends and acquaintances into a unit. They would undergo rudimentary training before heading off to border regions to protect the civilian population.

For the most part, civilians were not allowed to possess weapons in the Soviet Union with the exception of sport shooting clubs, therefore the main problem that the para-military units encountered was one of gaining possession of arms. Many creative methods were devised, including small weapons factories located in people's basements and buying or stealing weapons from the numerous Soviet troops stationed in Armenia. Very often, there were not enough weapons for every member of the unit and all were preoccupied with trying to figure out how and where to get more guns. The border regions of Armenia and all regions of Nagorno-Karabagh had village-based units which would be responsible for maintaining the security of their village and the surrounding countryside. There was not much coordination between units in this early period. These units traced their origins not to the present situation, but to the turn of the last century, when their ancestors were engaged in a liberation struggle against the Ottoman Empire as well as the tsarist authorities. *Fedayee*,the name that was adopted by the Armenian freedom fighters during the earlier period of struggle, now came to be used by the volunteer fighters as well as society as a collective identifier. Although many of the volunteer fighters at first hesitated to use a name that was considered sacred and associated with much revered heroes, the name became embedded in the popular imagination.[61]

Some scholars believe that there are certain break points in history, at which fundamental change occurs.[62] Previous patterns are fundamentally altered, whether they be behavioral patterns or political patterns. In this sense, the present struggle can be viewed as an historical and psychological break point. For the first time in many centuries, Armenians self-perceptions were changing. No longer satisfied to see themselves as victims of not only oppression but of circumstances and fate itself, they were now undergoing a period of reexamination and reappraisal. It has been observed that Armenians glorify defeat as much as victory.[63] For example, one of the major Armenian holidays commemorates the defeat of Armenian forces led by General Vardan Mamikonean by Persian forces intent on forcing Zoroastrianism on the Armenians. Vardan and most of his troops were slaughtered but the people were allowed to remain Christian. This type of Pyrrhic victory is also seen in "the cult of martyrdom" surrounding the victims of the 1915 Genocide. Although the majority of the inhabitants of Western Armenia were killed as a result of the Genocide, many attempt to portray this catastrophe as a symbolic victory for the faith. For having refused to convert to Islam and renounce both their Christianity and their Armenianness, they can claim some sort of victory over the barbarism of their enemies. The prominence of these events overshadows the commemoration of Armenian victories at the battles of Sardarabad, Karakilise and Bash Abaran, which stopped a Turkish invasion of Eastern Armenia and secured the creation of the first independent Republic of Armenia in May 1918.

Having either been forced by circumstances or by a conscious act of will, the Armenians of Armenia and Karabagh had decided on the path of armed struggle. No longer satisfied to emulate their ancestors, most of whom died without putting up resistance, the Armenians were in 1988 at a psychological crossroads. They perceived the situation as one of choice between submission and resistance. For a complex variety of reasons they chose the latter. When viewed within the context of a historical break point, the Armenian decision not to submit can be seen as the culmination of a historical process. The bitter lessons of the last hundred years had been learned by the Armenians. By the time of the outbreak of the current crisis, it would appear that the digestive process was well advanced.

Having committed themselves to resistance it was now necessary to formulate a strategy which could cope with a radically new situation. Unaccustomed to relying on their own resources, the Armenians found themselves in a predicament. New leaders emerged and argued for a reevaluation of Armenian history, stressing the necessity and ultimate benefits of relying on their own strengths.[64] It was repeatedly pointed out that Armenia found itself in its most serious predicaments precisely when it was forced to rely on outsiders to solve its problems. Old attitudes were hard to change, especially as they had been ingrained over decades of Soviet socialization and propaganda. But as Armenians delved into their past to find relevance for the present, they were constantly reminded that seventy years was merely an episode in a two thousand five hundred year continuum. This phenomenon affected not only the Armenian people, but was one that could be seen throughout the world as countries and peoples came to terms with their own identity in the aftermath of the Cold War. Lacking the unifying ideology of either Marxism or liberal democracy, many actors, both state and non-state, group and subgroup, struggled to define or redefine themselves. As the Armenians came to terms with their new situation, their attitudes towards themselves and others were a key factor in determining the direction in which the country developed. Throughout 1988 and 1989, the volunteer movement grew from a motley crew of disparate and uncoordinated units, each pursuing whatever course it thought best, into a more cohesive and disciplined nucleus of the future professional army. But the road from volunteer militia to professional army would be a long and arduous one. By the summer of 1990, these illegal armed formations had grown into powerful symbols of popular resistance and were viewed by the population as the only real guarantors of Armenian physical inviolability. There was a darker side as well, however, to the mission of national self-defense. As is inevitable in any mass social movement, the volunteer movement was infiltrated by darker elements who used the formation of armed units as a cover for their own criminal activity. Some men took advantage of the new-found status of the fedayee to enrich themselves at the expense of society. Such behavior seriously undermined public confidence and alarmed the local Armenian authorities, who had turned a blind eye to the movement from its inception.

When Gorbachev's decree on disarming all illegal armed formations was made known in Armenia, the newly-elected Parliament dominated by the

Armenian National Movement decided to use the opportunity to reign in the more unsavory elements and regain a certain measure of public safety. The immediate target became the Armenian National Army (ANA), headed by Razmik Vassilyan. The ANA was a mixture of tough, battle-hardened, and dedicated groups as well as adventurers who were creating a threat to public safety. Vassilyan had created a formidable fighting force but his leadership was viewed as erratic and as a threat to the predominance of the Armenian National Movement's armed units. In order to avoid bloodshed, the parliament began negotiations with Vassilyan in order to facilitate the disarming of the ANA. Vassilyan, however, was resistant and resentful, claiming that the sacrifices of the ANA should be rewarded by the creation of a regular Armenian Army, the nucleus of which should be the Armenian National Army, commanded by Vassilyan himself.

The crisis would be resolved only after the country reached the brink of civil war, the details of which will be discussed in the following chapter.

THE DEMOCRATIC MOVEMENT TRIUMPHANT

On August 4, Levon Ter-Petrossyan was elected Chairman of the Parliament. He won on the fourth ballot after defeating Vladimir Movsisyan, the Communist Party First Secretary. Although the coalition led by the Armenian National Movement had won a majority of the seats in the new parliament, they did not have an absolute majority. Defections from the Communist Party enabled Ter-Petrossyan to defeat his communist rival. These CP deputies feared the growing outside interference and polarization in Armenian society and wanted to avoid a civil war at all costs. They believed that only an ANM supported candidate could prevent the breakdown of order and keep Armenia away from the brink of catastrophe. In Ter-Petrossyan's political statement, he in essence presented the platform which the new authorities in parliament would follow. He laid out fourteen steps, which he claimed the other republics were following and giving priority within their own national boundaries. Among the steps were the development of a sovereign economic program; diversity of modes of property ownership; radical revision of obligations formulated with regard to the Union; ensuring the supremacy of the republic's constitution and laws; establishment of direct relations with foreign countries; creation of Armenia's own military and security forces; separation of executive, legislative, and judiciary powers; de-politicization of state institutions; and the establishment of a multi-party system and of full democratic freedom.

Although Ter-Petrossyan said that the above was not a political platform but more of a statement, it was nonetheless a clear signal that Armenia intended to follow the path of democracy and independence. The very thought of an independent Armenia just a few years previous would have been considered an unattainable dream, but events were moving quickly and those in the leadership of the ANM did not want to be caught as unprepared for independence as their predecessors in 1918. On August 23, the Parliament made a declaration of independence. This was not a declaration of full and complete independence as it was still premature to contemplate total separation from the USSR, but realizing that the days of the Soviet Empire were numbered, a long-term strategic plan was necessary to ensure the viability of Armenia. The declaration read, in part, that Armenia was starting the process of the establishment of independent statehood and that the Armenian SSR was renamed the Armenian Republic, with its own flag, emblem, and anthem. The Armenian Republic was a sovereign state vested with the supremacy of state power, independence, and authority and that only the Armenian Republic's Constitution and laws were in force in the entire territory of the Armenian Republic. In addition, citizenship in the Armenian Republic was conferred upon all citizens living in the territory of the Armenian Republic. Diaspora Armenians had the right to citizenship in the Armenian Republic. The Armenian Republic would establish its own armed forces, internal troops, and state and public security bodies subordinate to the Supreme Soviet to ensure its security and the inviolability of its borders and that the Armenian Republic has a right to its share of the USSR armaments and would itself decide the status of military service of its citizens. According to the declaration, army units and military bases and facilities of other countries could only be deployed or established on the Armenian Republic's territory through the decision of its Supreme Soviet, and the armed forces of the Armenian Republic could only be employed through the decision of Armenian Supreme Soviet. Armenia also asserted that, as an independent entity subject to international law, the Armenian Republic would conduct its own independent foreign policy and that all the resources of the republic were the property of its people. Furthermore, the Armenian Republic had the right to its share of the USSR's national wealth and would decide upon its economic management principles and status on the basis of diverse forms of ownership.[65]

Finally, the declaration stated that the Armenian Republic ensured freedom of speech, press, and conscience, and would establish a separation of legislative, executive, and judicial powers; a multiparty system and the equality of political parties; and the de-politicization of the security bodies and of the armed forces. In a bold and confident statement, the declaration proclaimed that the Armenian Republic would support efforts to bring about the international recognition of the Armenian Genocide.[66] Thus, the Armenian

Soviet Socialist Republic ended and the Republic of Armenia began. The great hopes and aspirations with which the republic was born were soon to be frustrated by the reality of the continuing conflict over Nagorno-Karabagh as well as the precarious and inherently contradictory nature of an Armenian Republic as part of the USSR. The years ahead would be filled with hardship and suffering, but for the time being the people of Armenia were given the opportunity to believe that with independence a new and better era would replace the bitterness of recent Armenian historical experience.

1   Lowell Tillet, *The Great Friendship: Soviet Historians on the Non-Russian Nationalities* (Chapel Hill, NC: University of North Carolina Press, 1969).
2   On the environmental problems in Armenia, see Armen Valesyan, "Armenia," in Philip Pryde, ed., *Environmental Resources and Constraints in the Former Soviet Republics* (Boulder, CO: Westview Press, 1995), pp. 221–234.
3   On the connection between environmentalism and nationalism, see Jane Dawson, *Eco-Nationalism: Anti-Nuclear Activism and National Identity in Russia, Lithuania, and Ukraine* (Durham, NC: Duke University Press, 1996).
4   Levon Avdoyan, Nagorno-Karabagh: An Historical Perspective," *International Journal on Group Rights* 3: 161–167, 1995.
5   Gerard Libaridian, ed. *The Karabagh File* (Cambridge, MA: Zoryan Institute, 1988), pp. 3–31.
6   Ibid, p. 34.
7   Ibid, p. 36.
8   On the Kurdish autonomous region, see Robert Krikorian, "Red Kurdistan and the Struggle for Nagorno-Karabagh," *Journal of the Society for Armenian Studies*, 6, 1992,1993, pp. 61–81.
9   Otto Luchterhandt, *Nagorny Karabagh's Right to State Independence According to International Law* (Boston, MA: Baikar Association, 1993), pp. 57–68.
10 Libaridian, *Karabagh File*, pp. 42–52.
11 For details on Heidar Aliyev, see Elizabeth Fuller, "Azerbaijan: Geidar Aliev's Political Comeback," *RFE/RL Research Report*, Vol. 2, No. 5, 29 January 1993.
12 Suny, *Looking toward Ararat*, p. 197.
13 Charles Furtado and Andrea Chandler, eds., *Perestroika in the Soviet Republics: Documents on the National Question* (Boulder, CO: Westview Press, 1992, p. 593.
14 Furtado and Chandler, *Perestroika*, p. 596.
15 Fiona Hill, *Report on Ethnic Conflict in the Russian Federation and Transcaucasia, July 1993* (Cambridge, MA: Harvard University John F. Kennedy School of Government, 1993), p. 71.
16 Furtado and Chandler, *Perestroika*, p. 596.
17 Mark Malkasian, *"Gha-ra-bagh!" The Emergence of the National Democratic Movement in Armenia* (Detroit, MI: Wayne State University Press, 1996, p.1.
18 Press Release, Zoryan Institute for Contemporary Armenian Research and Documentation, Cambridge, MA, 1989.
19 Nora Dudwick, "Armenia: Paradise Lost?," in Ian Bremmer and Ray Taras, eds. *New States, New Politics: Building the Post-Soviet Nations* (London: Cambridge University Press, 1997), p. 485.
20 Samvel Shahmuratian, ed., *The Sumgait Tragedy: Pogroms Against Armenians in Soviet Azerbaijan* (New Rochelle, NY/Cambridge, MA: Caratzas Publishers/Zoryan Institute, 1990), pp. 3–5.
21 Ibid.
22 For the most comprehensive account of the Sumgait massacre, see Shahmuratian, *Sumgait Tragedy*, which is a compilation of eyewitness accounts from survivors.
23 See Igor Nolyain, "Moscow"s Initiation of the Azeri-Armenian Conflict," *Central Asia Survey* (1994), 13 (4), pp. 541–563.
24 Furtado and Chandler, *Perestroika*, p. 597.
25 Ibid.

26 Ibid.

27 Krikorian, "Pariur Hairikyan," p. 12.

28 Furtado and Chandler, *Perestroika*, p. 599.

29 *Constitution (Fundamental Law) of the Union of Soviet Socialist Republics* (Moscow: Novosti Press Agency Publishing House, 1988), p. 29.

30 Furtado and Chandler, *Perestroika*, p. 601.

31 Ibid.

32 Ibid, p. 602.

33 Ibid.

34 Suny, *Looking Toward Ararat*, p. 188.

35 Furtado and Chandler, *Perestroika*, p. 605.

36 Ibid.

37 Ibid, p. 607.

38 Gerard Libaridian, ed., *Armenia at the Crossroads: Democracy and Nationhood in the Post-Soviet Era* (Watertown, MA: Blue Crane Books, 1991), pp. 127–129.

39 Nora Dudwick, "Armenia: The Nation Awakens," in Ian Bremmer and Ray Taras, eds., *Nations and Politics in the Soviet Successor States* (London: Cambridge University Press, 1993), p. 277.

40 Furtado and Chandler, *Perestroika*, p. 610.

41 Ibid.

42 Pierre Verluise, *Armenia in Crisis: The 1988 Earthquake* (Detroit, MI: Wayne State University Press, 1995), p. 31–32.

43 Ibid, p. 56.

44 Based on personal observations of Robert Krikorian, December 1988.

45 Furtado and Chandler, *Perestroika*, p. 612.

46 Press Release, Zoryan Institute, 1989.

47 Furtado and Chandler, *Perestroika*, p. 614.

48 Hill, *Report on Ethnic Conflict*, p. 71.

49 Furtado and Chandler, *Perestroika*, ibid.

50 Ibid, p. 619.

51 *Soviet Events of 1989 and 1990 as reported by the Express Chronicle* (New York: Center for Democracy in the USSR, 1991), p. 26.

52 Ibid.

53 Ibid, p. 27.

54 Hill, *Report on Ethnic Conflict*, p. 72.

55 For details of developments in Azerbaijan, see Tadeusz Swietochowski, *Russia and Azerbaijan: A Borderland in Transition* (New York: Columbia University Press, 1995), pp. 193–224.

56 For details regarding the January events in Baku, see Human Rights Watch/Helsinki, *Conflict in the Soviet Union: Black January in Azerbaijan* (New York, 1991).

57 Libaridian, *Armenia at the Crossroads*, pp. 47–50.

58 Furtado and Chandler, *Perestroika*, p. 630.

59 Robert Krikorian was present in Yerevan at the time of the incident and interviewed numerous eye-witnesses.

60 Ibid, p. 633.

61 For details on the formation of armed units, see Robert Krikorian, "From Swords to Plowshares...To Swords: The Recreation of Armenian Martial Identity," *The Annual of the Society for the Study of Caucasia*, Vol. 6–7, 1994–1996, pp. 23–38.

62 James Rosenau, *Turbulence in World Politics: A Theory of Change and Continuity* (Princeton, NJ: Princeton University Press, 1990), pp. 72–73.

63 See Khachig Tololyan, "Martyrdom as Legitimacy: Terrorism, Religion, and Symbolic Appropriation in the Armenian Diaspora," in Paul Wilkinson and Alasdair Stewart, eds., *Contemporary Research on Terrorism* (Aberdeen: Aberdeen University Press, 1987), pp. 89–103.

64 See Libaridian, *Armenia at the Crossroads*, for details.

65 Furtado and Chandler, *Perestroika*, pp.441–443.

66 Ibid.

Chapter 2

THE REEMERGENCE OF THE INDEPENDENT REPUBLIC OF ARMENIA

The new Armenian Supreme Soviet did not have any time to savor its democratic victory. Events in Armenia were moving too quickly. But had the newly elected parliament been able to assess the events of the last two and a half years, they would have had much to be proud of. Indeed, few would have imagined in February 1988 that the Communists would be defeated in Armenia at the ballot box. Accustomed as they were to unanimous voting for pre-approved candidates, most Soviet citizens would have scoffed at the mere mention of challenging the Communist monopoly of power. But that was what happened in Armenia. When the democratic movement began, few of the popular leaders had thought out any long-term strategy. In those heady days, Armenians quickly discovered hidden talents and strengths that few believed still existed in the Soviet Union. The loss of one generation of intellectuals in the Genocide and another during Stalin's purges had struck a blow at creativity and innovation. Up until this point, it appeared to outsiders, as well as many within the republic, that most Armenians had reconciled themselves to the notion that it was their inescapable destiny to be ruled by others.[1] But then something happened. When the first demonstrations took place and were not dispersed by force, the people discovered the power of collective action. The self-confidence and exhilaration that came about as a result was very significant. People began to think about the possibility of determining their own fate, if only to a limited degree.

THE TENTATIVE EMERGENCE OF CIVIL SOCIETY AND CONTINUING CRISES

During this early period, conversations turned constantly to political subjects. The cafes and squares were crowded with people discussing the latest political news. Newspapers sprung up everywhere and people waited in line at the kiosks to get the latest issues. The limits of debate were pushed to the maximum as a sense of urgency and immediacy pervaded public discourse. The experience of these first years was intoxicating and there was hope and optimism in the air. Of course numerous problems persisted. Many Armenians realized that the struggle for self-determination in Karabagh would a long and bitter one, but there seemed to be a consensus that it was a cause worth fighting no matter how high the costs. And within a short period of time the costs would mount dramatically. But the psychological barrier of reliance on "the third force," that is outside powers, had been broken for Armenia.[2] Its people were no longer content to trust its fate to others. The presence of history was all around and no one could fail to make the connection between past and present.[3] From the Genocide Memorial to the battlefield memorial at Sardarabad, the lesson was the same: those who were prepared to fight for what they believed in would be worthy to sit at the negotiating table as equals.

On August 29, the parliament declared emergency rule throughout the country as a result of the escalating crisis between the Armenian National Army (ANA) and the authorities. On that night an ANA unit attacked a Yerevan gas station which was being guarded by a unit of the Armenian National Movement, which was under the control of the Parliament. In the ensuing clash three ANM soldiers were wounded. A deputy of the Parliament along with a prominent fedayee commander went to ANA headquarters the next day in order to diffuse the crisis. For some unknown reason they were fired upon and killed. In connection with this incident, it was reported that ANA units opened fire simultaneously in various parts of Yerevan. These irresponsible and provocative acts prompted the Armenian Parliament to unanimously adopt a decree instituting a state of emergency and establishing a curfew. The Armenian National Army was also outlawed and its members were called upon to turn in their weapons or face prosecution.[4]

The next day the leaders of the Armenian National Army declared on national television that their supporters would comply with the decree and agreed to disband the ANA. This crisis came very close to unleashing a civil war in Armenia. The Armenians came to the brink of armed conflict and at the eleventh hour avoided what would have been a disaster for the country. The ANA had not wanted to subordinate itself to the legitimate elected authorities of the republic and had attempted to act with impunity. All other armed militia units operating on the territory of Armenia had agreed to subject themselves to the authority of the elected parliament with the exception of the Armenian National Army. With this crisis diffused, the authorities were able to gain a significant measure of control over the activities of the armed formations defending the borders of Armenia as well as operating in and around Nagorno-Karabagh. Most members of armed units and their leaders recognized the importance of coordination and governmental control and thus did not resist the authorities' attempts to nationalize the volunteer militias.

Following the victory of democratic forces within the republic, an uneasy truce developed between the central authorities in Moscow and the nationalist government in Armenia. Although the central authorities would have preferred to crack down on the democratic forces in Yerevan, they were constrained in their options. Unlike previous eras where the use of force and terror were standard operating procedure in the Soviet Union, Gorbachev's advent to power had changed both the internal and external environment. Although he was able to have the members of the Karabagh Committee arrested in the aftermath of the earthquake, he nonetheless was unable to hold them indefinitely or charge them formally. By 1990, Soviet-style democratic politics had developed in Armenia to the extent that the nationalist forces enjoyed the confidence of the people and to dislodge those forces would run the risk of alienating not only the Armenians, but other peoples such as the Balts who had also quickly developed alternatives to Communist authoritarianism. In order to maintain some sort of control more circumspect methods needed to be employed. Normally the republican Communist Party could be counted on to serve the interests of Moscow, but in the volatile atmosphere of the Transcaucasus even the Armenian Communist Party had taken a turn towards nationalism and there were no real forces calling for a more loyal Communist Party in Armenia. It seemed that even the Communists had come to realize the hopelessness of their situation and decided to work with the democratic forces in the republic in order to retain some influence.[5] Thus being deprived of an internal mechanism for pressuring the Armenian authorities, it was decided that forces outside the republic would have to be brought to bear. In this case, the central authorities in Moscow used Azerbaijan and the conflict over Nagorno-Karabagh to keep the new Armenian government off-balance. With Baku in the firm grip of the Communists, Gorbachev was able to play one side off against the other until a strategy to cope with the crisis could be developed. Any meaningful strategy, however, never really developed and up until the end of the Soviet Union, Gorbachev vacillated and wavered and thus increased the alienation of both sides. There was one issue upon which both the Armenians and the Azerbaijanis could agree: the manipulation of the tensions between the two republics by Moscow.[6]

OBSTACLES TO FORGING A DEMOCRATIC STATE

An important asset for Armenia in its development of democratic institutions of governance was its diaspora. Since the first demonstrations in February 1988, Armenians around the world fixed their attention on Armenia and Karabagh. Unable to make any meaningful contribution to the development of democracy in Armenia, Armenians abroad took advantage of the opening provided by the tragedy of the earthquake and began to render Armenia assistance in numerous spheres. Several diaspora Armenian organizations set up field offices in Armenia following the earthquake and through them information was passed in and out of the country with regularity. Either unable or unwilling to stop such flows of information, the authorities in Moscow in essence acquiesced. By 1990, regular shipments of humanitarian aid were being delivered to Armenia in order to mitigate both the impact of the earthquake and the effects of the conflict over Nagorno-Karabagh. In addition to humanitarian aid, diaspora Armenians sent non-lethal supplies to aid in the war-effort such as surplus uniforms and boots. Literature on democratic governance also made its way into the country. Many Armenians abroad were willing to lend their expertise to the newly-created parliament and soon advisors were finding their way into the republic.

Throughout fall 1990, internal and external problems persisted for Armenia. Externally, an intermittent economic blockade imposed by Azerbaijan paralyzed the Armenian economy. With negligible fuel supplies making it into the republic, many enterprises were working at much reduced capacity while the airport was frequently inoperable due to lack of fuel. Many homes used natural gas as their primary means of energy and as a result of the blockade poverty-stricken areas were particularly hard-hit.[7] Added to this economic blockade was the chaos that resulted from frequent disruptions of harvesting and stealing of livestock by Azerbaijani raiding parties that took place along the Armenian-Azerbaijani border. Constant shelling of Armenian border villages was further destabilizing an already fragile situation. There were numerous reports of Soviet MVD and Army troops participating in these assaults on the side of the Azerbaijanis.[8] It was clear to the Armenians that such tactics were intended to intimidate and terrorize them and force them to abandon the struggle for Nagorno-Karabagh. These clashes "reflected Moscow's determination to reinforce its control over Azerbaijan and to frustrate Armenian moves toward full independence."[9] According to one informed source, "a decision had already been taken, evidently at the level of the USSR Security Council, to proceed with operations specifically designed to attain these complementary goals."[10]

Taken together, these internal and external threats delayed, but could not prevent, the process of developing democratic structures in Armenia. The democratic forces in Armenia realized that in order to maintain peace and stability internally, they would have to consolidate their gains and demonstrate to the people that the democratic movement was worthy of their trust. As the democratic movement gained momentum throughout 1990, the Armenian Communist Party was becoming increasingly isolated and irrelevant. Its inability to solve the Nagorno-Karabagh conflict and institutionalized corruption had tarnished the image of the Communist Party beyond repair. Their ability to influence the central authorities or even intercede on behalf of the people of Armenia and Karabagh was negligible. It had become painfully obvious that few people still supported the Communists and even fewer people had any confidence in their ability to solve the numerous problems of the republic. Unlike many of the other republican Communist Parties, the Armenian Communist Party did not have large numbers of Russians in their ranks who could reach out to the center for support, such as in Ukraine or the Baltic states. This relative homogeneity of the party, as indeed of the country as a whole, denied the authorities in Moscow a critical lever with which to manipulate the course of events. In an obvious attempt to arrest their declining importance in Armenia, the Central Committee of the Armenian Communist Party appointed S. Poghosyan to replace V. Movsisyan as First Secretary of the Communist Party. All these maneuvers would be in vain for the initiative had gradually but inexorably slipped away from the Communists and no amount of cadre replacement could make up for their past behavior.

By the end of 1990, democracy had made considerable progress in Armenia. Throughout the autumn, various legislation was passed, including the legalization of private property and a resolution to depoliticize state institutions, factories, educational institutions and military units. The winter of 1990 saw the adoption of legislation on agricultural communes and privatized farming as well as on the principles of privatization. Another important step in the transition to democracy was the decision to adopt legislation on political parties, establishing a multi-party system in Armenia. Not only had the Communist Party been removed from power through the ballot box, but the country pulled back from the brink of civil war and began the slow and deliberate process of reform and democratization. Political pluralism was a hallmark of the growth of democracy in Armenia. In addition to the Armenian Communist Party and the Armenian National Movement, which grew out of the Karabagh Committee, also active in Armenian politics were the Christian Democratic Union (CDU); the Republican Party, led by the former dissident Ashot Navasardyan; the Union of Constitutional Rights, a nationalist party which opposed the Karabagh Movement; and the Union for National Self-Determination, led by Pariur Hairikyan. To this heterogeneous group must be added small but active groups of members of political parties based in the diaspora, such as the Armenian Revolutionary Federation (ARF); the Social Democratic Hunchakian Party and the Democratic Liberal Party (Ramyavar).[11]

Political pluralism was evidenced by healthy yet heated debate about issues that had never been discussed in Armenia previously, such as national defense, economic reform, freedom of the press and religious rights, etc. One of the bulwarks of the new democracy was the flourishing of the independent press. Numerous dailies, weeklies and other periodicals began to appear in the kiosks throughout the country. With a rich literary and journalistic tradition from which to draw, Armenians quickly took advantage of the new freedoms regarding the press. The most significant problems that they encountered were the chronic shortage of electricity, paper and ink due to the disruption of supplies because of the Nagorno-Karabagh conflict. These newspapers and periodicals acted as guardians against abuses, governmental and otherwise, as well as a mouthpiece for every conceivable political conviction. In this early period there was a healthy respect for the power of the printed word. Previously forbidden subjects were broached and intense debates which emanated from the mass media outlets began to circulate within the larger society. In the official paper of the Armenian Writers' Union, *Hai Grogh*, there began to appear articles about previously controversial subjects such as the suspicious car accident in the 1970s that took the life of the beloved writer Pariur Sevak. Of equal significance for the process of reclaiming the past, were numerous articles and books dealing with the years of Stalinist oppression. Among the favorite topics at the time was the life and work of the famed poet Eghishe Charents, who lost his life at a young age during the Great Purges of the 1930s.[12]

As 1991 began, although the conflict over Nagorno-Karabagh still continued, there was reason for optimism as Armenia began to develop as a pluralistic and democratic society, albeit within the confines of the Soviet Union. The vulnerability of the new Armenian democracy was emphasized in January, as Soviet troops cracked down in Lithuania where they attempted to stage a coup in order to overthrow the democratically elected government. This bold move served as a violent wake-up call for democratic forces throughout the Soviet Union. The possibility that the new democratically elected leaders would end up either in jail or up against a firing-squad was becoming increasingly likely.

ARMENIA OPTS OUT OF THE USSR

In March, an All-Union referendum took place in nine of the republics of the USSR which was designed to preserve the USSR. Armenia boycotted the referendum and instead determined that it would hold its own referendum on September 21, 1991. On the day after the All-Union referendum, a public opinion poll was conducted in Armenia which indicated approximately 80% of the population of Armenia supported secession from the USSR.[13] This defiance of Moscow did not go unnoticed. Soviet special purpose troops (OMON), also known as "black berets", had been dispatched to the region at the start of the conflict over Nagorno-Karabagh. Their mission in Nagorno-Karabagh was

> to bully Armenians into leaving the area for Armenia. During winter and spring 1990–1991 the black berets engaged in continuous acts of harassment against Armenian villages in the enclave, including raids on collective farms and the destruction of various communal facilities. Their purpose was to break the Armenian population's spirit and to encourage them to leave the area or, at least, abandon any hope that NKAO would ever be ceded to the Armenians.[14]

In April, Azerbaijani OMON attacks on Armenian villages increased and Armenian units responded to these provocations. In this atmosphere of increased hostility, "Operation Ring" was conceived and carried out by the central authorities and the Azerbaijani Communist Party leadership. The goals of the operation were the deportation of Armenians living in villages in Azerbaijan adjacent to the Armenian–Azerbaijani border, the elimination of the threat of attacks from Armenia in a five-kilometer strip along the border which would be controlled by Soviet armed forces, and the expulsion of Armenians from Karabagh, especially targeting those most strongly advocating for self-determination.[15] A combined operation of Soviet and Azerbaijani forces first struck in the Getashen district of the Khanlar region northwest of Nagorno-Karabagh. Unfortunately for the Armenian villagers, they had decided to ignore an earlier order to abandon their villages and seek refuge in Armenia.

MVD troops backed up by Soviet Army tanks and armored personnel carriers encircled the villages and then went about systematically deporting the inhabitants. Although resistance was put up by the local Armenian self-defense units, they were outgunned. One by one, the villages of the region were emptied of their Armenian inhabitants. This collusion between the central authorities and the Azerbaijanis was a bitter blow to the Armenians. Up until this point they had still held out some slight hope that Moscow could still see itself clear to act as an honest broker in the conflict between Karabagh and Azerbaijan. They realized that this was an increasingly remote possibility as long as Azerbaijan retained a Communist leadership and Armenia did not. Even this slight hope was dashed as news of "Operation Ring" reached Armenia. The government and people of Armenia realized that from now on they would be fighting two enemies simultaneously, Azerbaijan and the reactionary forces of the center.

Throughout the summer, the forces of reaction were strengthening their hand in Moscow and this could only bode ill for all democratic forces in the

Soviet Union. There was a sense in Armenia that sooner or later the pressure would be stepped up to such an extent that a showdown would take place in Moscow that would have repercussions in the Transcaucasus. In August, a coup attempt by conservative elements in the Party and state apparatus against Gorbachev was launched while he was away vacationing in the Crimea. Ostensibly it was timed so as to prevent Gorbachev from signing a new agreement regulating relations between the center and the republics and would have resulted in far more autonomy and independence for the republics. This was considered to be going too far by the coup plotters and in their view threatened the very foundations of the USSR.

Levon Ter-Petrossyan immediately denounced the coup and threw his support behind the democratic forces then emerging under the leadership of Boris Yeltsin, President of the Russian Federation. The entire nation was transfixed on events in Moscow, for Armenia knew that its fate would be decided there and not in Yerevan. If the coup had succeeded, it would have only been a matter of time before "law and order" were restored in Armenia and Karabagh on the points of Soviet Army bayonets and the democratic experiment would end in disaster. The volunteer militia units were especially concerned because the coup leaders had announced that all illegal armed formations would have to be disarmed. If this were to happen, then the civilian populations of both Armenia and Karabagh would be left to the mercy of the Azerbaijani and Soviet security forces. Units serving in the field at the time gathered around their radios to listen to the latest news from Moscow. In at least one instance, the commander of a unit serving on the Armenian-Azerbaijani border gathered his troops together to explain the situation and to solicit their opinions as to what the best course of action would be. Before he could even finish, the entire unit pledged their fidelity to the cause of Armenia and Karabagh and would only be parted from their weapons by death.

The coup collapsed within days. The armed forces refused to fire upon the people and either stayed in their barracks or went over to the side of the democratic opposition. With the end of the coup came the end of the Soviet Union. In early September, all Communist Party property in Armenia was nationalized thus further weakening the already-crippled party. In the aftermath of the coup and the ultimate discrediting of both the idea of preserving the USSR and the Communist Party the results of the upcoming referendum were a foregone conclusion. On September 21, 1991, 95% of the eligible population of Armenia turned out to vote and an overwhelming 99% voted in favor of secession from the Union of Soviet Socialist Republics.[16] Two days later the Parliament of the Republic of Armenia made a declaration of independence. It was now official; the Republic of Armenia, after several years of delicately trying to balance the interests of the center with those of its citizens, now unequivocally chose the path of independence and left the USSR behind.

THE BURDENS OF STATE-BUILDING

Within weeks of the declaration of independence, presidential elections took place in Armenia, with the chairman of the Parliament, Levon Ter-Petrossyan being elected with 84% of the vote.[17] Other prominent candidates such as the writer and activist Zori Balayan; Sos Sarkisyan, an actor and the candidate of the Armenian Revolutionary Federation; and Pariur Hairikyan, leader of the Self-Determination Union and long-time Soviet era dissident also ran but received little support. In the first flush of independence, most people took it for granted that the organization which was largely responsible for bringing Armenia its independence, the Armenian National Movement (ANM) would also lead its first independent government. This popular mandate would be necessary to shepherd Armenia through the difficult path of establishing an independent and democratic state with a free market economy. The tasks that faced the new government were overwhelming. The Communist-era infrastructure had been seriously damaged by the on-going conflict with Azerbaijan and the latter's blockade of most imports and energy supplies. Now that independence had come to the republics of the Transcaucasus, a new dynamic was at work, one which necessitated relations between sovereign states.

The government inherited Communist-era governmental structures and ministries as well as a well-educated population. It was to be expected that Armenian National Movement supporters would be appointed to all key positions but the difficult part would be deciding which old cadres should be kept in place and which should be removed. This was a problem in the republic because most of the trained cadres were associated with the Communist Party and to remove them all at once would have a disastrous effect upon the functioning of enterprises and ministries. A compromise would have to be sought between the new ruling elite and the old elite. In the early days, efficiency was compromised for the sake of political loyalty as the new government first and foremost sought to install people whose commitment to the new regime would be unquestioned. Gradually, however, these ideologically driven policies would have to give way in the face of the shear enormity of running an entire country. In this experiment with democracy, Armenia chose a presidential system of government, with the President being elected by direct popular vote. Presidential powers included the appointment of the Vice-President and Prime Minister, the latter being subject to parliamentary approval. In addition, there was a national security council, which comprised the President, Vice-President, Prime Minister, Defense Minister, and Interior Minister. The President was responsible for the formulation of policy whereas the Prime Minister was in charge of the daily operations of government and directly answerable to the chief executive. The Prime Minister also reported to Parliament and presided over the Council of Ministers, which was comprised of the Prime Minister and the heads of regular ministries. The members of the Council were appointed by a joint decision of the President and Prime Minister, who were then to be approved by Parliament.[18]

The highest levels of the new leadership of the Republic of Armenia had not, for the most part, been tainted by association with the old Communist regime. Many of the new leaders in fact had been active in the opposition, and more than a few had been arrested during the Communist regime. The group of leaders responsible for creating a viable Armenian democratic state was well-educated and seemingly up to the task. The President of the Republic, Levon Ter-Petrossyan, was born in Aleppo, Syria in 1945. His father was one of the founders of the United Communist Party of Syria and Lebanon and decided to repatriate to Soviet Armenia in 1946. Ter-Petrossyan graduated from Yerevan State University as an Orientalist and philologist and worked at the Institute of Literature at the Armenian Academy of Sciences as well as being the Scientific Secretary of the Manuscript Library (Matenadaran).[19] Ter Petrossyan's choice for vice president was economist Gagik Harutyunyan. Harutyunyan had been a professor of economics as well as having worked as an economist for the Armenian Communist Party since 1982. He was widely travelled and had studied market economics in the West.[20] In November 1991, he was appointed prime minister after the resignation of Vazgen Manukyan.

The legislative branch was represented by a single-chamber parliament, with deputies elected by district. The Parliament was elected in 1990, and although the Armenian National Movement won a majority, there were also independent candidates and representatives of the other political parties as well. The Parliament was to convene sessions twice a year in the spring (early February to late June) and fall (late September to late December). Extraordinary sessions could be convened at the discretion of the Parliament's Presidium, a third of the parliamentarians, the Chairman of the Parliament, or the President. The parliament, which consisted of 259 deputies, was the scene of both lively debate and increasing conflict.[21] The Parliament had more than a dozen registered blocs of political factions, parties and independents. There were also 120 members of the parliament who were officially independent, but were mostly the remnants of the Armenian Communist Party, which had been legalized. Armenia was one of the few republics of the former Soviet Union not to have banned the Communist Party, but most members were not yet prepared to declare their affiliation openly. One of the most pressing concerns in Armenia was the lack of a constitution and it was feared that without clearly defined and delimited powers, conflict would be inevitable. Although society in general was pro-reform and in large measure had approved the changes that had occurred thus far, their morale was being drained by the on-going conflict with Azerbaijan and the blockade, and this situation was being exacerbated by increasing conflict between the executive and legislative branches.

In this early period, special emphasis was put on the development of the judicial branch of government with the intent that the rule of law could be quickly established and many of the abuses of the previous regime could be avoided. Accordingly, two types of courts were envisioned: district courts and the Supreme Court. Both courts were to have jurisdiction over criminal and civil cases, whereas the Supreme Court was intended to make final decisions on appeals and exercise general legal control over the district courts. It was also intended to give the Supreme Court a higher profile in the judicial system and therefore it was to have original jurisdiction over complex and important civil and criminal cases. Special courts for the arbitration of commercial disputes involving state enterprises were also established.[22] The area of human rights was to be protected by the judicial branch as well.

The new government not only had to learn to govern the country but it also now became necessary to establish relations with foreign countries as well as its diaspora. The foreign relations of Armenia will be discussed in greater detail in Chapter Four, so let it suffice here by briefly discussing the relationship between the Republic of Armenia and the diaspora at the onset of independence. As previously mentioned, the diaspora had been intimately involved with Armenia since the earthquake of December 1988, when Armenia had been part of the Soviet Union. The onset of independence caught the diaspora off-guard in many respects. Never dealing with an independent Armenia, diaspora Armenians in their enthusiasm thought that they would be welcomed unreservedly and with open arms. Although diaspora Armenians had been guaranteed the right to citizenship in the parliamentary declaration on independence, no mechanisms existed to implement this right and indeed many in Armenia doubted the wisdom of granting full citizenship to people who were not living in the republic and in fact had never lived in Armenia.

Would these overseas Armenians be allowed to run for office, would they be obligated to serve in the military, would they be allowed to buy property which would most likely remain vacant and unoccupied for the majority of the year only to be used for a few weeks or months during the summer? These and other questions needed to be answered before any decisions were taken on the matter of who was eligible for Armenian citizenship and who was not. On an emotional and abstract level the people of Armenia were devoted to the idea of one Armenian nation and one Armenian people no matter where Armenians lived, but on a practical level concerns were raised about what was the proper role for these expatriates.

Whatever suspicions and concerns existed in the minds of the people of Armenia, diaspora attitudes and actions did little to ameliorate the situation. From the outset, one must be very cautious when talking about the diaspora as if it were a united entity. Diaspora communities in such disparate places as Beirut, Tehran, Paris, Buenos Aires or Los Angeles had little in common with each other let alone a country that most had never seen and in fact had been separated from for many generations. Many Armenians abroad no longer spoke Armenian and had integrated and assimilated into their host societies. This diversity was compounded by ideological splits in the diaspora mostly revolving around attitudes towards and acceptance of Communist rule in Armenia. Not only were communities ideologically divided on the issue of Soviet Armenia, these divisions and controversies even permeated the Armenian Apostolic Church and resulted in parallel churches and community structures throughout much of the diaspora. Cold War politics played a very large role in exacerbating these controversies and keeping old wounds from healing. Although the animosity between competing factions was more muted among the younger generation, the older generation still clung to their ideological blinders.

In a move widely hailed among certain circles in the diaspora, President Levon Ter-Petrossyan appointed a diaspora Armenian as the first foreign minister of the republic. In November 1991, he announced the appointment of Raffi Hovannisian to the post of foreign minister. A lawyer by training, Hovannisian had worked in Armenia for several years as the representative of a diaspora organization. Many saw the appointment as a signal that the diaspora would play a pivotal role in the political, social, economic and cultural life of the republic, while others saw it as an indication that Armenia's foreign policy priorities would be oriented toward the West. Hovannisian was not the only diaspora to be appointed. In addition, energy specialist Sebouh (Steve) Tashjian, a Jerusalem-born Armenian from California was appointed State Minister of Energy and Fuel and was given major responsibility for helping Armenia survive the almost total blockade that was strangling the country. Also, Gerard (Jirair) Libaridian, a Lebanese-born historian who ran an institute for contemporary Armenian Studies in Boston, and had been active in helping Parliament was appointed as a presidential advisor.

On the domestic front, the new government had a host of serious issues to confront. Organizing opposition to Communism was far different than actually being responsible for the well-being of the entire country. Armenia's new rulers were hardly alone in their lack of administrative expertise. As in the case of all the other former Soviet republics, administrative expertise was in the hands of trained bureaucrats, the overwhelming majority of whom were either members of the Communist Party or somehow affiliated with it. The task now was to prepare new cadres for the myriad responsibilities associated with effectively governing the republic. The immediate tasks were so pressing that few members of the elite had the time or the energy to devise any long-term strategy for the transition away from Communism and towards a democratic republic with a free and open market. The day-to-day operations of the government absorbed the energy, attention and resources of the government. A tremendous amount of effort would be required to build the kind of civil society that everyone in the republic at least paid lip service to. With little or no long-term democratic tradition to draw upon, the leadership of Armenia was largely unprepared for the challenges facing them

STABILITY AT ALL COSTS

Although the Republic of Armenia was born with high hopes and expectations, the reality of life as an independent country at war and surrounded by neighbors either hostile or in chaos was enough to make the government of Armenia reassess its priorities. Survival became the overriding priority of the new government. Governing would be a great responsibility for any group of leaders but in the case of Armenia, the responsibility was further increased by the burden of history and the psychological pressure of knowing that the price of failure would be catastrophic for the entire nation. Bearing in mind the historical legacy of oppression, deportation and genocide that the Armenian people had suffered, it was not surprising that the survival of the republic had to take precedence over other issues. Learning from the past, the Armenian leadership determined that stability was the highest priority for the country and that no forces, either internally nor externally would be allowed to threaten the integrity of the state.

The need for stability was justified by the government on the grounds that all resources had to be harnessed for the conflict over Nagorno-Karabagh and internal discord could have disastrous effects not only on Armenia but on Karabagh as well.[23] The experiences of other republics, such as Georgia which was being torn apart by civil and ethnic strife, was a stark reminder of the dangers present in the post-Soviet era. In order to obtain the needed internal stability, the enforcement of law and order was essential. The problem was which laws and whose order should be enforced. The process of legal, political, social and economic reform was far from complete and there was considerable confusion regarding what laws were in force and who was responsible for their enforcement. One of the main concerns of the government was the control of organized crime. Armenian criminal organizations had always been a presence on the Soviet scene and with the implosion of the USSR, the field of opportunity broadened considerably throughout its former territory. Numerous gangs infiltrated the Armenian economy and took over entire sectors such as gasoline and consumer goods. Under the conditions of blockade and severe economic hardship, the "mafia," as all criminal organizations were called in the Soviet and post-Soviet era, was becoming extremely powerful. Within a short period of time, the mafia was also able to infiltrate the government and allegations of high level corruption became rampant. In order to control the spread of mafia influence, the government determined that a strong hand was necessary, and President Ter-Petrossyan appointed Vano Siradeghyan, an old colleague from his days in the Karabagh Committee, to head the Ministry of Internal Affairs which would be responsible for the enforcement of law and order in the republic.

In addition to the economic crimes committed by the mafia, the streets were no longer safe as rival groups battled for control of turf. Murders, bombings and drive-by shootings were not uncommon. In addition, there were plentiful supplies of arms because of the war in Karabagh, and these were frequently being used against fellow Armenian citizens. Soon the Ministry of the Interior and its head Vano Siradeghyan, simply known as Vano, acquired a reputation for heavy-handed albeit effective methods. The citizens of Yerevan would jokingly say that there were no longer "any unexpected killings" on the streets of the capital. Rumors began to circulate among the population that in order to clean up organized crime in the republic, Vano decided to take over these criminal operations for himself. A common refrain heard throughout the country was "what better way to control crime than to nationalize it." Many also felt that the President of the Republic of Armenia, Levon Ter-Petrossyan, was aware of the activities of his Interior Minister but had acquiesced for a variety of complex reasons. In the conspiratorial atmosphere of post-Soviet Armenia, some said that the Minister of the Interior had gathered compromising material on the president and therefore the president was powerless to control Vano for fear of being exposed himself. Others, perhaps more accurately, argued that the internal stability was an absolute priority for the new government and it was willing to overlook some of the more questionable activities of the Interior Minister if it meant that law and order would be enforced and internal stability guaranteed. Other allegations singled out the President's brother as a leading figure in high-level corruption, as well as members of the President's immediate circle. Some of these allegations came from former members of the Karabagh Committee and the Armenian National Movement.

Whatever the truth to these and other allegations, the fact that the population began to believe them was indicative of a change of mood in Armenia. After several years of hardship and turmoil, the population was tired and frustrated and wanted to reap some of the benefits that it thought would be accrued as a result of independence. The economy was floundering as a direct result of the blockade imposed by Azerbaijan, corruption was rampant and the standard of living was falling sharply. The once enthusiastic masses of people that crowded Opera Square and demonstrated for the unification of Karabagh with Armenia and the end to the corrupt rule of the Communist Party had by now become apathetic and almost wholly absorbed by the struggle to put food on the table and survive with a modicum of dignity. Of course, many of the problems, both real and perceived, were beyond the control of the government. Nonetheless, Levon Ter-Petrossyan and his administration were held accountable. With internal dissatisfaction and external dangers threatening the existence of the republic within its first few years, many analysts questioned the long-term viability of the state. The regime was concerned with the state, but they defined the state in terms of their rule and equated the state with their regime. As has been the case in many other states dealing with the legacies of Communism and colonialism, the consolidation of the state became a secondary priority to consolidating the regime in power.[24] The development of a civil society and the establishment of the rule of law was pursued with less vigor than the pursuit of consolidating ANM control over the levers of state power. Many of the bureaucrats and officials of the state were more concerned with their own well-being than with the smooth and efficient running of the state apparatus. This is not to say that there were not any dedicated and efficient officials, for in fact there were many, but their ability to effect change in the entrenched and corrupt bureaucracy which itself was an outgrowth of the previous Communist system was severely restricted.

Despite the slowness of state consolidation, the new regime was active in attempting to legitimate its rule. In some respects this was made easier by the on-going conflict with Azerbaijan over the status of Nagorno-Karabagh.

With an external enemy equated in the popular imagination with the Turk, it was not difficult to portray the present struggle as one of survival and a continuation of the age-old confrontation between Armenian and Turk in which the Armenian was usually the victim. With the perceived threat of annihilation hanging over the people, the government was largely able to keep the opposition to verbal, non-violent assaults. This of course was done with the tacit acceptance of the opposition as well, because no political force in Armenia was willing to take the risk of inciting internal political instability and thus present an opportunity for Azerbaijan to take advantage of the resulting chaos. There was a consensus among all political forces in Armenia that the stakes were too high to gamble with the security of the state and thus the nation.[25]

In its attempt to create order and discipline in the chaos of post-Soviet Armenia, the state reached out to the Armenian Apostolic Church, the national church to which the overwhelming majority of Armenians both in Armenia and in the diaspora belonged. Throughout history, the Armenian Church had been a unifying factor in the life of the Armenian people.[26] It played an especially important role during those times when Armenia had been deprived of independent statehood. Its influence among all strata of Armenian society was immense, even among those not actively practicing their Christianity. Its symbolic role as protector of the Armenian nation, language and culture was imbedded in centuries of tradition. The Church also played an important role abroad in the eyes of the diaspora. The Soviet authorities took advantage of the loyalty to the Church among the majority of the diaspora to improve its image in the overseas Armenian communities. By portraying the Church in Armenia as an autonomous entity entitled to operate freely inside Soviet Armenia, the authorities were able to undermine some of the more negative stereotypes regarding Soviet rule. The Communist Party coopted the Armenian Church, which it used as an instrument of state policy.[27] On the other hand, the Armenian Church cooperated with the state in order to ensure its survival in a generally hostile environment. Both sides viewed the other with suspicion, but each served a purpose for the other. With the advent of the democratic movement, the Church was put in a precarious position by the Soviet Armenian authorities. The Church was called upon to step in and counsel caution to the democratic activists. It did so on many occasions and as a result, many viewed it as an instrument of the state and anti-democratic. With time, the Church distanced itself from the authorities and came to be seen again as an instrument of national consolidation and reconciliation. Not everyone within the republic was pleased with the prominent role of the Church, however. Attacks on non-Apostolic believers have taken place throughout the republic with the tacit knowledge, if not the support, of the government.

As the process of building viable state structures slowly continued it was inevitable that the issue of creating regular armed forces should be raised. Thus far, Armenia had sufficed with the units of volunteer militia which guarded the frontiers and fight in Karabagh but lacked the coordination necessary for a regular army. It was only in March 1992 that the Defense Minister Vazgen Sargsyan announced that Armenia needed to establish a regular army of 30,000 to ensure the safety of the population and satisfy the national security requirements of the republic.[28] This came in response to increasing hostility along the borders of the Armenian republic. The creation of an army demanded financial resources, something which the state lacked. The creation of an armed force in the Republic of Armenia was aided by the fact that many Armenians received commissions in the officer corps during the Soviet period. These Armenian officers returned to Armenia to serve the new armed forces and instill in them a high degree of professionalism. The combat experience of Afghanistan and more recently Nagorno-Karabagh provided a necessary base from which to develop a highly-trained and professional armed force. But time and resources would be necessary to provide the training necessary to bring the Armenian armed forces up to world standards. In terms of esprit de corps, the Armenians had a distinct advantage over their Azerbaijani counterparts. The Armenian armed forces understood their mission of defending the country and the need to stay above politics. Although many in the officer corps were supporters of the ANM, nonetheless, they viewed themselves as Armenian officers first and only partisans of the ANM second. Political education was also carried out among the ranks in order to prevent any sentiments of praetorianism from developing. The formation of the armed forces was considered crucial by the regime as a tool for political socialization and service was compulsory just as it had been during the Soviet period. Despite attempts by the government to encourage enlistment, the general population still viewed the armed forces through the prism of the Soviet era, when service was equated with abuse and abhorrent standards of living. With the added factor of the continuing war over Nagorno-Karabagh and constant shelling of Armenian border positions, it was not surprising that few young men were enthusiastic about joining. There were numerous reports of the government rounding up young men from cafes and public transportation and sending them off for military training, regardless of exemptions.[29]

The brightest news on the horizon came from the mountains of Karabagh. In May 1992, Azerbaijani forces were defeated and expelled from two key strategic locations. The first to fall was the city of Shusha, (Shushi in Armenian), the last Azerbaijani stronghold in Karabagh. From the commanding heights of Shusha, Azerbaijani forces had been unleashing punishing GRAD rocket attacks against the Karabagh Armenian capital of Stepanakert. It was viewed as a strategic necessity to neutralize Shusha. Quickly following on the heels of this resounding victory, Karabagh Armenian forces also captured Lachin, the strategic corridor separating Karabagh from Armenia. This victory now allowed supplies to arrive directly by road from Armenia as well as shifting the front to give the Armenians a more advantageous position. The news of these stunning victories were warmly greeted in Armenia and helped boost the popularity of the government somewhat, as it was an open secret that support from Armenia was vital to the victories of the Karabagh Armenians. One of the major architects of the Karabagh Armenian victories was an American-born Armenian, Monte Melkonian. After spending many years in the Middle East in the 1980s as a key member of the Armenian Secret Army for the Liberation of Armenia (ASALA), Melkonian broke with the organization over tactics and strategy to found an offshoot, ASALA-RM (Revolutionary Movement). Incarcerated in a French prison for several years, Melkonian arrived in Armenia in fall 1990. Within a relatively short period of time, Melkonian offered his services to the military establishments of Armenia and Karabagh. It was in Karabagh that he was able to put his vast military experience to good use. His inspirational leadership and harsh discipline was soon recognized by the leadership of Karabagh and he was given command of one of the regions of Nagorno-Karabagh. Melkonian played an instrumental role in organizing the Karabagh Army and turning it into a first-rate fighting force. His adoration by the populations of Armenia and Karabagh was evident in 1993, when he was killed in action in Karabagh. His funeral in Yerevan was attended by all the leading officials of Armenia ; he was given full military honors and buried in the martyrs' cemetery on the outskirts of the city. The region he commanded was renamed Monteapert in his honor.[30]

Despite the victories in Lachin and Shusha in the summer of 1992, the government of Armenia still had much opposition and distrust to overcome. The government attempted to turn the increasing dissatisfaction and disaffection with the regime outward towards external targets. By the judicious promotion of certain nationalist themes, such as patriotism and love of the fatherland, nation and church, the regime was able to engage in considerable damage-control at minimal cost to itself. By summer 1992, the regime came to feel increasingly embattled and isolated, and it began to search for a way out. It was being attacked by the opposition for a number of alleged short-comings, including issues of corruption and the government's handling of the Nagorno-Karabagh conflict. Among the most vociferous critics of the government was the Armenian Revolutionary Federation (ARF). In what appeared as a retaliatory move, President Ter-Petrossyan went on national television in late June to announce that the ARF was trying to undermine the government and in a startling move also claimed to have information that the organization had links to the KGB. He then ordered the chairman of the bureau of the ARF, Hrair Maroukhian, to be deported from Armenia within 48 hours.[31] This move on the part of the government indicated a high level of insecurity and their resort to Bolshevik-type methods further weakened their stature in the eyes of both the public and the international community.

DISSENSION WITHIN THE RANKS OF THE ANM

As the Karabagh Committee developed into a broad-based political movement in the late 1980s and early 1990s, it was perhaps inevitable that strains would begin to appear both within the Committee as well as in the democratic movement as a whole. The Karabagh Committee began as an umbrella organization for the democratic movement, containing many diverse elements with differing strategic and tactical visions for the future of Armenia. In a gradual process which began as early as 1988, the Karabagh Committee evolved into what later came to be the Armenian National Movement. During this evolutionary process, the Karabagh Committee coalesced around a leadership core that contained, among others, Levon Ter-Petrossyan, Vazgen Manukyan, Ashot Manucharyan, Hambartsum Galstyan, Vazgen Sargsyan and Vano Siradeghyan. Throughout the early years of the development of the democratic movement, from 1988 to about 1990–1991, differences in personality, style and vision were subordinated to the common struggle for the self-determination of the Armenians of Karabagh as well as the drive to democratize Soviet Armenia. It slowly became clear, however, after the Armenian National Movement came to power in 1990, that differences of opinion existed among the ruling elite of the ANM, and that these differences of opinion could lead to serious discord in the ranks of the ANM. Even prior to the accession to power, the Karabagh Committee had either excluded or been rejected by such personalities as Igor Muradyan, Pariur Hairikyan, and Zori Balayan. The slowly-emerging rifts between members of the Karabagh Committee itself was seen as something qualitatively different by the rank and file of the movement as well as many outside observers.

Within the first few years after Armenia became independent, the cohesion of the original Karabagh Committee would dissolve, with various members creating rival political parties and becoming vocal members of the opposition, while others enjoyed the fruits of power, and tragically Galstyan would be gunned down in Yerevan in 1994. While Levon Ter-Petrossyan became President of Armenia, his allies Babgen Araksyan became Chairman of Parliament, Vazgen Sargsyan, Minister of Defense, and Vano Siradeghyan, Minister of the Interior and then Mayor of Yerevan. Vazgen Manukyan would create his own opposition political party, as would Ashot Manucharyan and David Vardanyan. The leadership of the Karabagh Committee did not survive its democratic victory intact.

THE WORKINGS OF GOVERNMENT

Debate in Parliament was beginning to heat up. Calls for the resignation of the government over its alleged mishandling of the Nagorno-Karabagh conflict were heard by opposition deputies along with the demand that Armenia recognize the self-proclaimed Republic of Nagorno-Karabagh.[32] Ter-Petrossyan refused to do so, arguing that to recognize the independence of Karabagh would amount to a de facto declaration of war against Azerbaijan and this was a step that he was not going to take under any circumstances. In August, the Armenian village of Ardzvashen, located just inside Azerbaijan, and its surrounding territory was captured by Azerbaijani forces. The fall of Ardzvashen renewed demands that the government resign and opposition rallies took place in Yerevan denouncing the military defeats.

In response to the uproar, Ter-Petrossyan finally agreed to hold an emergency session of Parliament. The session was supposed to consider the President's proposal to hold a national referendum on his presidency but confronted with growing demonstrations outside the parliament building, no decision was reached. Enraged by the turn of events, the president accused the opposition of attempting a coup and threatened to dissolve parliament.[33] The president was increasingly being criticized for policy mistakes and breaches of democratic norms. As the crisis escalated, the rhetoric on both sides grew increasingly shrill. In order to offset some of the recent criticism of his administration and its handling of the war in Karabagh, President Ter-Petrossyan appointed former prime minister Vazgen Manukyan to the post of State Minister for Defense in September. Manukyan would answer directly to the Minister of Defense Vazgen Sargsyan. Barely a month later, Manukyan was appointed Minister of Defense, replacing Sargsyan, who was named as a special advisor to the president and the envoy to the Armenian districts bordering Azerbaijan. The administration understood how volatile the mood of the population was at this time of desperation and did not want to ignite any spark that could potentially sweep them from office. The economic situation became so desperate that the government announced its intention, in December, to formally request that the parliament agree to the reopening of the nuclear reactor, which had been closed since the fall of 1988. Even the safety system of the nuclear power plant had been shut down due to a lack of electricity. According to the law, once the parliament gave its assent, then a national referendum would have to take place for Medzamor nuclear power plant to be reopened. At the same time, the ruling Armenian National Movement even called a press conference in which they criticized the government for its "inadequate response to the grave crisis."[34] A few days later, the President announced that new parliamentary and presidential elections would be held following the adoption of a new constitution, which was being drafted by a parliamentary commission. As the winter of 1992/1993 began in earnest the country was on the brink of collapse. With sub-zero temperatures, industry was at a standstill, fuel almost nonexistent and the population remained indoors huddled around makeshift stoves fueled by anything wooden, including door frames and furniture. The atmosphere was one of the utmost severity and depression.

The debate regarding the constitution was becoming more acrimonious. The opposition called for a special constitutional assembly which would be empowered to draft a new constitution instead of the current parliamentary commission. The President responded by claiming that the parliament was fully entitled to act as such a commission and added that the parliamentary form of government was a threat to the stability of the country and therefore a strong presidential system was best suited to Armenia's needs. Political debate in Armenia was interrupted by reports of an Azerbaijani offensive against the Lachin corridor. This offensive was defeated in April and Karabagh Armenian forces undertook a counteroffensive which resulted in the capture of the strategically important area of Kelbajar, north of Lachin between Armenia and Karabagh. Its capture meant the elimination at a stroke of hundreds of kilometers of frontline for both Armenia and Karabagh and significantly enhanced the security of Armenia's eastern borders and Karabagh's western front. With his position strengthened by the recent events in Karabagh, President Ter-Petrossyan requested a meeting in mid June with the principal opposition parties, the Armenian Revolutionary Federation and the Liberal Democratic Party. He castigated them for not supporting his policies, especially those regarding Karabagh. The President and his supporters felt that the activities of the opposition were undermining the credibility of the government and thus hindering its operation.[35] The procedures of democratic governance had not quite struck firm roots in the country yet, and in general the political factions in Armenia did not deal well with criticism. Politics was personal and any criticism levelled against a particular policy was viewed as a personal affront to the initiator of that policy. Soviet political theories and practices did not allow room for much dissent. The concept of a loyal opposition which would criticize the government when necessary in order to act as a brake on government excesses was alien to those raised in the Soviet milieu.

On July 1, 1993, the parliamentary constitutional commission officially announced that it had completed a draft constitution which it was going to present to the full parliament and then prepare it for a national referendum. According to the draft constitution, a new "National Assembly," made up of one hundred members elected for five year terms, would replace the old parliament and be subject to dissolution by the president, who would also be directly elected by the people for a five year term in office.[36] The issue of a new constitution to replace the old Soviet constitution would prove to be a major divisive factor in relations between the ruling ANM and the opposition. Ter-Petrossyan supported a strong presidential type of system which would have strengthened his position against the parliament which he viewed as obstructionist. Many of the deputies, especially those belonging to the opposition, viewed the parliamentary system as the best guarantee against governmental abuse of power and argued for a more evenly distributed system of checks and balances. In September, a coalition of six main opposition parties presented an alternative draft of the constitution which particularly stressed the separation of powers between the executive and legislative branches.[37]

Other evidence of discord was also becoming apparent. In July, Vazgen Manukyan resigned as Minister of Defense. Although Manukyan was ill and subsequently went to Paris for medical treatment, his resignation was seen to be the result of a falling-out with Ter-Petrossyan. The popular Manukyan, who had been called upon by the President to serve in a number of capacities, was viewed by some people close to the President as a man with perhaps too much popularity and a potential rival for power at some point in the future. Personality differences and clashes over policy formulation did nothing to ease to rivalry between the two leaders of the democratic movement. Following the resignation of Manukyan in July, National Security Advisor Ashot Manucharyan resigned from his post in August.[38] This was the latest example of increasing conflict between the President and his former colleagues and supporters. Manucharyan, who had been involved with the Karabagh Committee from the outset and had been a strong advocate of democratic politics, became disillusioned with the policies and intrigues of the ANM ruling elite. Both he and Manukyan were soon to become some of the President's fiercest critics and challengers in the political arena.

In late August, President Ter-Petrossyan appointed Serge Sargsyan as the new Defense Minister. Sargsyan, a deputy in the parliaments of both Armenia and Karabagh, was also extremely involved in the Karabagh State Defense Committee. He actively participated in the planning of strategy for the conduct of the war and was well-respected by the soldiers at the front as well as the politicians. His appointment came as a surprise to many observers of the Armenian political scene. The Armenian government had been adamant in its denial of any involvement in the Karabagh conflict and remained firm in its stance that the conflict was between Azerbaijan and Nagorno-Karabagh and that Armenia was only an interested third party. But with this appointment, in effect Armenia was acknowledging its direct role in the conflict and was thus unable in the future to claim with any credibility that it was not involved in the war.

Although there were problems with democratization in the political sphere, even more serious socio-economic problems were threatening the fabric of traditional Armenian society. As living standards plummeted, due to the Azerbaijani blockade as well as the general dislocation resulting from the collapse of the Soviet Union, increasing numbers of people were slipping below the poverty line. The most vulnerable groups included the large refugee population, the elderly and children. According to one study:

> Traditionally, visible poverty was stigmatized as the result of laziness and incompetence. Today, people analyze their predicament in two ways. When they compare their present with the past state, they universally label themselves "poor." When they compare themselves with their neighbors, they hesitate to use this label, but prefer to stress their impoverishment as a process rather than a state, and are quick to point out those even needier than themselves. Informants agreed that while the overwhelming majority of people can no longer afford clothes, furniture, or travel, the main criterion of poverty was inability to maintain basic nutrition. People experience their new poverty as humiliating, and often try to hide its extent from each other for fear it will diminish the respect for the family and harm their children's prospects. Despite the strength and importance of kinship, reciprocity, people are less able to help relatives, and the flow of cash and goods is increasingly confined to parents, children and siblings.[39]

In February, the government Statistics Department released the results of a poll it had conducted in Yerevan in December regarding the attitudes of the population towards the performance of the government. According to the poll, only 3% of the residents of the capital supported the ruling ANM, while 13.7% supported the Communist Party and 11.3% supported the ARF. Most striking was the fact that almost 50% of respondents supported no party while 15% even refused to answer any questions at all.[40] At a press conference called by the ARF, the party announced that several other opposition parties supported the ARF's call for the formation of a temporary coalition government, which would prepare for an eventual constitutional assembly to draft a new constitution. According to the proposal of the ARF, new parliamentary and presidential elections would be held, after which the temporary government would be dissolved.

In mid-February, former presidential national security advisor Ashot Manucharyan accused several high-ranking members of the Ter-Petrossyan administration of corruption, abuse of power and other illegal acts.[41] Specifically, Manucharyan accused Interior Minister Vano Siradeghyan of illegally profiting from his position as well as orchestrating a campaign of repression and intimidation against the opposition parties in Armenia. In response to these serious allegations, the parliament debated forming a special commission to investigate the allegations, but the proposal was defeated. The increasing allegations of corruption in high places were beginning to seriously undermine the credibility of the government. Coming from such high-ranking officials, these accusations were even more damaging, although many people had become cynical and apathetic, viewing such revelations as a "falling-out among thieves." In April, the parliament's Commission on Governmental Abuse and Corruption continued hearings into charges of widespread corruption throughout the government. Various high-ranking officials were called before the commission, including former Yerevan mayor Hambartsum Galstyan, but the commission was also strongly criticized because of the prominent role of Interior Minister Vano Siradeghyan, himself accused of numerous charges of corruption and abuse of power.[42] In addition to the increase in allegations of corruption and official malfeasance, violent crime was also on the rise. In April, Vardges Petrossyan, a former president of the Armenian Writers' Union and ADL Ramkavar Party parliamentarian was assassinated by unknown gunmen.[43] Speculation was rife as to the reasons behind Petrossyan's murder, some claiming political motivations while others were sure it was related to organized crime. Politically motivated arrests and detentions were also on the rise as was political in-fighting, accompanied by violence. In May, a former presidential advisor on national security Vahan Avakyan, who had been a deputy to Ashot Manucharyan, was arrested in Moscow. Avakyan's wife had been arrested in February for possession of computer diskettes which allegedly contained state secrets. The government claimed that Avakyan was engaged in espionage for a foreign government. In October, the Avakyan proceedings were closed to the public on orders of the presiding judge, after the defendant implicated several high-ranking members of the administration including the president himself in corruption scandals. He pleaded guilty and was sentenced to four years imprisonment.[44]

In June, an assassination attempt was made on the chairman of the Armenian Justice Ministry's Special Investigations Board, Vladimir Grigoryan, who was responsible for investigating allegations of governmental corruption. According to the Armenian General Procurator's preliminary investigation, two of the four gunmen accused of trying to assassinate Grigoryan were members of the Interior Ministry's special police detachment.[45] This of course implicated the controversial Interior Minister as well as raising questions about a number of other unsolved murders, including the former KGB chief of Armenia, the head of the state railway administration, the chairman of the Chamber of Commerce and Vardges Petrossyan. Vano then dismissed two Interior Ministry officials who were participating in the investigation of the attempted assassination of Grigoryan, which brought the total number of employees of the ministry who had been dismissed recently to almost thirty. Although the Commission on Corruption and Abuse of Power rejected the charges of corruption against Vano in July, the chairman of the commission appealed to the president to reconsider his appointment of Siradeghyan, citing evidence gathered during the course of the investigation.[46] The evidence was beginning to mount against the Minister of the Interior yet the president stubbornly refused to discipline him. Members of the government began to complain that the minister was undermining their authority and interfering with the performance of their duties. Vano was implicated in numerous illicit events throughout the republic, yet he still retained the confidence of the president.

The only event on the political horizon of Armenia which caused satisfaction for both the government and the opposition was the signing of a cease-fire between the armed forces of Azerbaijan and Nagorno-Karabagh in May 1994. It was heralded by some as the prelude to a peaceful settlement of the conflict, while others viewed it merely as a breathing space for the exhausted troops to recuperate before trying to solve the conflict militarily. In fact, all sides in the conflict were exhausted and casualties had been enormous. Although the Azerbaijanis had taken the brunt of the casualties, many of whom died senselessly in human-wave assaults reminiscent of the Iran–Iraq War or the trench warfare of World War I, the smaller population of Nagorno-Karabagh made peace equally essential. In May, 1994 the guns fell silent although everyone remained alert as so many other previous cease-fires had failed to hold. But at least for the time being, the soldiers and civilians hoped for the best so that perhaps some day they could try to resume normal lives again.

As the government consolidated its hold on power, the opposition parties sought ways to counter the growing strength of the ANM. Believing in the power of strength in numbers, yet not wanting to give away any organizational autonomy, members of the opposition parties began to think of new strategies. Meetings between the leaderships of various parties were held and, in an attempt at serious cooperation, a new opposition coalition was formed called the National Coalition Alliance, comprised of the Armenian Christian Self-Determination Union, the Armenian Democratic Party, the ARF, the Constitutional Rights Union and the National Democratic Union.[47] The political situation was deteriorating rapidly, however, and within a matter of weeks a new set of rules, dictated by the government and not to the liking of the opposition, would be in play. The government's hand was being strengthened and the fragmentation of the opposition prevented any concerted efforts at containing their growing power. In December, the political climate in Armenia deteriorated considerably. Early in the month, opposition figure Hrant Markaryan was arrested on unspecified charges and when several opposition parties attempted to pass a motion requiring an explanation from the Interior Ministry, this motion was blocked by Edward Yegoryan, the chairman of the ANM parliamentary caucus.[48] A confrontation between the authorities and the opposition seemed increasingly likely as the government continued to harass members of the opposition. In a shocking turn of events, the former mayor of Yerevan Hambartsum Galstyan was murdered in mid-December, worsening the political atmosphere within the republic.[49] Although the motive for the murder was unknown, many rumors began to circulate, most prominent of which were Galstyan's alleged ties to organized crime and his well-known conflict with Vano. Two days later, three parliamentarians, including former Prime Minister Manukyan and parliamentary foreign affairs committee chairman Vardanyan resigned their seats in protest after the parliament refused to call for a report from the president on the current unstable situation in the republic and the deterioration of public order. This was a serious blow to the government as both Manukyan and Vardanyan were founding members of the Karabagh Committee and well-respected in society at large.

Within the next few days, another thirteen deputies resigned, and the Armenian Revolutionary Federation, the National Democratic Union, the National Progressive Caucus and independent deputies announced their formal suspension of activities and participation in parliament. In order to coordinate their activities, they formed a Representative Council. The situation escalated out of control on December 28, 1994 as President Ter-Petrossyan went on national television and announced the banning of the ARF, prohibiting it from operating inside Armenia. He alleged that the ARF was engaged in criminal activities, including drug smuggling and murder. He further accused the ARF of having a secret organization, codenamed Dro, within the party which was responsible for such activities as well as planning the overthrow of the government.[50] The president failed to provide any evidence against the ARF, however. In the meantime, forces from the Interior ministry conducted raids against ARF and affiliated organizations, arresting several ARF leaders and confiscating computers, fax machines, files and other office equipment. Finally, several major news organs were shut down, including the widely read paper, *Erkir*. The next day, the ministry of justice announced that it was upholding the ban on the ARF. The crisis now passed the point of no return and polarization reached a new level in society. Within a matter of a few short years, Armenia, which had prided itself on its internal cohesion and stability, was facing a crisis which threatened to tear the country apart and ignite civil war.

The Supreme Court of Armenia determined that the ARF should be banned temporarily for six months but decided not to pass judgement on the other charges, citing a lack of evidence at the present time. Suspicions were aroused about the political motivations of the authorities because the six month ban effectively would prevent the ARF from participating in the upcoming parliamentary elections scheduled for May 1995. Demonstrations and strikes took place against the government, some of which were broken up by security forces. One of the defense attorneys of the accused was beaten and harassment by government operatives increased. A campaign of intimidation was stepped up and then on May 16 it was announced that Artavazd Manukyan, one of the accused, had died while in custody.[51] He had medical problems and was not allowed to see a physician or receive the proper medical treatment despite repeated requests and his death scandalized the country, causing alarm among human rights advocates both in Armenia and abroad. The government's explanation of events proved to be unconvincing which further alienated it from society.

In the midst of the this turmoil, the Armenian Church was also undergoing its own internal restructuring. In August 1994, Vazgen I, Catholicos of All Armenians, passed away after being in office since the mid-1950s. According to the rules of the Church, an assembly of clerical and lay delegates from around the world would have to gather to cast ballots for the new Catholicos. This was the first time that such an event would take place in an independent Armenian republic. The position of Catholicos has always been closely tied to the political currents of the times and the present situation was no exception. There were several candidates for the office, including the archbishops of Jerusalem and Karabagh, as well as the current Catholicos of the Holy See of Cilicia, which although ecclesiastically under the jurisdiction

of the Catholicos of All Armenians, based at Etchmiadzin, was in fact autonomous. It was thought by many that if Catholicos Karekin I of Cilicia was to be
elected Catholicos of All Armenians, this would help heal a rift in the Church
which came about as·a result of events in the 1930s and had been a festering
wound in the diaspora. Apparently President Ter-Petrossyan also felt this
way, because he publicly announced that in his opinion the delegates should
elect Catholicos Karekin I as the new Catholicos of All Armenians. This
statement was viewed by many as an unacceptable interference in the work-
ings of the Church and a breach of the separation between Church and State.
As predicted, Karekin I was elected Catholicos of All Armenians.[52]

The parliament decided to move the elections from May to July 5, 1995.
They also later announced that they were preparing the final draft of the constitution for a national referendum which would coincide with parliamentary
elections in July. In June, the Central Election Commission (CEC) voided the
participation of candidates from the National Coalition Alliance-ARF due to
invalid signature gathering. Ten opposition parties then formed a new multi-
party council in response to the activities of the CEC. Vazgen Manukyan was
chosen to head the coalition until a governing body was elected. On 26 June,
the Supreme Court announced that it would initiate trials against 11 of the
ARF members being detained. The trials were scheduled to begin on July 7,
after the conclusion of elections. The timing of the trial was significant in
that the government was accused of not wanting the trial to interfere with
elections and therefore purposefully scheduled them for after July 5. The
July parliamentary elections and constitutional referendum took place in an
atmosphere of confusion and suspicion. According to the law, at least half
the eligible voters had to participate in the referendum for it to be considered
valid. The Central Election Commission declared that the referendum on the
constitution was approved by the electorate.[53] The passage of the constitution would greatly strengthen the executive branch at the expense of the
legislative and judicial branches and many feared that it effectively elimin-
ated most of the checks and balances that were necessary for a true separation
of powers. According to the new constitution, presidential elections would
have to be held fifty days prior to the expiration of the current term of office,
thereby setting the next election date for September 21, 1996, the fifth anniversary of the referendum on the independence of Armenia.

The final results of the parliamentary election were announced and came
as little surprise. The Republic Bloc, led by the ANM, garnered at least two
thirds of the seats in the new 190 seat National Assembly. An allied women's
party, Shamiram, gained eight seats, while the Communist Party gained six
seats. The National Democratic Union and the National Self-Determination

Union each garnered enough votes for three seats. The other opposition parties did not receive enough votes to participate in the proportional system. The National Assembly of Armenia had 190 seats, 150 of which were elected on a majoritarian system in single-mandate constituencies, while thirteen parties/blocs competed for the remaining 40 seats. According to a report prepared by the staff of the Commission on Security and Cooperation in Europe (OSCE), who acted as international observers during the elections:

> Voter turnout and the involvement of the many local observers in polling stations testified to the electorate's active participation in the political process. Nevertheless, the ban imposed previously on the opposition party Armenian Revolutionary Federation (ARF, or Dashnaks) cast a shadow over the election and the referendum The ban on the ARF was one factor in the OSCE Parliamentary Assembly observer delegation's assessment of the Armenian election and referendum as "free, but not fair." The evaluation also cited many reports by opposition candidates of intimidation and pressure to withdraw their candidacy, the Central Election Commission's arbitrary registration of candidates, and the pro-constitution position of the state-run mass media…
>
> Armenia has so far, in the most difficult economic circumstances, impressively managed to combine stability, political pluralism and economic reform. But apprehensions are growing about realizing the high hopes this success has engendered.[54]

The opposition cried foul and believed that the integrity of the entire process had been compromised and that the results of both the parliamentary elections and the referendum were in doubt. Only 141 deputies attended the opening session, in which parliamentary chairman, Babken Araktsyan was reelected to his post. As the opposition was reeling from what it considered a clear breach of democratic practices, the situation in the republic took a turn for the worse. In a bizarre twist and clear escalation of tension, the government arrested Vahan Hovhannesyan of the ARF and eight others and accused them of conspiring to assassinate the president and other high-ranking government officials. Eventually the number would rise to 31. In the aftermath of the elections, the population turned its attention to two riveting trials that simply became known as the "Dro Trial" and the "Trial of the 31."

In February 1996, the National Assembly elected Vice President Gagik Harutyunyan to the post of chairman of the newly created nine-member constitutional court. Five members of the court were to be appointed by the president and four members by the parliament. This move caused even further suspicion from the opposition as Harutyunyan was a high ranking member of the government and thus, they claimed, did not possess the necessary independence to act as chairman of the constitutional court. The opposition also pointed to the overall problem of the lack of separation of powers among the executive, legislative and judicial branches in Armenia, a problem which was recognized long ago but which little could be done about given the current political climate inside the country.

During the spring of 1996, the country was still debating the results of the previons year's elections and referendum but focus increasingly shifted towards the upcoming September 1996 presidential election. The various opposition parties were deciding on their candidates and the National Self-Determination Union had already nominated its candidate, Pariur Hairikyan as had the National Democratic Union, choosing Vazgen Manukyan. There were discussions and some attempts to unite forces in order to defeat the incumbent, Levon Ter-Petrossyan who was the candidate of the Armenian National Movement, but for the most part the opposition parties followed their own separate paths. Over the next few months, further candidates were put forward by their parties, including Aram Sargsyan for the Democratic Party of Armenia, Sergei Badalyan for the Armenian Communist Party, Ashot Manucharyan for the Scientific-Industrial and Civic Union, and Lenser Aghalovyan of the "Artsakh-Hayastan" group. The Armenian Revolutionary Federation was still banned. Many people realized how difficult it would be to defeat the incumbent, especially considering that he was in control of the resources of the state, including the state-run media, thus having a distinct advantage over his opponents. The man in charge of Ter-Petrossyan's campaign was his old ally and chairman of the National Assembly, Babken Araktsyan. As September approached and the opposition candidates continued their election campaigns against President Ter-Petrossyan, observers believed that none of the candidates would be able to garner enough votes to unseat the incumbent. But then the unexpected happened. Three of the opposition candidates, Pariur Hairikyan, Aram Sargsyan and Lenser Aghalovyan withdrew their candidacies in favor of Vazgen Manukyan, and although banned, the ARF also gave it support to Manukyan.[55] Thus, overnight the presidential race became a serious contest essentially between two men and former allies, Levon Ter-Petrossyan and Vazgen Manukyan. Just weeks before the election, this news was greeted with some trepidation by the government. As a figure with a certain popular appeal, having been a founding member of the Karabagh Committee as well a former prime minister and minister of defense, Manukyan was in a position to give the president serious opposition. Manukyan's platform entailed formulating state policies based on national values, formation of a new government of national accord by the allied opposition parties, new parliamentary elections, and the adoption of a new constitution strengthening the legislative and judicial branches of government to better balance power against the strong executive branch. Manukyan also pledged to crack down on organized crime and corruption and direct special attention to social programs which would help ease the negative effects of reform and privatization.

On September 22, President Ter-Petrossyan claimed victory as early returns showed him in the lead over his rivals. In order to prevent a second round run-off election, one of the candidates must receive at least 50% of the vote. The opposition staged a demonstration to protest what it viewed as massive fraud. They claimed that the government falsified the results and that in fact Manukyan won over 50% of the vote. For three straight days, protesters demonstrated peacefully against the government and finally on September 25 a rumor circulated that Vazgen Manukyan and others had been arrested while trying to file a petition. The crowd then forced open the gate to the National Assembly building and were met by security forces who fired over the heads of the crowd. Nonetheless, the crowd broke into the parliament's chambers and physically assaulted the chairman Araktsyan and his deputy Sahakyan, who required hospitalization for their injuries. President Ter-Petrossyan held emergency meetings with his ministers and issued orders banning all movement into the city, at the same time deploying armored personnel carriers and troops throughout the city's intersections and around government buildings.[56]

The next day the National Assembly voted unanimously with only two abstentions to lift parliamentary immunity on opposition deputies implicated in the riot in order to pursue criminal proceedings against them. The immunity of Vazgen Manukyan and seven others was lifted and warrants for their arrests were issued.[57] Manukyan and many others went into hiding as the crisis threatened the stability of the country. When the final results were announced Ter-Petrossyan would claim 51.75% while Manukyan was credited with 41.29%.[58] Eventually Manukyan would give himself up and request to the courts to be held accountable for the disturbances which occurred outside of the National Assembly building on September 25. He also lodged an official protest to the Constitutional Court which was eventually rejected. The opposition in addition to claiming fraud also decided to boycott municipal elections which were to take place in November. The polarization of the Armenian polity was now almost complete. The government realized that the situation had been handled badly and sought ways to ameliorate the situation although many thought that it was far too late for that. In any event, in the coming months, President Ter-Petrossyan would initiate a series of government reshuffles intended to appeal to the population. In early November, Prime Minister Bagratyan resigned his post and was replaced by Armenia's Ambassador to the United Kingdom Armen Sarkissyan.[59] This move was widely viewed as an attempt to ease the volatile internal political situation. Bagratyan had been appointed in February 1993. He was largely responsible for the implementation of the economic reform program and was well-liked by the international lending community. Sarkissyan announced that he would continue the reforms of his predecessor and try to initiate dialogue with all segments of the Armenian population. His speeches struck a responsive cord as the population hoped that his appointment signalled the beginning of a change in course for the Ter-Petrossyan administration.[60]

The resignation of Bagratyan was quickly followed by the replacement of the interior and foreign affairs ministers, Vano Siradeghyan and Vahan Papazyan. Both were close to the president and the ruling ANM. Siradeghyan was appointed as mayor of Yerevan while another confidant of the president Defense Minister Vazgen Sargsyan retained his post.[61] In a further cabinet reshuffling, the President appointed the Ambassador to the United Nations Alexander Arzumanyan to the post of Minister of Foreign Affairs, Ambassador to Canada Garnik Nanagulyan as Minister of Trade and Tourism and former Communist Party leader Vladimir Movsisyan to the post of Minister of Agriculture.[62] By bringing in these men, who were either serving outside of Armenia and therefore not viewed as being as tainted by corruption as those who served inside Armenia or in the case of Movsisyan who was not associated with the ANM in any way, the President hoped to forestall further criticism. These measures at reconciliation were hampered by other events such as the verdicts passed in the "Dro" trial. After many months, numerous delays in the trail, and widespread allegations of violations of both procedure and human rights, three of the defendants were sentenced to death on charges of terrorism, drug trafficking and crimes against the state. The sentences were immediately appealed. The remaining eight defendants were given sentences ranging from three to fifteen years imprisonment and confiscation of property by the state. ARF leader Hrant Markaryan, however, was only found guilty of possessing multiple passports and an unregistered firearm but not guilty of involvement with the "Dro" group, which many viewed as in fact exonerating the ARF of any responsibility for the activities of the alleged "Dro" group.[63] Shortly thereafter, in a further attempt to ameliorate the disastrous political situation in the republic, Prime Minister Sarkissyan met with leaders of the ARF to discuss ways of involving all political parties in the political process and of resolving the current crisis. These attempts also failed to create any breakthroughs as the Ministry of Justice determined that the ARF had not sufficiently reformed its internal organization to warrant a lifting of the ban. In February, a trial of five people charged with crimes related to the events which took place on September 25, following the presidential election began in Yerevan. The defendants were charged with inciting mass disorder and unrest and attempting to forcibly seize the parliament building.[64]

In March, Prime Minister Sarkissyan travelled to London to undergo surgery. While hospitalized, he announced his resignation citing his current health condition. A week later the President startled both the country and the international community by announcing the appointment of Robert Kocharyan, President of the Republic of Mountainous Karabagh as his new Prime Minister.[65] This bold move caught both the population of Armenia and the international community off-guard. The appointment was denounced by Azerbaijan and many other members of the international community as a move designed to complicate the negotiations for a peace settlement in the Nagorno-Karabagh conflict. President Ter-Petrossyan realized how fragile and unstable the situation in Armenia had become since the presidential elections the previous September. Internal discord and polarization were threatening the very foundations of the state and thus also threatening the hold of the ruling Armenian National Movement on power. By appointing the popular and trusted Kocharyan as Prime Minister, Ter-Petrossyan hoped to be able to stabilize the situation internally and give the process of reconciliation a jump start. Kocharyan was not only respected by the people of Armenia and Karabagh, he was also respected by the opposition and especially the ARF. In early April, Kocharyan held a meeting with leaders of the ARF, who congratulated him on his appointment. He in turn expressed his commitment to working towards national unity as well as improving Armenia's relations with its diaspora.[66]

In an attempt to recover from the repeated traumas suffered over the last few years, the opposition announced the creation of the Union for National Accord which was a coalition of several opposition groups and called on the government to agree to new parliamentary elections. The former Prime Minister Hrant Bagratyan also announced his intention to form a new political party, the Freedom Party, which would represent the interests of property owners and producers. Some analysts predicted that he would use this party as a vehicle to propel him into the presidency in the wake of Ter-Petrossyan's announcement that he would not run for another term in 2001. The political landscape in Armenia remains clouded and there is much uncertainty regarding which way the country will develop in the coming years. Meanwhile, the Armenian National Movement itself was undergoing serious internal turmoil. Factions were emerging within the ANM which threatened to split the movement. President Ter-Petrossyan announced his support of

Vano Siradeghyan as the new chairman of the ANM, replacing Ter-Husik Lazaryan, the cleric turned political activist. Vano was opposed by Edward Yegoryan, who was considered the ANM ideologist and a proponent of changing the structure of the ANM to reflect a more inclusive approach to politics. During the days preceding the July annual congress of the Armenia National Movement, there was much speculation that the election of Vano would induce a split in the movement, with Yegoryan and his supporters breaking away from the ANM to form their own party. Vano was elected chairman yet it remains to be seen what repercussions this will have on the functioning of the party.[67]

POLITICAL AND SOCIAL CHALLENGES TO STATE-BUILDING IN ARMENIA

The Republic of Armenia currently faces several serious challenges as it tries to create a democratic state. The next two chapters will discuss the economic and geo-political challenges confronting Armenia, but the republic also faces serious internal problems that need to be overcome before the processes of democratization and state-building can succeed. On the societal level, one of the major challenges is integrating the hundreds of thousands of refugees who have arrived in Armenia as a result of the conflict with Azerbaijan. Armenia was not prepared to accept the vast numbers of refugees who surged into the countries after pogroms in Sumgait, Kirovabad and elsewhere beginning in 1988. The country was not equipped to handle such large numbers because the infrastructure was notoriously stretched even to meet the needs of the citizens of the republic. Many residents of Yerevan had been put on waiting-lists for housing years ago and still had not received an apartment and now thousands upon thousands of Armenians from Azerbaijan were arriving with no place to stay and no other place to go. The government took over hotels, youth hostels, and even government dachas to try to accommodate the huge influx. But unfortunately, the Soviet system was incapable of handling such a situation and as a result, the refugees by and large remained outside the care of the government and were largely dependent upon their own resources to make do as best they could.[68]

These refugees can be roughly placed into two categories: villagers from Karabagh and surrounding regions and city-dwellers predominantly from the Azerbaijan's capital Baku and its second-largest city, Kirovabad (now Ganje). The first group of refugees has proven to be less of a problem for the Armenian government. Since their arrival beginning in 1988, many of the villagers have been resettled in formerly Azerbaijani-populated villages in the rural regions of Armenia. Many returned to Karabagh as soon as their native regions were liberated from Azerbaijani control, while others slowly continue to repatriate to the present day. Those that have remained have been more or less integrated into the economy and society. Being native speakers of Armenian, even if it is the dialect of Karabagh, has made the transition easier. Also in the rural regions the sense of community and mutual dependency is more well-developed than in the cities. Their adjustment into a rural environment similar to the one they left behind has also speeded their integration. The urbanized Armenians of Baku and elsewhere have presented significant challenges to the Armenian government as well as society as a whole. As city-dwellers, their resettlement in rural regions proved to be a serious impediment to integration. The large masses of Baku Armenians could not be entirely resettled in Yerevan due to lack of apartments and other facilities. The government in Yerevan tried to resettle many of these urban refugees in the same abandoned rural villages previously occupied by Azerbaijanis. The problems the refugees encountered were enormous. In Baku, they had lived affluently by Soviet standards and now they were being resettled in villages and had no idea what to do or where to begin. Their problems were exacerbated by the fact that many of the refugees spoke only Russian and did not know any Armenian, which further alienated them from their rural neighbors. Many tried to stay in Yerevan and preferred to live in squalor in the city than to risk living in an environment that was so alien to them.

In addition to the divisions present between refugee and native Armenian, there is a further dichotomy between those Armenians and their descendants who repatriated to Soviet Armenia during the decades of Soviet rule and those Armenians who were native to the republic. This division was much more pronounced in the decades following World War II and is slowly beginning to close partly due to the fact that the first people allowed to emigrate out of Armenia in the 1970s and 1980s were the repatriates and their families thus lessening their numbers in Armenia. It should also be mentioned that with independence has come new attitudes in the republic towards the diaspora. The Soviet government propagandists are no longer around to stir up mistrust towards the foreign-born Armenians as they did during the Soviet period. With Armenia struggling to survive in what it views as a generally hostile neighborhood, it makes little sense to divide the Armenian people even further. The lessons of collective strength have begun to sink into the psyche of the average citizen.

With regard to minorities in the Republic of Armenia, the small Greek, Assyrian, Kurdish, Russian and Jewish communities are facing the same economic hardships as the majority Armenian population, but they face the added burden of trying to preserve their cultural identity. Armenia is over 95%

Armenian and thus Armenian culture predominates inside the republic. The minorities have their own schools, newspapers, and cultural centers, as well as a governmental body devoted to minority affairs. Overt discrimination against non-Armenians does not appear to be a problem and those that choose to emigrate usually do so for economic reasons.

Corruption and organized crime are high on the list of social and economic problems in Armenia. Soviet-era corruption in Armenia was well-known throughout the Soviet Union and many Armenians drew a curious sort of satisfaction from their ability to cheat the Soviet system. A commonly-heard refrain from the Soviet era was that the system denied the people their freedom and ability to prosper legally, so why not try to take advantage of whatever opportunities presented themselves to provide for one's family. Corruption in the republic has reached such proportions that by the government's own admission between 40% and 53% of the economy is controlled by organized crime, which means the actual figure is probably even higher.[69] In addition to the economic impact of this corruption, the social impact may have even more far-reaching ramifications. The people have become demoralized by the pervasive corruption and the seeming venality of some public officials. It is often commented upon that there is no difference between the mafia and the government for they are one and the same. It is a commonly held belief in Armenia that most public officials serve the state in order to enrich themselves and for no other reason. Of course, this is little different than other developing countries, but Armenia has set itself a higher standard according to its own pronouncements. Until the government takes serious and demonstrable steps to crack down, it can expect little in the way of public enthusiasm for either the state or for state service. There are some recent indications, however, that the new Prime Minister, Robert Kocharyan is serious about eliminating corruption. It remains to be seen whether he is able to achieve this goal.

1   This theme is elaborated upon by Libaridian, ed., *Armenia at the Crossroads*.
2   Libaridian, *Armenia at the Crossroads*, pp. 9–39.
3   For the important role that history plays in Armenia, see Richard Hovannisian, "Historical Memory and Foreign Relations: The Armenian Perspective," in S. Frederick Starr, ed., *The Legacy of History in Russia and the New States of Eurasia* (Armonk, NY: M.E. Sharpe, 1994), pp. 237–276.
4   *Soviet Events*, p. 32.
5   Suny, *Looking toward Ararat*, pp. 235–236.
6   Nolyain, "Azeri-Armenian Conflict," p. 561.
7   *Soviet Events*, p. 32.
8   See David Murphy, "Operation 'Ring': The Black Berets in Azerbaijan," *The Journal of Soviet Military Studies*, Vol. 5, No. 1 (March 1992).
9   Murphy, "Operation 'Ring'," p. 80.
10 Ibid.

11 For details on the political parties in Armenia, see Rouben Adalian, ed., *Armenia and Karabagh Factbook* (Washington, DC: Armenian Assembly of America, 1996), pp. 20–34.

12 See *Goyamart* 12 (18), June 1991.

13 Dudwick, "Armenia: Paradise Lost?," p. 502.

14 Murphy, "Operation 'Ring'," p. 82.

15 Ibid, p. 84.

16 Claire Mouradian, *L'Armenie* (Paris: Press Universitaires de France, 1995), p. 99.

17 Shireen Hunter, *The Transcaucasus in Transition: Nation-building and Conflict* (Washington, DC: Center for Strategic and International Studies, 1994), p. 37.

18 For the structure of the Armenian government, see Rouben Adalian, ed. *Armenia Factbook* (Washington, DC: Armenian Assembly of America, 1994), pp.4–12.

19 Embassy of the Republic of Armenia to the United States, "Armenia: An Emerging Democracy," 1994, pp. 4–6.

20 Ibid.

21 Adalian, *Armenia and Karabagh Factbook*, p. 5.

22 Ibid, pp. 10–11.

23 Hunter, *Transcaucasus*, p. 39.

24 On the transition from authoritarianism, see Juan Linz and Alfred Stepan, *Problems of Democratic Transition and Consolidation* (Baltimore, MD: Johns Hopkins University Press, 1996).

25 Hunter, *Transcaucasus*, p. 39.

26 Suny, *Looking toward Ararat*, pp. 10–11.

27 Sarkis Atamian, *The Armenian Community: The Historical Development of a Social and Ideological Conflict* (New York: Philosophical Library, 1955), pp. 424–447.

28 Armenian National Committee of America, *Transcaucasus: A Chronology*, April 1992, p. 3.

29 For the development of the Armenian military, see Jonathan Aves, "National Security and Military Issues in the Transcaucasus: The Cases of Georgia, Azerbaijan and Armenia," in Bruce Parrott, ed., *State Building and Military Power in Russia and the New States of Eurasia* (New York: M.E. Sharpe, 1995); Elizabeth Fuller, "Paramilitary Forces Dominate Fighting in Transcaucasus," *RFE/RL Research Report*, Vol. 2, No. 25, 18 June 1993; Richard Woff, "The Armed Forces of Armenia," *Jane's Intelligence Review*, September 1994.

30 For biographical information on Melkonian, see Markar Melkonian, ed., *The Right to Struggle: Selected Writings of Monte Melkonian on the Armenian National Question* (San Francisco, CA: Sardarabad Collective, 1993).

31 *Foreign Broadcast Information Service Daily Report: the Soviet Union* [henceforth FBIS–SOV], 92–126, 30 June 1992.

32 Rouben Adalian, "Armenia's Foreign Policy: Defining Priorities and Coping with Conflict," in Adeed Dawisha and Karen Dawisha, eds., *The Making of Foreign Policy in Russia and the New States of Eurasia* (New York: M.E. Sharpe, 1995), p. 314.

33 FBIS–SOV–92–161, 19 August 1992.

34 *Transcaucasus: A Chronology*, January 1993.

35 FBIS–SOV–93–118, 22 June 1993.

36 FBIS–SOV–93–125–A, 1 July 1993.

37 FBIS–SOV–93–174, 10 September 1993.

38 FBIS–SOV–93–156, 16 August 1993.

39 Nora Dudwick, "A Qualitiative Assessment of the Living Standards of the Armenian Population: October 1994–March 1995," Draft of *Armenia Poverty Assessment Working Paper No. 3*, Washington, DC, June 1995, p. iii.

40 *Transcaucasus: A Chronology*, March 1994.

41 FBIS–SOV–94–031–A, 15 February 1994.

42 Armenian Assembly of America, *Monthly News Digest of News from Armenia* [henceforth *Monthly Digest*], May 1994.

43 Ibid.

44 *Transcaucasus: A Chronology*, November 1994.

45 Ibid, July 1994.

46 *Monthly Digest*, August 1994.

47 *Transcaucasus: A Chronology*, November 1994.

48 Ibid, January 1995.

49 *RFE/RL Daily Report*, No. 238, 19 December 1994.

50 *Transcaucasus: A Chronology*, January 1995.

51 Ibid, June 1995.

52 Krikor Maksoudian, "Religion in Armenia Today," lecture delivered at the Library of Congress, May 1997.

53 For a comprehensive account of the elections, see the report entitled *Technical Assistance to Armenia: July 5, 1995 National Assembly Elections and Constitutional Referendum* compiled by the International Foundation for Election Systems (IFES).

54 Commission on Security and Cooperation in Europe, *Report on Armenia's Parliamentary Election and Constitutional Referendum*, August 1995, pp. 1–2.

55 *Transcaucasus: A Chronology*, October 1996.

56 Elizabeth Fuller, "The Fall from Democratic Grace," *Transition*, 15 November 1996, pp. 41–45.

57 Ibid.

58 Ibid, p. 42.

59 Emil Danielyan, "A Crisis of Legitimacy in Armenia," *Transition*, 7 February 1997, p. 85.

60 Ibid.

61 Ibid.

62 *Armenpress*, 9 November 1996.

63 *Transcaucasus: A Chronology*, January 1997.

64 Ibid, March 1997.

65 Ibid, April 1997.

66 Ibid, May 1997.

67 Emil Danielyan, "Is Armenia's Ruling Party About to Split?," *RFE/RL Daily Report*, 23 June 1997.

68 The discussion of the situation of refugees in Armenia is based upon several years of field work carried out between 1989–1991 by Robert Krikorian.

69 *Noyan Tapan*, 30 June 1997.

Chapter 3

THE ARMENIAN ECONOMY

The state of the Armenian economy in the immediate post-Soviet period was more a test of survival than for any other Newly Independent State (NIS). If there was ever a period in which the zeal of nationalism and independence was tempered by the reality of a new paradigm in economic relations, the case of Armenia is a prime example. In 1991 the newly independent Armenian state found itself in a situation which the ANM could never have anticipated. The belief that an educated, entrepreneurial society with a large diaspora spread throughout the developed world would be able to integrate itself with the West and become part of the world economy, was shattered by the reality of the geopolitical situation Armenia found itself a part of with the collapse of the Soviet Union.

While Armenia's geographic location creates the impression of a nerve center in what could possibly be an extensive system of trade and regional cooperation, its reality has left it landlocked and isolated. The Soviet economic infrastructure which was left in place had a disproportionate effect on a nation lacking resources and geographically isolated. The interconnectedness of the former Soviet economy coupled with the collapse of the system of intra-republic trade, laid the groundwork for a dramatic decline in the Armenian economy. However, while natural decline was inevitable for all of the former Soviet states, given the adjustment from a command economy to a market economy, rebuilding of former trading systems and the establishment of new ones, removal of the welfare state, etc., Armenia suffered the additional strain of environmental disaster immediately preceding the collapse of the Soviet Union and then the onset of conflict which furthered its isolation. The Nagorno-Karabagh conflict and the resultant blockades by Azerbaijan and later Turkey, coupled with the near total collapse of the state in Georgia from 1992 to 1994, presented an added challenge which made Armenia's existence an exercise in survival.

How Armenia's economy was altered from one of the relatively affluent republics in the former Soviet Union to becoming a test case in survival, and how it has attempted to cope with the challenge of independence and conflict is the focus of this chapter. The format that this discussion will take is to study specific periods prior to and following the collapse of the USSR, and highlight certain aspects of the Armenian economy. Issues to be covered are the nature of the economy prior to the collapse of the Soviet Union, energy, privatization of agriculture in 1990 and of industry in 1994, trade routes, foreign investment, the role of international financial lending institutions, and humanitarian assistance. Finally, the social impact and its effect on recent political developments will be considered.

INTERDEPENDENCE OF THE ARMENIAN ECONOMY

Armenia's economy prior to the collapse of the Soviet Union, like most other former republics, was heavily dependent upon intra-republic trade. Both its exports and imports represented 50% of Gross Domestic Product (GDP) in the 1980s. Its role in the USSR was to process intermediate goods and materials procured from other republics and to supply a wide range of consumer and non-specialized producer goods.[1] Armenia had a substantial light industry capacity and a moderate heavy industry which produced vehicle tires, caustic soda, synthetic rubber, and a large quantity of electric motors, cables and metal cutting machine tools. In order to produce these goods the country was heavily dependent on imports of energy, agricultural and chemical supplies, wood, paper and other intermediate goods. Armenia also had a large share, disproportionate with its size, of the Soviet military industrial complex, supplying high technology lasers and electronics.

The extent of Armenia's dependence on trade prior to independence in 1991, can be indicated by the fact that in 1990, the two largest import items were oil and gas (17%) and machinery (25.56%). With regard to exports, Armenia's two largest products were machinery (40.50%) and light industry (23.92%).

ENERGY INFRASTRUCTURE

Armenia's energy system was heavily dependent on oil and gas. Armenia had three steam generating plants which produced 1744 megawatts (MW) of power or 49% of Armenia's electrical capacity which totaled 3,553 MW.[2] The bulk of this energy came from Azerbaijan where two major pipelines carrying oil and gas originated. Once the Nagorno-Karabagh conflict escalated to outright warfare in 1992, Armenia began to feel the results of Azeri control over almost 50% of its energy capacity. Armenia was forced to rely on a limited amount of natural gas (400 MW) on another pipeline which originated in Turkmenistan, but traveled through Georgia, as well as Uzbekistan and Russia, en route to Armenia. This pipeline would also become the target of saboteurs during the conflict which resulted in major interruptions to Armenia's remaining gas supplies.[3]

Armenia was also the only former Soviet state outside of Ukraine, Lithuania, Belarus and Russia to possess a nuclear power plant. The Medzamor nuclear plant produced 23% of Armenia's electrical capacity.[4] The plant also afforded Armenia the ability to have a cadre of trained nuclear scientists and specialists. Following the 1988 earthquake, Medzamor would be closed following protests by Armenia's green movement and concerns about the plant's location on a fault line. The closure of the Medzamor plant, combined with Armenia's oil and gas crises, would further hinder Armenia's economy during the worst period of fighting in the Karabagh conflict.

Finally, the remaining 28% of Armenia's energy capacity came from hydroelectric power. Armenia has an abundance of fast flowing rivers and waterfalls. Prior to independence there were five major hydroelectric facilities. However, the infrastructure of these facilities were old and in need of refurbishment or replacement. The largest facility, on lake Sevan, which produced 55% of the total hydroelectric capacity would eventually be forced to operate at a reduced capacity because of its excessive drain on the water levels of the lake. Again this is a result of increased use stemming from the energy crises which would begin after the cut off of Azeri oil and gas.

TRANSPORTATION INFRASTRUCTURE

As with energy, Armenia's transportation links with the outside world are also heavily dependent on either the good will or stability of its neighbors. Prior to independence and the Nagorno-Karabagh conflict, Armenia had two railroad connections running through Azerbaijan, one through Georgia, and another through Turkey. There were no railroad ties with Iran nor any permanent structure crossing the Arax river into Iran.

Armenia has two main roads connecting it with Georgia and two with Azerbaijan. One of the routes through Georgia is parallel with the railroad over the chokepoint of the Khram river bridge in Georgia's Marneuli region. This bridge, in addition to the pipeline, was the target of Azeri saboteurs during the conflict.

Armenia was heavily reliant on seaports in Georgia, in particular Batumi, for trade with the European states of the USSR and the West. While for trade with Central Asia, Armenia relied upon Azerbaijan's railroads and ports on the Caspian Sea.

PRIVATIZATION OF AGRICULTURE

Armenia began its privatization program before the collapse of the Soviet Union. While the Armenian government hoped to carry out widespread privatization early on, the first facet of the economy to be privatized was agriculture. In the summer of 1990, Armenia began to implement market reforms, beginning with the law on private property. This resulted in the adoption of the land code on January 30, 1991. Within two months 80% of Armenia's arable had been privatized.[5]

The speed with which land reform took place signaled a willingness on the part of Armenia's new post-Communist leadership to transform Armenia into a market economy. Armenia surpassed all other former Soviet states in the extent of its privatization. The Armenian National Movement (ANM), led by Levon Ter-Petrossyan also had political motivation behind its decision to implement land reform. In order to create a market economy it was necessary to begin placing property in the hands of the people. Allowing individuals to own land displayed the government's seriousness in making the transition. However, the ANM, whose strength lay in the cities, chose to use the process of privatization as a method of breaking the strength of the Communist Party in the countryside.[6]

The net result of the privatization of land was greater output as agricultural production increased by 15% in 1991. Yet problems arose given the pace of privatization and the inability of Armenia's legislative and financial system to follow in kind. Farmers were placed in the position of not having access to, nor the liquidity to purchase, critically needed inputs. Since land was divided into small plots, many farmers were left without machinery and the ability to purchase other necessities such as fertilizer.[7] Furthermore, as Armenia's transportation system with the outside world began to deteriorate, as a result of conflict with or instability within its neighbors, the cost of farming inputs began to rise because of shortages and overall transportation costs. This led to a large scale loss of livestock in 1991 and 1992.[8]

The Armenian government's early decision not to liberalize crop prices enhanced the cost squeeze for farmers, since their output could not keep pace with the rising prices of the various inputs required. In addition, the nature of land reform created a problem with irrigation. Plots were divided in parallel nature, away from sources of water, while irrigation systems were in need of repair. This left farmers without water. However, even with this shortcoming, a new taxation system would eventually be created which helped to address this problem by assessing taxes based on the potential production of the arable land owned by each farmer. Another major shortfall of the land reform program was the inequality it created amongst farmers capable of using tractors. They were allowed to receive plots of land when collectives were privatized amongst the farming families. This allowed tractor drivers the opportunity to receive fees from non-mechanized farms which required their assistance.[9]

Even with the problems which accompanied privatization, the role of agriculture in Armenia continued to grow. Whereas agriculture accounted for approximately 18% of both net material production (NMP) and employment during the 1980s, the sector accounted for 46% of NMP and over 25% of total employment in 1992.[10] Agriculture would take on an even more prominent role in 1993, as the economy continued to worsen. By 1994 agricultural production accounted for almost half of Armenia's national income.

A critical shortfall in furthering the success of Armenia's land reform program was the continued state ownership and control of the distribution system for agricultural inputs and agro-processing plants. This has caused a major delay in the program's further growth.

THE ROLE OF HUMANITARIAN AID

After the widespread privatization of land, Armenia expected to move rapidly into the next major stage towards a market economy, the privatization of small, medium and large scale enterprises. However, this process was delayed as the conflict in Nagorno-Karabagh worsened. Other priorities took center stage and the concern over the resultant effects of mass privatization of industry without a stable market for investors no doubt slowed this process down.

Armenia's economy took a major turn for the worse. The energy shortage caused by conflict with Azerbaijan and instability in neighboring Georgia further isolated Armenia. By November-December 1992, Armenians were on the edge of starvation. Industries were closing, basic necessities were running short, homes were left without heating during one of the region's worst winters, and bread was scarce.

This situation was compounded by the added stress of caring for almost 300,000 people who had been left homeless as a result of the destruction of Armenia's second largest city, Gyumri (formerly Leninakan) during the 1988 earthquake. Many of these people were still living in metal shipping containers, had been out of work for years, and were forced to rely upon humanitarian assistance. The collapse of the Soviet Union ended their immediate prospect of having their lives restored as construction projects came to a halt. The Armenian government had no resources to continue funding the reconstruction in the earthquake zone. This situation was compounded by the influx of almost 300,000 Armenian refugees who had been driven from Azerbaijan as a result of the escalating conflict. It is with this human crises, and with a larger crises looming on the horizon, that the Armenian leadership began in earnest to push its plans to open a dialogue with Turkey.

The Armenian government, hoping to open a new chapter in its relationship with Turkey, negotiated a number of agreements with the Turkish government in which the supply of electricity was critical.[11] Turkey agreed to supply Armenia's energy starved system by linking its electrical grid with Armenia. As a result of protest from Azerbaijan, Turkey reneged on this agreement. Furthermore, by November 1992, the Armenian government had asked the United States for emergency supplies of flour because Yerevan's supply of bread would run out within days. President Bush responded by authorizing an emergency airlift of wheat to Armenia.

The shortage of wheat, for producing a simple staple like bread, led to a large scale European Union financed program of shipping 100,000 tons of wheat to Armenia. This would become the first in a large scale program of humanitarian assistance. This is critical in understanding the situation that Armenia had to confront. One year after independence, the nation which had grand dreams for its future was now forced to move from a relatively, by Soviet standards, high standard of living to subsistence survival.

The cash strapped government of Levon Ter-Petrossyan could not afford to pay for the wheat and was forced to ask for credits or outright humanitarian shipments in order to keep its people from starving or fleeing a worsening situation en masse. Furthermore, given the nature of Ter-Petrossyan's government, its popularity, democratic credentials, and strongly Western orientation, it became in the West's interest to assist Ter-Petrossyan, not only on humanitarian grounds, but to also maintain the stability of the government. Armenia was extremely vulnerable to all of its neighbors, and more importantly for Western nations like the United States, the concern over Armenia's relationship with Iran and US desires to promote an Armenian–Turkish relationship combined with a large and active Armenian diaspora community in America, furthered the US role in assisting Armenia and its government.

While the first major shipment of humanitarian assistance was supplied in the form of 100,000 tons of EU wheat, it was decided that the most rational route to ship the wheat to Armenia was through its neighbor Turkey. Georgia was considered too chaotic while the Turkish route was perceived as leading to the development of better relations between Armenia and Turkey and towards creating a western link for Armenia to Europe. This plan was well received by Armenian officials because of the belief that if commerce between the two states could develop on serious level, with open corridors for humanitarian assistance being the first confidence building measure, then Armenia would have the closest possible link to the west.

However, this project collapsed as the cash-strapped Armenian government paid for the shipment of the donated wheat and then had to accept lower grade Turkish wheat which was replenished by the European Union's wheat. Finally, the delivery schedule of 1,000 tons a day was never reached. The deliveries were erratic, of low volume, and eventually came to a halt (Only 40–50,000 tons of wheat, when the Turkish government decided in the beginning of April 1993 to close its border with Armenia. Essentially Armenia was blockaded on two sides, and the hoped for development of a western link was dashed on the rock of geopolitics. Turkey decided that, until Armenian forces withdrew from the Kelbadjar region of Azerbaijan, it had no other choice it but to assist Azerbaijan by closing its border to the delivery of all goods including humanitarian assistance.

The hoped for development of links between Armenia and Turkey may have been naive on the part of the Armenian leadership. However, in this early period following independence, Armenia's policy was driven by the hope that the United States would intervene diplomatically and alter Turkish policy. While the US certainly did advocate this position in Turkey, the precedent upon which the EU wheat deliveries would fail had been set during the previous August, when US airforce planes carrying medical supplies to Armenia through Turkish airspace were forced to land in Turkey for a "prolonged inspection." Turkey's growing hard line towards Armenia was indicated when Red Cross parcels to be shipped via Turkish roads and railroads were stopped entirely until they could be delivered to Greece and sent to Armenia by Greek cargo planes.

From 1992 to early 1994, when Armenia's humanitarian difficulties reached their peak and the fighting in Nagorno-Karabagh continued to escalate, Georgia became increasingly important as a lifeline for Armenia. Trade was not the issue during this period, the survival of the Armenian people was at stake. The economy had taken such a substantial downturn that GDP had declined by 63% while industrial output dropped by 75%.[12] These figures, combined with the energy and transportation blockades, painted a very grim picture for Armenia in the short term.

All of the Transcaucasian states were in a similar predicament, but Armenia was in a far worse position. Armenia's absolute reliance on the safety of the Georgian transportation system necessitated that its neighbor's stability be of the highest priority. The ports of Poti and especially Batumi became extremely important along with the security of the railroad and highways from these ports to Armenia.

The assistance which Armenia received, after President Ter-Petrossyan declared Armenia on the verge of a national disaster in December 1992, elicited a serious response from Europe, but more importantly the United States. The role of the Armenian–American community must be underscored in advocating the US decision to assist the besieged nation in the Caucasus. Humanitarian assistance from the US in 1992 and 1993 equaled approximately $150 million. In addition, the United States paid transportation costs for shipments of goods supplied by Diaspora Armenians valued at almost $60 million during this period.[13]

Armenia not only suffered from the inability to pay for food or its delivery, but it also lacked the ability to provide heat for its population during some of the worst winters in the region's history. The US Agency for International Development (USAID), through numerous subcontractors, provided kerosene heaters and kerosene for thousands of Armenians in the most vulnerable sectors of society. Without this assistance many would have undoubtedly perished. The heating program also entailed long term storage of heating fuels for the future. The cost could not have been met without international assistance, of which large portions came from the United States.

In order to see that these programs were successfully implemented, the United States created a Caucasus Logistics Advisory Unit (CLAU) through the UN in order to react to crises on the road and rail networks from Georgia to Armenia. The CLAU also repaired damage caused by natural disasters, sabotage, disrepair and conflict along these routes.[14]

By May of 1994, a Russian mediated cease-fire had been negotiated and by July 27, the defense ministers of the three participants to the conflict signed a formal cease-fire. With the end of the fighting, the country was finally able to focus on other issues needed to improve the economy and bring forth the hoped for economic prosperity. However, given Armenia's lack of capital, the country was still reliant on large amounts of humanitarian assistance. The United States continued to provide shipments of wheat and kerosene to keep the country's population alive and warm during winter months. In 1994 alone, Armenia received 230,000 tons of wheat and 50,000 tons of kerosene. This assistance would be critical to providing the underpinning for Armenia's further economic reforms, which would begin in earnest in 1994. However, the extent of the aid's impact on the reform process is better understood when looking at the amounts provided in 1995 and 1996.[15]

In 1995 the United States provided 138,000 tons of wheat and 20,000 tons of Soybean. This assistance coupled with that of previous years has reached some 1.5 million people in Armenia. Half of Armenia's remaining population has been forced to rely upon outside assistance. Kerosene and mazout (low grade fuel oil) shipments in 1995 equaled 25,000 tons and 81,000 tons respectively. USAID estimates that 210,000 of the most poverty stricken families in Armenia, especially in the earthquake zone, have been the beneficiaries of the US sponsored heating program. As Armenia's situation improved in 1996, the US provided 64,000 tons of wheat and continued to supply kerosene and mazout in large enough amounts to support the most vulnerable segments of Armenian society. More importantly, by 1996 USAID under a memorandum of agreement with the Government of Armenia (GOA) allowed for the monetization of the wheat by permitting the GOA to sell the wheat to mills and bakeries. The proceeds from the sales would allow the government to purchase additional wheat.[16]

From 1994 to 1996, Armenia's economy began to show steady growth, yet as we have seen the country still received large amounts of assistance. This aid allowed the Armenian government to cover expenses for critical imports, and take the risks necessary in order to carry out its ambitious economic reform program. Without the aid, stability may have been in question regardless of Armenia's ethnic homogeneity, which many have cited as the primary reason for its stability. Armenia would have certainly experienced some social disorder had it not received this aid, and its current leadership may not have remained in power. It is expected that Armenia will continue to receive large amounts of assistance, especially in the humanitarian realm, to help offset the cost to the government of critical imports such as wheat and kerosene. Much of this aid will come from the United States, as the US government appropriates money and the Armenian-American community lobbies the United States Congress to press the executive branch of government to appropriate higher levels of assistance.

While Armenia no longer suffers from the threat of starvation or national disaster, the lasting legacy of this period is that the combination of war, a lack of the most basic necessities needed for survival and the still unrepaired devastation left by the 1988 earthquake forced large numbers of citizens to leave the country. Officially Armenia has a population of 3.7 million. The real numbers may in fact be just below 3 million. The population adjustment may have made it easier to provide for the people, but nevertheless Armenia suffered the loss of some of its most technically skilled citizens. In a situation where industry had been brought to a standstill and funding for advanced scientific centers had dried-up, combined with the possibility of being drafted, Armenians were forced to flee for simple economic reasons rather than invading armies.

In fact many of these people went to Russia where job opportunities were better or to other countries in the West in order to send money home to their families. It is estimated that $8 million worth of remittances flows back into the country monthly to support families.[17]

RISING INFLATION AND THE INTRODUCTION OF THE DRAM

Following the collapse of the Soviet Union, Armenia continued to use the Russian ruble as its currency remaining part of the ruble zone until November 1993. The ruble continued to devalue following the break-up, and as Russia reintroduced new rubles, the old rubles continued to flow in large numbers to the former-Soviet Republics. Essentially Russia kicked the non-Russian republics from the ruble zone and furthered the process of inflation in Armenia and other non-Russian republics.

However, it would not be accurate to characterize Armenia's growing inflation rate in 1993 as solely due to an influx of old Russian rubles. Armenia did not implement significant reforms that would effect the large and ineffi-cient social safety net, bloated government services, and lack of fiscal respon-sibility on the part of the government. Deficits were high and monetary policy was not under control, especially after the introduction of the Armenian cur-rency, the Dram, in November 1993. While its official exchange rate was 14 dram to the US $1, it soon began to lose value as unofficial rates began to skyrocket and the situation was worsened by the lack of any significant for-eign currency reserves.[18]

The inflation rate grew and by the final quarter of 1993 average monthiy inflation was 150%. By the first six months of 1994 average monthly infla-tion stabilized to 40%. It needs to be reiterated that the gradual stabilization of the Armenian currency would not have been possible without the assistance granted Armenia by outsiders and in particular US humanitarian aid. With-out the commodities brought into the country, prices would have risen much faster and to a higher level.

The Armenian government, realizing that inflation needed to be brought under control and desperately wanting the assistance of the interna-tional financial institutions, began implementing tighter monetary policies and exercising fiscal restraint. A large portion of the credit for bringing infla-tion down goes to the policy of the Bagrat Asatryan, the Chairman of the Central Bank of Armenia (CBA). He carried out a total reorganization of the CBA staff and was given complete independence from the government and cabinet. Mr. Asatryan refused to continue supporting inefficient government enterprises with cheap credits and pressured commercial banks to increase their reserve requirements. Asatryan combined the pressure on the banks by sacking 80% of the government regulators of the banking center because of concerns over corruption which allowed pyramid schemes to pose as commercial banks. Mr. Asatryan's austere monetary and regulato-ry policies would eventually make Armenia a model of macro-economic stability.[19]

Control of inflation was furthered by the spring and summer harvests in 1994 which helped bring down the price of food. The combination of these policies along with seasonal increases in the food supply brought monthly inflation from June to September back into single digits. In August 1994, president Ter-Petrossyan came to the United States on a state visit and during his stay he met with World Bank and IMF officials to discuss loans to further what would become a major move in privatization and denationalization.

In order for the World Bank and IMF to become involved in projects in Armenia, two key criteria had to be met. The first which Armenia had met by July of 1994 was the formal signature of a cease-fire agreement with Azerbaijan. The World Bank and IMF had no intention of providing assistance to a nation involved in a conflict. With the first criteria met the door was open for large scale assistance which required that Armenia now meet a set of standards of fiscal restraint, tight monetary policies in order to control inflation, reduction of the bloated civil service and implementation of a host of other austerity measures which the IMF prescribed.

THE 1994 PRIVATIZATION PROGRAM

Prior to the escalation of the war in Nagorno-Karabagh, Armenia was beginning to make progress with its privatization program. As stated earlier, Armenia began widespread privatization of agriculture in 1991. However, the next more ambitious phase of this program did not materialize. While the National Assembly passed a privatization law in June 1992, little progress was made in the two years that followed. However in 1993 the government was able to begin the process of privatizing small retail stores. This helped pave the way for the creation of hundreds of new small businesses which furthered the growth of free enterprise.[20.]

In addition, during 1993, ownership of residences was transferred to inhabitants and in its aftermath new construction of private housing increased. Critical to the growth of free enterprise and creating a framework for harnessing the Armenian proclivity for business, the Armenian parliament passed the "Business Law" in March 1992 which applies equally to citizens and non-citizens. It created a climate conducive to foreign businessmen who want to register new businesses in Armenia. It also established a simple to understand legal framework. Unlike other CIS states, it was not complex, and reflected the comfort and desire with which the government of Armenia views free enterprise. While the law has many gaps, it certainly allows room for future amendment. It also is a reflection of the immediate need of the Government to encourage foreign investment.[21] The business law which contains provisions for "freedom of transferability in corporate and other entities shares" led to the emergence of an active and growing stock market.[22]

Nevertheless, privatization still had not gone very far, nor had the growth of free enterprise progressed at the hoped for pace. The primary cause for the less than anticipated growth was the conflict in Nagorno-Karabagh. The effects of the conflict caused capital flight, strained government budgets, depleted the population's savings and thus prevented the generation of credit to finance government or private investment projects.

With the conflict continuing to loom in the background, the government under the efforts of the reform minded economist, Prime Minister Hrant Bagratyan, managed to pass legislation on January 12, 1994 known as the "Program for Privatization and Denationalization of State Enterprises and Non-finished Construction." This program amended the 1992 Privatization Law giving it the backbone needed to carryout a significant program in which the government would be removed from the business sector.

Even with the passing of the amendment it would not be until the summer, following the formalization of the cease-fire in the Karabagh conflict, that real progress would take place. This also coincided with Ter-Petrossyan's visit to the United States and meetings with the World Bank and IMF.

What did the 1994 Amendment do that was so significant? To use the words of Armenia's President " We are just giving back to the people what used to belong to them."[23] Ter-Petrossyan's statement is far more simple than what really began to take place with the implementation of this program. Privatization and denationalization are different. Privatization is the outright transfer of state property to Armenian and foreign citizens and firms. Denationalization is not an outright transfer of title, but is a lease or management contract on state property. Denationalization has certain advantages over privatization. For example, privatization requires the agreement of a government approved privatization program while denationalization can be initiated by an investor contacting the relevant government agency.[24]

The 1994 program of privatization and denationalization called for a total of 4,700 state-owned enterprises and unfinished construction sites to be privatized based on the 1992 originating legislation. The program targeted primarily small and medium sized businesses. The larger enterprises were not included in the initial wave of the program. There was also a concern that foreign investors might be put in the position of investing in an enterprise that had no hope of surviving in the difficult business climate. However, these concerns were allayed in part by the fact that the crisis situation in Armenia which prevailed in the previous two years forced a "survival of the fittest" and thus only the most profitable enterprises survived. This might be an overly optimistic assessment, but it held true in a number of cases.[25]

The scale of the transfer of state-owned assets was large, by Armenian standards, leaving only 5,000 in the hands of the government. The remaining state owned enterprises were by far the largest. While the fact that Armenia is a small country allowed the government the luxury of rapidly implementing land reform, it was thought that this ambitious program would benefit from the same circumstances. The belief that the state could withdraw from 4,700 enterprises by the end of 1994 proved overly ambitious. By August 1995 only 1,093 small scale enterprises were privatized. This phase of the plan was on track, while the privatization of medium scale entities was far behind. Some 35 medium-scale enterprises were offered for sale, but only 26 were privatized as of November 1995.[26]

The problems encountered with the privatization program were assuaged with the assistance of the World Bank. The intervention of the international financial lending institutions dovetailed with the actual implementation of the privatization legislation allowing Armenia to receive not only the financial assistance, but the technical expertise in carrying out the program, marketing strategies, Western methods of doing business and planning.

With World Bank assistance in 1995, the government worked out a monthly plan which set targets for the privatization of small, medium and large-scale enterprises. This new one was just as ambitious as the previous one in that it called for the privatization of 3,000 small scale, 700 medium-and-large scale enterprises and 600 unfinished construction sites by the end of 1995.[27]

THE ROLE AND PROJECTS OF THE INTERNATIONAL FINANCIAL LENDING
INSTITUTIONS

Armenia's initial involvement with the World Bank began in January 1992, when it applied for membership of the World Bank group, which includes the International Bank for Reconstruction and Development (IBRD), International Finance Corporation (IFC), International Development Association (IDA) and the Multilateral Investment Guarantee Agency (MIGA). In order to become a member of the World Bank Group, Armenia had to apply for membership of the IMF.[28]

Eight months later Armenia joined IBRD, the main lending arm of the World Bank. Armenia's first major lending projects were received from the World Bank in 1993 and 1994. The first was a $12 million loan for a an institution building project, the objectives of which were to facilitate conversion to a market economy by building programs in four functional areas: (a) economic management, (b) resource mobilization, (c) enterprise reform, (d) financial sector reform. In line with World Bank's mission it was geared at laying the groundwork for a hoped for long term project aimed at future loans for converting Armenia's economy.[29]

This project was aimed at providing technical assistance in order to pave the way for future World Bank activity. The loan was for 20 years, including a five year grace period, with a variable interest rate. The project was implemented by the Armenian Ministry of the Economy, and completion was set for 1996.[30]

The second World Bank Project was an earthquake zone reconstruction project. The northwest portion of Armenia, centering around the city of Gyumri still remained in a complete state of disrepair and poverty resulting from the 1988 earthquake. Little assistance had been provided to this hardest hit region since the collapse of the Soviet Union. On February 1, 1994 IDA, the soft loan arm of the World Bank which provides long term loans at concessional interest rates to the poorest countries, approved a $28 million dollar credit to Armenia.

Project goals were to provide financing for housing, municipal services, completion of factory shells for profitable industries and technical assistance. The IDA loan has a maturity of 35 years and a grace period of 10 years. As with the first loan, the Ministry of Economy was the implementing agency.[31]

The earthquake reconstruction project provided badly needed assistance for a region which had been in total depression for almost four years. However, it was only enough to begin what would be a long and continuous process of rehabilitating the region.

The Nagorno-Karabagh conflict continued to prevent assistance from the IMF, whose aid was needed for the short term macro-economic stabilization of the country. Even though Armenia became a member of the IMF in 1992, and the IMF conducted two missions in 1994 to the country, it was reluctant to provide major assistance to Armenia because of the conflict. In December of 1993 the President of the IMF, Michael Camdessus, wrote to Armenia's President and informed him of the IMF's refusal to support Armenia at the time, given his concern over regional conflicts and their continuing threat to any possible application of "a successful...implementation of a growth oriented stabilization and systemic reform program." Camdessus went on to say that support from major international donors would be "...difficult to mobilize under present circumstances." The IMF's president urged Ter-Petrossyan to intensify his efforts towards finding a peaceful solution to the conflict. All other major financial institutions followed the IMF's lead. The Fund's only involvement in Armenia was through a resident advisor to the Central Bank of

Armenia. Major assistance would not take place until the cease-fire was formalized on July 27, 1994.[32]

As stated earlier, Armenia's president arrived in the United States in August 1994 and held meetings with representatives of the World Bank and IMF in Washington, D.C. The results of these meetings paved the way for what would become large scale assistance from both institutions. With a cease-fire in hand, and Armenia's government moving forward with large scale privatization and ready to accept IMF austerity measures; (which by December 1994 would lead to the liberalization of bread prices, electricity subsidies, tax reform and deep cuts in the government's fiscal policy) the Consultative Group for Armenia of the World Bank on November 22, 1994 made financial commitments of $265 million for 1995. This represented 75% of Armenia's financing needs for the following year.[33]

The support shown for Armenia by the Consultative group came from the following attendees: France, Germany, Italy, Japan, the Netherlands, the Russian Federation, the European Bank for Reconstruction and Development (EBRD), the World Bank and the IMF. A major turning point was reached at this meeting as Armenia was set to receive aid that would assist with conversion to a market economy, but more importantly the critical credits and grants to purchase critical imports needed to maintain stability by assisting those citizens most in need and thus able to implement, with some degree of safety, economic reform without setting off a social explosion.[34]

The IMF became intimately involved with the Central Bank of Armenia and the Ministry of Economy in implementing programs needed to enhance long-term macro-economic stability. Its first major loan was in December 1994 when the Fund provided a $23.6 million loan to support Armenia's balance of payments. This Systemic Transformation Facility (STF) was accompanied by credits from the World Bank and EBRD. All of this assistance was geared at macro-economic stabilization. The requirements for the assistance were standard for IMF supported efforts. The requirements were "liberalization of prices, foreign trade, and the foreign investment climate; reduction of budget deficits; tight monetary policy; and institution building through privatization and passage of legislation on property rights, contracts, and accounting."[35]

The IMF, the World Bank and the Government of Armenia developed a program for 1995 and 1996 which would create the conditions for sustainable economic growth while simultaneously raising the living standards of the population. This program envisaged the following: reduce inflation to around 30% during 1995, and to 19% during 1996; increase real GDP by at least 5% in 1995 and by an even higher rate in 1996; ensure that the CBA's reserves are bolstered.[36]

The policies followed by the Government of Armenia, with strong IMF backing had remarkable success during the 1994–1996 period. In 1994, Armenia registered 5.4% growth in GDP while in 1995 growth went beyond 6.9% and 4.3% in the first eight months of 1996. By February 1996 the IMF approved its largest credit to Armenia , a three year, $148 million enhanced structural adjustment facility (ESAF). The first tranche of $25 million being released at the end of February. The recent agreements with the IMF and World bank call for total growth in 1996 to equal 6.5% and to reach 8% by 1998. The growth in GDP is to be accompanied by a reduction of inflation to 8% by 1998.[37]

Armenia's macro-economic policy has earned substantial praise from the international financial lending institutions and major donor countries. Throughout these institutions and Western capitals, Armenian government officials are described as making enormous strides and great progress which far exceed their neighbors and many other states of the former Soviet Union. However, serious concerns exist, which are not voiced publicly given the tendency of officials to encourage positive developments. Armenia's precarious geographic location places it in a position of potential isolation and renewed conflict. A World Bank "Country Brief" stated the following in March 1996:

> Armenia's reform program faces four important risks. First there is the serious risk of a resumption of hostilities over Nagorno-Karabagh, and the consequent continuation of Armenia's economic isolation. This could have serious implications for creditworthiness, investment and growth. However, the current peace negotiations continue to move in a positive direction and economic recovery is increasing popular support for peace. Second, there is a risk of stabilization and structural reform being undermined by sociopolitical opposition if economic recovery does not proceed fast enough to satisfy rising expectations (presidential elections are to be held in September 1996). However, this will be mitigated by improving targeting of social assistance and by continued humanitarian assistance from donors and the Armenian diaspora. Third, the implementation of the reform program could be undermined by institutional deficiencies, although the ongoing reorganization of the public administration and the provision of technical assistance by the World Bank Group and by other donors will help to counteract this risk. Fourth, an additional risk is that aggregate demand will recover only slowly in Armenia's FSU markets, and that access to non-traditional export markets would be undermined by protectionism.[38]

The assistance of both bilateral and multi-lateral donors has allowed Armenia to maintain a high level of critical imports which would have been too cost prohibitive given the high price of transportation, and inability to finance the debt. In addition, investment in infrastructure is difficult without the support of external financing. There is little domestic savings and the government cannot rely on local sources of finance.

Multi-lateral investment in Armenian infrastructure and industries primarily came from the World Bank and the EBRD. In 1994 and 1995 the World Bank began a series of project appraisals and implementations which included a $42 million loan for irrigation rehabilitation project. Much of the irrigation system necessary to successfully follow-through on land reform was in disrepair. Three quarters of Armenia's agricultural production comes from irrigated lands. The Bank recognized that Armenia was striving towards self-sufficiency in a number of aspects of agriculture. In addition, Armenia has growing prospects of being able to export agricultural products.

While financing the irrigation project through IDA the World Bank simultaneously approved a $13.7 million credit to improve Armenia's electricity supply. This project would create additional power units, but would repair and upgrade current power generation and distribution facilities. Both loans were again based on a concessionary basis.

THE EUROPEAN BANK FOR RECONSTRUCTION AND DEVELOPMENT

The role of the European Community and in particular the European Bank for Reconstruction and Development should also be emphasized. Since Armenia is a member of the Organization for Security and Cooperation in Europe (OSCE) and considers itself to be European country, its future links with Europe are going to grow in importance. It is already integrated into the OSCE structure and is relying upon the OSCE Minsk Group to negotiate a settlement in the Nagorno-Karabagh conflict. Armenia is currently being considered for membership in the European Parliament.

These political links go hand in hand with a hoped for economic integration with Europe. European countries have provided large amounts of humanitarian assistance and the role of the EBRD will undoubtedly grow in the future, so long as regional political developments do not destabilize the situation. The EBRD has essentially been involved in three major types of projects in Armenia which primarily reflect Armenia's most pressing problems. These projects involve energy, transportation and agriculture.

EBRD initiatives are initialing being targeted towards public sector projects which will help relieve disincentives to foreign investment in what is a hoped for future growth of the private sector in Armenia. By focusing on energy and transportation, the EBRD believes that it will be able to create more efficient use of Armenia's current energy supply and expand transportation capacity to facilitate movement of goods. The two key projects which the EBRD is involved in are the Hrazdan 5 power station and the cargo terminal at Zvartnots airport.[39]

The Hrazdan 5 power unit is being supported by a $57.4 million dollar loan from the EBRD to construct a new 300 MW gas-fired power station. The loan was approved in April 1993 and the project is expected to be complete by 1999. The overall project includes technical assistance beyond construction, such as reform regulations in the energy sector, electricity tariff reform, and installation of modern accounting systems. When the project is complete, plans are being put into place to privatize the facility as part of an overall plan to begin privatizing the energy sector in Armenia.[40]

The EBRD's second major project is to enhance Armenia's only form of transportation not completely reliant on the goodwill or safety of bordering nations, the Zvartnots cargo terminal. Armenia relies inordinately on air transportation since the collapse of the Soviet Union and Zvartnots, the largest airport in the country which is in the capital, has been hamstrung by not having modern cargo handling facilities. In November 1994 the EBRD approved a $22.8 million loan to finance modern landing and loading facilities. This project will allow Western cargo operators to provide services to Armenia.[41]

Unlike the two previous public sector projects which the EBRD has financed, its third major project has a large private sector component. Not surprisingly this project is in the agricultural sector, the first aspect of the Armenian economy to undergo widespread privatization. The project known as the Armenia Whole Sale Market Company (WMC) has as its objective to create a market-driven distribution system for fresh food. The WMC will have a large central market in Yerevan and six smaller collection and assembly markets in rural agricultural zones. The EBRD provided a $15 million loan in December 1995 for the WMC. The loan will provide $11.5 million for upgrading an existing building for the market and to pay for the six collection markets. The remaining $3.5 million will be provided to Agrobank, Armenia's second largest bank which services the agricultural sector. The money will be used to provide loans to private businesses such as farmers, wholesalers and transport companies.[42]

Other areas which the EBRD would like to become involved in include the creation of financing intermediaries. There are very few credit worthy banks in Armenia which are capable of intermediating significant amounts of money for project financing. The EBRD and other multi-lateral technical assistance projects are in the process of creating such a system . They are also encouraging a downsizing in the number of banks which exist in Armenia and hope that this will lead to a system of stable, credit-worthy banks.

The problem in banking has also made it difficult to assist small private enterprise projects which the international financial lending institutions are not able to support because project start-up will outweigh the cost of the project overall. Large scale projects are needed and this is why both the EBRD and the International Finance Corporation (IFC), the lending arm of the World Bank which supports private enterprise, have been unable to find projects to assist. Ordinarily IFC would take part in a project to the order of $25 million, but given Armenia's unique situation they were involved in a $7 million dollar project.

FOREIGN INVESTMENT

Since 1995, the issue of foreign investment has been high on the agenda for the Armenian government. Armenia's National Assembly has passed sweeping legislation in order to create as favorable a business climate for foreign investors as possible. This has been recognized by many, but it has yet to bring in the kind of large scale foreign investment which the country needs to revitalize its economy. While over 55% of the country's GDP comes from the private sector, this still has not stimulated large foreign investment and interest in purchasing large government enterprises offered for privatization.[43]

There is a lot of hope generated by the large Armenian diaspora, but to date the overwhelming majority of diaspora money has been in humanitarian assistance. The amount of diaspora aid is in the tens of millions, not an insignificant sum, but the government and the international financial lending institutions would like to see more plans developed by the diaspora for investment. This is not to say that there has not been any diaspora related investment, because there is, but it is not of the scale desired, given the size of the diaspora and the amount of money in their possession, especially given the amount that has been provided in humanitarian aid.

Nevertheless, there have been a handful of large foreign investment projects that do show promise for the future. Four of them are Global Gold Armenia mining project, ArmenTel, Coca-Cola Bottlers Armenia and Midland Armenia bank. The Midland-Armenia bank is critical in that it is the first foreign bank to open a branch in the Republic of Armenia. The Bank has charter capital of $10 million dollars, with 30% of the capital provided by Vatche Manougyan, an Armenian entrepreneur from England, which is larger than any Armenian bank. It is hoped that Midland-Armenia will lead to a consolidation of Armenian banks and greater acceptance of Western standards to create a truly professional banking system.[44]

Global Gold is an Armenian-American venture which has a start-up investment of $10 million. The project aims to mine an estimated 18 tons of gold and search for additional deposits throughout the country. It is estimated that investment in this project could rise as high as $200 million in the future, thus making it the largest foreign investment in the country. This project will also make Armenia the 13th largest producer of gold in the world. If the Global Gold project succeeds it will become a pilot project for other foreign investors who wish to become involved in the sphere of non-ferrous metallurgy, such as copper and molybdenum of which Armenia has large deposits.[45]

The ArmenTel Armenian-American enterprise is involved in a major project of upgrading and restructuring the Yerevan City telephone network and the international telephone network of Armenia. The project has been so successful that the German company Siemens has provided another $55 million loan in addition to its previous $75 million loan. This project totals $130 million and is the second major foreign investment project in the country. When completed, Armenia will have a state of the art telecommunications system which, while improving communications for Armenia's citizens, will also be an added incentive for foreign investment especially in the fields of high technology and communications, areas in which Armenia has enormous potential, given its history of providing communications equipment prior to the collapse of the Soviet Union.[46]

In the realm of private investment projects, Armenia has potential in Agrobusiness, bottling, fruit juice processing and mini-hydro power projects. The government, as part of a future scheme to privatize the hydro-power industry, has begun a project in which small scale hydro-power units totaling 12 MW have been put to tender. This is the first step in a larger project in which Armenia will give foreign investors an opportunity to develop a learning curve in understanding privatization in Armenia's energy system. Following this initial phase the government plans the privatization of larger scale power facilities.[47]

TRADE LINKS AND REGIONAL COOPERATION

The Armenian government is concerned with the precarious transport and trade routes which exist with its neighbors to the north, east and west and has sought to foster new ties and trade links with other states. Armenia has expanded its trade relationship with Iran. While the development of trade ties with Iran is a problem for the United States, which provides a large amount of assistance to Armenia, it is generally understood that Armenia has little choice in this matter given its geographic location and the political situation with its neighbors Turkey and Azerbaijan.

Armenian trade links with Iran grew slowly in the first few years following independence, but have developed at a brisk pace since the signing of the cease-fire. The incremental nature of relations with Iran, especially regarding trade and transportation routes, was symbolized by the time taken to complete the bridge over the Arax river linking the two states. Since the completion of the bridge in December 1996, this trade route has been busy with vehicle traffic. Armenia has a large trade imbalance with Iran, but it is also one of Armenia's largest trade partners. Trade shows are regularly conducted between the two countries and high-level delegations have traveled to each others capitals. Armenia sees its economic relations with Iran growing especially to provide it with access to both the Persian Gulf and the rest of the Middle East, and to Central Asia.

The recent connection of the railroads of Iran and Turkmenistan have ameliorated some of the difficulty in transporting Armenian goods to Turkmenistan. It has also become an additional link in reducing reliance upon the northern transportation system that Armenia needs in order to facilitate trade with Turkmenistan and Central Asia as whole. While it does not appear that there are plans to expand the railroad from Iran to Armenia in the near future, certainly as relations continue to develop, and if outside financing can be found, this will become a reality.

Armenia has recently linked itself with the Iranian power grid. The completion of this project is part of a larger plan for the country to create redundant power sources and give it greater energy self-sufficiency. The linking of the power systems is part of another wider plan to eventually build a natural gas pipeline from Iran to Armenia. Again the issue of foreign financing is a problem which overshadows many arrangements with Iran, given its pariah status in the international community and pressure placed by the US government on any US company or its subsidiary from getting involved in deals which invest in the Iranian oil and gas industry.

Nevertheless, these projects or even discussions show a forward looking thinking on the part of the Armenian government to find solutions out of their current dilemma. The economic relationship with Iran and the expansion of transportation links is also part of a strategy to cement its relations with Turkmenistan, its major supplier of natural gas. Turkmen gas is critical to Armenia's continued economic growth especially for providing power to its gas generated electrical grid. Armenia provides Turkmentistan with precious stones and non-ferrous metals in exchange for natural gas.

The three countries have recently formalized their relationship by establishing a joint transportation company based in Ashkhabad, Turkmenistan. This trilateral venture essentially represents 27% of Armenia's imports valued at $250 million, while Armenia has exported goods to Iran and Turkmenistan valued at $66 million or 21% of its total exports for 1996. The trade is likely to grow and may soon include Russia as part of this growing economic integration process. Armenia and Iran are also in the process of bringing Greece into another trilateral arrangement.[48]

The Armenian leadership is also trying to become more involved in recent discussions over regional integration. In particular, the Armenian delegation at a recent meeting of the Black Sea Economic Cooperation Council (BSEC) proposed that with the reopening of the Medzamor Nuclear Power plant, they could now begin selling excess electrical capacity to members. Whether or not Armenia currently has excess capacity, it did sell this excess capacity prior to the collapse of the Soviet Union. The likely customers of this electricity would be Georgia and Turkey. In addition, Armenia offered itself as a major trading route. More specifically as the "Fourth European Corridor." Levon Zurabyan, the President's spokesman, said that the BSEC countries should look to Armenia to become a nexus for road, rail and pipeline traffic. However, the key to the proposal was that investment of as little as $4 million can facilitate the movement of 37 million tons of cargo of which two thirds would be for transit and the remainder for Armenian consumption.[49]

While the proposal itself may not lead to anything, Armenia is placing regional cooperation in forums in which its neighbors, in particular neighbors it is in conflict with, are being asked to take on a new kind of relationship where trade and economic development would hopefully sideline political differences. The government appears to truly believe that it can pursue a policy in which war-weariness, combined with the potential of economic growth, may eventually lead to an interest in avoiding future conflict.

THE SOCIAL COST

Armenia's growing efforts to solve its economic problems all take place within the framework of potential social disorder. Armenia, more than any other former Soviet state, has had more than its fair share of disasters. For a small country it has carried a heavy burden, while at the same time, because of its small size, it has been able to implement certain projects with little difficulty.

The combination of the 1988 earthquake, challenges faced by an economy in transition, conflict, closure of borders, breakdown in trade routes, and loss of most of its energy in addition to major flows in population has placed an inordinate amount of strain on the Armenian people. While macro-economic stabilization has been achieved through the influx of large amounts of humanitarian assistance, loans and the aid, the population has faced enormous challenges in survival. It is at the popular level that the economic changes are most felt and where they will either succeed or fail. The perception of positive change, in the mind of the people, is critical for the reforms to succeed.

Without getting involved in a discussion of the political situation in Armenia, the government of President Levon Ter-Petrossyan and the ruling Armenian National Movement (ANM) has not explained its policies well. The reclusive president has often allowed false impressions over policies to be taken on by the population at large and this has led to a resultant distrust of the economic program.

Improvement of the lives of some of the people has been at best incremental. For almost five years much of the population was forced to live with little electricity, running water and other basic necessities. Education has been seriously disrupted for many, especially children. Life for almost 500,000 people in the earthquake zone has hardly improved, with few opportunities for the population of that region. Many are still residing in shipping containers known as "domigs" which freeze during the winter. If it were not for the large shipments of kerosene heaters from outside the mortality rate of these people would have made the situation untenable.

For such a small country with a population of 3.7 million the effects of the post independence period have been significant. In 1993 Armenia had a labor force of 1.7 million people. While official government statistics show an unemployment rate of 9.5% for 1996 the reality certainly does not correspond with this number.[50] For example, 1993 government statistics reported an unemployment rate of 5.4% but a January 1994 UNICEF report stated that 59% or a million people were either unemployed or on involuntary forced leave.[51]

Many of those who are not formally unemployed have remained on payrolls so that they can continue to receive state sponsored health benefits and other basic items that are provided to employees. Nevertheless many of those who do remain employed receive their diminished salaries late and at times are paid in goods instead of cash.

The level of poverty among Armenians is high. Over 80% of the population lives below the poverty line established by the World Bank at $1 per person per day. The level of humanitarian assistance to Armenia combined with the social networks which exist amongst Armenians within Armenia and with extended families outside of the country have assisted many families.[52] Even with this assistance the social dislocation has effected almost the entire population.

Armenia has become a heavily stratified society. The poor do not just reflect uneducated and rural families. "The Poor" in Armenia is comprised of "most workers, school teachers, most local community doctors, engineers, the overwhelming majority of scientists, as well as small scale retailers." The huge expanse of the population which represents both highly educated and uneducated citizens has created a perception within Armenia of the poor representing the mass of society while "they" represent the ruling elite. This perception, which in many respects is based on reality, has developed into belief that state structures favor the ruling elite which is made up of the ANM and its adherents. The remainder of the population or "the poor" have little or no confidence in the state and many who are both educated and poor have no hope for a future.

This situation has lead to a large outflow of the population. The Armenian government accepts the statistics that some 677,000 people have left the country since 1991, with the largest amount leaving in 1993. Other sources estimate the numbers to be higher. The breakdown for the population which has left is disturbing. Of the officially accepted number of emigrants, 55% represent individual migration, where one member of the family has left to support the remainder of the family, which continues to reside in Armenia. The difference represents family migration, in which the entire family has left the country and will eventually detach themselves from Armenia.[53]

Some 75% of those who have migrated come from urban areas. Most of these people worked in industry or research institutes and once the economy contracted, as it did following the imposition of blockades etc., these people were subsequently without work. The level of education amongst the migrants is high. Emigration was highest amongst those who were specialists. Armenia lost one third of its specialists in the humanities and the natural and technical sciences. This brain drain has hurt Armenia, as these are the very same people that Armenia wants to keep in the country when the anticipated economic recovery begins and Armenia hopes to become a center of high technology design and production.[54]

Based on income the majority of those who have left the country are of moderate means of which 67% have settled in Russia and 15% have gone to the "distant abroad." Migration became an accepted coping strategy for dealing with the hardships imposed upon them by the absence of work, geopolitical instability and poor living conditions. While the high level of migratory activity is common throughout much of the Commonwealth of Independent States (CIS), for such a small country as Armenia the impact has been enormous. Almost 20% of the population has left the country.[55]

The migration of Armenians is expected by some to continue for another decade. While the numbers of those leaving will diminish it will still remain significant. The projected figures run as high as 50,000 annually. This means that another 500,000 people could leave within the next decade. These figures, if accepted, mean that Armenia will have well under 3 million people within ten years. While some have posited that Armenia is already populated by less then 3 million, there will be no doubts in the near future. The migration will not stop until economic growth begins to be felt by all of the population. It is also expected that the outflow of Armenians will be furthered by the consolidation of farms. As many of the more than 200,000 farms created as a result of land reform begin to decrease, many people from the rural regions of the country will leave for the cities. The cities will not be able to accommodate these people and hence will continue to drive the migratory process.[56]

The dramatic effects felt by the population, following the collapse of the Soviet Union, has created deep divisions and more importantly a sense of political apathy . While this situation held true for some years following the difficult reality of independence, it changed dramatically in the fall of 1996.

THE IMPACT OF THE ECONOMY IN THE 1996 PRESIDENTIAL ELECTIONS

Many Armenians grew tired of politics and politicians after the hardships incurred during the 1990s. Those who had the means left the country. Those Armenians who could not leave concerned themselves with trying to carve a new niche in the transition of the economy or, as with most of the population, survival. The parliamentary elections in 1995, which gave the ruling ANM overwhelming control of the National Assembly, left many people completely apathetic about the state of political affairs in the country. The perception of unfair electoral practices combined with perceived and actual widespread corruption amongst the ruling elite finally converged in the 1996 Presidential elections.

Most Armenians continued to remain apathetic about politics and had little faith in the opposition until they rallied around one candidate, Vazgen Manukyan. Up until August 1996 the majority of Armenians and much of the world, to include the critical support of the international financial institutions, believed that there was no viable opposition to Levon Ter-Petrossyan and that he would win with no problems. His re-election would undoubtedly mean stability and the continuation of the macro-economic policies which his government and the IMF planned. When in September the opposition parties coalesced around Vazgen Manukyan with a platform calling for an attack on corruption and a change in social policy to support those most effected by the economic dislocation of the last five years, concerns were finally raised within the government and outside of the country.

Members of the government stated that if Manukyan won the financial support from outside would dry-up. Armenia's small gains would be lost as the opposition tried to rebuild the welfare state with money that did not exist. The opposition effectively capitalized on the stresses which the population had felt for the last five years. When the election took place on September 22, and Levon Ter-Petrossyan was able to avoid a run-off election under highly suspected circumstances, the feared social explosion took place. Fortunately for Armenia, it did not take on the nature of events which unleashed themselves in her neighbors such as Georgia and Azerbaijan.

However, the fact that the President had to rely upon the Army to maintain control following the outburst in the Armenian capital meant that some kind of re-evaluation had to take place. The Armenian nation had become so pressurized in the last few years that the condition of the people could not be ignored. At the same time the government had to be concerned about the effect that perceived instability would have on potential foreign investors, international financial institutions, and the level of humanitarian assistance received from Armenia's benefactors, most importantly the United States.

Once the situation was back under control in Yerevan, the President began to make changes. Whether these changes will have a major impact on the state of the people still remains to be seen. However, in a post election speech Levon Ter-Petrossyan spoke at length about the problems of corruption within the government, and promised that means would be taken to help the people. The importance of his speech in the midst of this crises was critical and the fact that he addressed head-on the issue of corruption within his own government was important.[57]

For many, corruption became a major bottleneck in the growth of the Armenian economy. In order to get anything done it became necessary to bribe or give kickbacks to certain individuals within the power ministries. In particular, the Defense Ministry run by Vazgen Sargsyan was the target of numerous allegations of corruption.

The month following the elections, the President appointed a number of Armenian Ambassadors to the West in important ministries to include the Prime Minister, Ministry of Trade and Tourism and the Foreign Ministry.

The new Prime Minister Armen Sarkissyan, the former Ambassador to Great Britain, took the government's message overseas. That message was that Armenia would continue on its path of macro-economic stability, making as favorable a climate for foreign investment. Sarkissyan also went one step further by openly discussing the social polarization created in Armenia as a result of capital accumulation in the hands of a few. He went on to address corruption in government and the need to implement laws to take corruption out of the civil service.[58]

The governments economic policy was now being geared to address the concerns of two constituents. The first being the population of Armenia and the second being the international financial community which it could not afford to offend for fear of losing the financial support Armenia had received since 1994.

CONCLUSION

Armenia has a long way to go before it can finally turn the corner and begin to achieve the kind of economic growth which will have tangible effects on the lives of the people. So far the government has coped well by achieving macro-economic stability with the assistance of the international financial lending institutions, the United States, Western Europe and other developed nations.

However, it is obvious that Armenia will not be able to sustain the reforms without continued assistance. This aid will remain critical as such time as the blockades of Armenia are lifted and the energy problem is finally solced. The government has made significant strides in assuaging the latter issue. Deals with Iran, the restructuring of the energy system in the country and the reopening of the nuclear powerplant have done much towards addressing this serious problem which almost brought Armenia to the brink of disaster in the winters of 1992 and 1993. Armenia has every intention of becoming an energy exporting nation as it was in the 1980s.

That day may not be as far off since the Armenian President tabled this possibility in Turkey at the BSEC conference in April 1997. Yet even with the energy issue being addressed the problem of unreliable links to the outside world still exists. Throughout this entire chapter there has been one major theme and that is the fact that future Armenian prosperity will rely upon peace in the region and access to the outside world. The country cannot be supplied by air nor can it achieve sustainable economic growth without a long and uninterrupted period of peace.

Armenia is also in the difficult position of having to compete for very limited resources being offered by the international community. Armenia does not have major natural resources like its neighbor Azerbaijan nor does it have the seaports of its northern neighbor Georgia. Analysts have said that the level of interest in neighboring Georgia is three to four times higher than for Armenia. In the case of Azerbaijan, world class oil reserves drive the interest in that state and hence all of the subsidiary industries which support the extraction of oil. Armenia on the other hand, as is so often stated, must rely upon its human resources and the ability of the government to make as hospitable an investment atmosphere as possible. Unlike Azerbaijan, which which will have high investor interest over its oil regardless of the speed of privatization or legislative reform, Armenia cannot afford to do the same.

Armenia needs to market itself and needs the assistance of its diaspora which has become extremely successful in the nations that have become their homes. The government must communicate its need for foreign investment with the diaspora, but at the same time allow them to take a more active part in the future of the country. The bonds of blood can go only so far unless they are given a stake in the well being of their ancestral homeland.

Armenia needs to cope with migration, which could very well turn into a major problem in tapping into a human resource base of skilled technical people who may not be there when the next phase of economic growth is anticipated.

The very tenuous nature of the current growth and macro-economic stability is not readily apparent to those who do not follow the region closely. So much of Armenia's future is dependent upon continued peace in the region. All of the nations are continuing to arm themselves and defense spending in Armenia is still very high. With the continued regional arms race, albeit at a very low level relative to other regional arms races, a new conflagration in the region can lead to a loss in all of the gains made since 1994. It is in the interest of Armenia that conflict not break out again. It is Armenia that stands to lose the most should an outbreak of fighting turn for the worse.

---

1 *Armenia Country Economic Memorandum*, World Bank, Report No. 11274–AM, Vol. 1, (Washington, D.C.), March 24, 1993, p. 1.
2 Rouben Adalian and Joseph Masih, eds., *Armenia and Karabagh Factbook*, (Washington D.C., Armenian Assembly of America), July 1996, p. 50.
3 Ibid.
4 Ibid.
5 KellyAnn Szalkowski, "On the Way to the Market: Armenia's Policies of Land Reform," *Special Report on Armenia*, No. 1, August 1993, p. 1.
6 Ibid, p. 8.
7 Ibid, p. 12.
8 Ibid, p. 13.
9 Chrystia Freeland, "Blockade Belies Increase in Stability," *Financial Times*, June 7, 1995, p. 3.

10 *Armenia: The Challenge of Reform in the Agricultural Sector*, (Washington, D.C., The World Bank), 1995, p. 1.

11 *Armenian Assembly of America Daily Report*, February 25, 1993, p. 1.

12 Michael Wyzan, "Impatient Despite Successful Economic Reforms," *Transition*, November 15, 1996, p. 46.

13 United States Department of State, Office of the Coordinator of U.S. Assistance to the NIS, *U.S. Assistance and Related Programs for the New Independent States of the Former Soviet Union: 1993 Annual Report*, (Washington, DC; U.S. Department of State, January 1994), section 6, pp. 1–3.

14 Ibid, section 6, p. 1.

15 United States Department of State, Office of the Coordinator of U.S. Assistance to the NIS, *U.S. Assistance and Related Programs for the New Independent States of the Former Soviet Union: 1994 Annual Report*, (Washington, DC; U.S. Department of State, January 1995), p. 9.

16 United States Department of State, Office of the Coordinator of U.S. Assistance to the NIS, *U.S. Government Assistance to and Cooperative Activities with the New Independent States of the Former Soviet Union: 1996 Annual Report*, (Washington, DC; U.S. Department of State, January 1997), p. 5.

17 Wyzan, p. 47.

18 Freeland, p. 3.

19 Ibid.

20 Van Z. Krikorian, "New Wave of Privatization to Hit Armenia," *CIS Law Notes*, June 1994, p. 1.

21 Van Z. Krikorian, "Armenian Law Creates Favorable Climate for Business Operations—Part III," *CIS Law Notes*, October 1993, p. 3.

22 Van Z. Krikorian, "New Wave of Privatization to Hit Armenia," *CIS Law Notes*, June 1994, p. 1.

23 Ibid.

24 Ibid, p. 2.

25 Ibid, pp. 3–4.

26 "Republic of Armenia—Recent Economic Developments," *IMF Staff Country Report*, No. 95/111, (International Monetary Fund, Washington, D.C.), November 1995, p. 12.

27 Ibid.

28 "Armenia Applies for Membership in World Bank," *World Bank News Release*, No. 92/S29, January 13, 1992; "Armenia Joins World Bank," *World Bank News Release*, No. 93/S14, September 16, 1992.

29 "Armenia: Institution Building Project," *World Bank News Release*, No. 93/78, April 1, 1993.

30 Ibid.

31 "World Bank Approves Earthquake Reconstruction Project for Armenia," *World Bank News Release*, No. 94/35ECA, February 1, 1994.

32 Michel Camdessus, Managing Director of IMF, Washington, D.C., to President Levon Ter-Petrossian, Yerevan, Armenia, December 17, 1993, regarding Armenia's request for IMF support.

33 "Meeting of the Consultative Group for Armenia," *World Bank Press Release*, November 22, 1994, p. 2.

34 Ibid.

35 Wyzan, p. 47.

36 "Republic of Armenia: Policy Framework Paper, 1996–1998," prepared by Armenian authorities, IMF, and World Bank, January 22, 1996, p. 2.

37 Wyzan, p. 47.

38 "Armenia," *World Bank Country Brief*, March 1996, p. 6.

39 "EBRD Activities in Armenia," *European Bank for Reconstruction and Development*, July 2, 1997, p. 3.

40 Ibid.

41 Ibid.

42 Ibid.

43 Stuart Parrott, "Armenia: Economic Growth Deemed 'Remarkable? by EBRD," *Radio Free Europe (RFE)/Radio Liberty (RL)*, April 16, 1997, p. 2; United States Department of State, Office of the Coordinator of U.S. Assistance to the NIS, *U.S. Government Assistance to and Cooperative Activities with the New Independent States of the Former Soviet Union: 1996 Annual Report*, (Washington, DC; U.S. Department of State, January 1997), p. 5.

44 "Georgia, Armenia, Azerbaijan Country Report," *The Economist Intelligence Unit*, First Quarter, 1996, p. 26.

45 Vahan Hovanissian, "Armenia: Joint Venture to Boost Gold Production," *RFE/RL*, April 3, 1997, p. 1.

46 "Siemens Increases Credit to ArmenTel Up to $130,000,000," *Noyan Tapan Daily Information Bulletin for Groong Readers*, April 29, 1997, p. 1.

47 "Armenia Privatizes Eight Hydro-Power Plants Through International Tender," American Embassy, Yerevan, Armenia, December 19, 1996, pp. 1–3.

48 Vahan Hovanissian, "Central Asia: Growing Links Improve Economies," *RFE/RL*, April 23, 1997, p. 2.

49 "Armenia Offers BSEC Countries Energy for Sale," *Noyan Tapan Daily Information Bulletin for Groong Readers*, May 1, 1997, p. 3.

50 "Macro Economic Data for Armenia," *Investment Climate of Armenia: Facts and Figures,* Enterprise Development and Foreign Investment Promotion Armenian Agency (EDIPA), January 1997, Fact Sheet No. 3, p. 1.

51 Wolf Scott, "Emergency and Beyond: A Situation Analysis of Children and Women in Armenia," *UNICEF Geneva*, January 1994, Section 22.

52 "Caucasus Update: Georgia, Armenia, Azerbaijan," *United Nations High Commissioner for Refugees (UNHCR) Information Bulletin*, July 1994, p. 8.

53 *1996: Armenia Human Development Report*, United Nation Development Program (UNDP), May 1996, p. 14.

54 Ibid.

55 Ibid.

56 Ibid, p. 15.

57 Armenian President Levon Ter-Petrossian's Address to the Nation Upon His Reelection to the Presidency of the Republic of Armenia, September 30, 1996.

58 Armenian Prime Minister Armen Sarkissian's Center for Strategic and International Studies Speech, Washington, D.C., January 10, 1997, pp. 2–4.

Chapter 4

ARMENIA'S FOREIGN POLICY

Throughout the contents of this book, and specifically the chapter on Armenia's economy, the geographic isolation of Armenia is a common theme. This isolation, while profoundly effecting the economic development of the country, also has a major impact on the security perceptions of the Armenian people and its leadership.

At its simplest and most basic all one needs to understand the effect of geography on Armenia is to look at the map. It is a nation which is land-locked, lacking in strategic depth, in possession of few natural resources and with a transportation infrastructure reliant upon the goodwill of its neighbors. Moving beyond this basic observation one sees that Armenia is a nation whose traditional enemy, Turkey, lays across its border, with the second largest army in the North Atlantic Treaty Organization (NATO). Even geographically, Armenia's border with Turkey contains no real natural barriers.

The republic remains blockaded on two sides by Turkey and Azerbaijan. From 1992 to 1994 Armenia's primary access to the outside world was through the ports of Batumi and Poti in the republic of Georgia. This route frequently was unreliable because of sabotage and internal instability in Georgia.

Armenia entered its period of independence handicapped by its role in the conflict in Nagorno-Karabagh. While it would be incorrect to state that the Armenian National Movement (ANM) and the leader of the first government of independent Armenia, Levon Ter-Petrossyan, had no interest in the conflict over Nagorno-Karabagh it is correct to say that they did not anticipate that the movement to free the Armenians of Nagorno-Karabagh Republic (NKR) from Azerbaijan would come at such a high cost. The ANM, while readily using the conflict to further its own ends of ultimately coming to power in Armenia, perhaps never realized that six years after independence they would still be involved in serious negotiations over the status of the enclave.

While there are many aspects to the foreign policy of the Republic of Armenia, all are in some way related to the conflict in NKR and all, whether they be economic or political, seek in some way to circumvent or alleviate the effects of that conflict. While this chapter does not attempt to be a thorough explanation of that conflict, it will repeatedly use the conflict as a point of departure for explaining how the conflict effected attempts at breaking new ground in foreign policy. It will also explore and analyze how the conflict has come to dominate the internal dynamic within Armenia which in turn has had an effect upon Armenia's foreign policy and security perceptions.

The period leading to the referendum on Armenian independence on September 21, 1991, and the following months which witnessed the collapse of the Soviet Union in December of that year was a time marked with nervous excitement. Armenians finally had an independent republic. The new era was dominated by the collapse of totalitarian dictatorships, the flourishing of democracy, the primacy of the rule of law in international relations and a new role for international governmental institutions like the UN and CSCE.

Unfortunately, as has often been stated, the new world order into which Armenia, and the other former Republics were born, was more like a new world disorder. The incompatibility of competing nationalist aspirations between Armenia and its neighbors and the belief that some how the country could conduct a foreign policy exclusive of these ethnic conflicts was naive. Nevertheless, Armenia's leaders attempted to keep their relations with their neighbors separate from the conflict in Nagorno-Karabagh. When this policy failed, the Armenian government decided that their survival as a state and as a political movement within Armenia hinged upon a union of the nationalist cause with the hard issues of security and geopolitics.

ARMENIA AS PART OF A REGIONAL SYSTEM

As Armenia moved towards independence the security issues which predominately figured in their calculations were how Armenia would conduct its relations with its immediate neighbors and, most importantly, with two states with whom they were historically at odds: Azerbaijan and Turkey. In addition, Armenia had to contend with its southern and northern neighbors, Iran and Georgia. Its next level of priority was Russia and then the countries possessing large Diaspora populations. This is not to say Russia, for example, was less of a priority than Georgia, because Armenia does not share a common border with Russia. However, the layers of the onion, so to speak, are merely a framework for understanding the structure of Armenia's relations. This can be said for the majority of the states of Caucasia or Central Asia.[1]

In order to further understand the atmosphere in which the foreign policy of Armenia developed, it is important to acknowledge that Armenia is part of a regional system which is unique as a result of its peculiar economic and political development as well as its position within a region caught in competition among three regional powers: Russia, Turkey and Iran. To ignore this regional dynamic is to lose sight of how the small Caucasian states of Armenia, Azerbaijan and Georgia are in many ways forced into limited policy choices; to pursue an independent policy will have a disproportionate effect upon the neighboring state. This goes hand-in-hand with the significant impact that seemingly internal developments in one Transcaucasian state can have upon a bordering state. In the Transcaucasus this phenomena is heightened given the interdependence of all three states through, trade, infrastructure, and ethnic groups living on both sides of borders.[2]

As this chapter progresses it will be seen how Armenia's leadership early on during its independence realized these limitations and began to work within this unique regional system to alter its position in the Nagorno-Karabagh conflict.

RELATIONS WITH TURKEY

As the Soviet Union began to collapse and it became obvious that Russia wished to shed its links with the states of the former Soviet South and orient itself towards Western Europe, the Armenian leadership began to analyze pragmatically the situation with which it was confronted. Russia was not the only state which sought to reorient itself with the West. All of the Transcaucasian states saw an opportunity to reorient themselves and believed that assistance would readily flow to their countries. This shift towards the West did not necessarily take on the desire for direct aid, for example, from the United States. Once the Elchibey government came to power in Baku they looked westward, but did not go beyond Ankara where they saw significant cultural and linguistic ties. However, Azerbaijan would have to rely upon the investment of international oil companies which would primarily come from Great, Britain, the US, France, etc.

In the case of Armenia, in order to develop strong ties with the West they had to create a relationship with Turkey. The ANM realized that Russia was beginning to distance itself from the Transcaucasus and that Armenia's relationship with Azerbaijan was continuously deteriorating as the conflict in Nagorno-Karabagh worsened. They watched as the infrastructure which held the former Soviet states together began to unravel making their links to Europe through that system tenuous. In light of the above, the decision by the ANM and its leader Levon Ter-Petrossyan to try to radically alter the environment in which Armenians and Turks perceived each other was momentous.[3]

As stated in previous chapters, the memory of the Genocide committed by the Ottoman Empire upon the Armenians was strongly felt throughout Armenia, but more so in the Diaspora. The Armenian government believed that if they could develop relations with Turkey based on economic ties, meaning that Armenia could use Turkey as a link to Europe and Turkey could do the same with Armenia for the Central Asia Republics, as well as increasing the rate of trade between the two states, then the bitterness associated with the horrible events of the past could be overcome.

The new Armenian government did not seek to press the issue of the Genocide or the question of former Armenian provinces in Turkey. Upon joining the CSCE in 1992, Armenia in essence agreed not to press territorial claims. The Armenian government had made a bold step which would put it at odds with its own population, but also the Diaspora which Armenia would rely upon as the trials of independence increased.[4]

Turkey at this time allowed its territory to be used for the transshipment of humanitarian assistance to Armenia. Its airspace, railroads and ports were available for facilitating the movement of these goods. The possibility that this kind of goodwill would grow into a more meaningful relationship led to talks in which Armenian–American representatives operating with the tacit approval of authorities in Yerevan began negotiations over the expansion of port facilities in the Turkish city of Trabzon on the Black Sea. This port would be used to accomodate increased Armenian trade with Europe. While the scheme to build-up the port of Trabzon collapsed, other agreements would be reached between the two states.[5]

During the second half of 1992, Armenia was just beginning to feel the full effects of the blockade by Azerbaijan. At the same time, the Armenian hand in Nagorno-Karabagh was severely weakened by a large-scale Azeri offensive which began in early June. During this period Armenia's border regions with Azerbaijan came under heavy shelling while its links through Georgia, which included the gas pipeline and railroad, were being sabotaged.[6]

The Armenian economy was brought to a virtual standstill. Armenia's economic ties with Iran were not well developed and the country was relying upon large amounts of humanitarian assistance from the United States and Europe. The need for a secure link to the West through Turkey was evident and so there was an added impetus to improve relations with Turkey. The tenuous situation which Armenia was in led to negotiations with Turkey over the supply of 100,000 tons of European Union wheat and the supply of electricity to Armenia by linking the Armenian power grid with Turkey's.[7] These agreements held out the promise that Armenia and Turkey would gradually develop a mutually beneficial relationship, which would eventually lead to normal diplomatic relations. Furthermore, the Armenian government hoped that this would bring them one step closer towards integration with the economy of Western Europe.

While Yerevan believed that they could separate their relations with Turkey from the worsening situation in Nagorno-Karabagh they failed to take into account the differing opinions within Turkey regarding its relations with Armenia. First, there were those within Turkey who believed that the collapse of the Soviet Union would usher in a new period in which Turkey would be ascendant in the Transcaucasus and Central Asia. This faction believed that they should support their Turkish brothers in Azerbaijan. Turkish President Turgat Ozal was a proponent of this ideology. By the fall of 1992 Azerbaijan's offensive began to run out of steam and the Armenians of Nagorno-Karabagh were beginning to drive the Azeri's out of the enclave. These events strengthened the hand of the Pan-Turkists.[8] The other faction believed that Turkey could forge links with Armenia because of Armenia's need for an outlet to the west. They believed that they would be able to develop strong economic relations with Armenia. At this time Armenia was considered to be the only stable former Soviet State on its border. The Turks also believed that they would be able to moderate Armenia's position on the Nagorno-Karabagh issue.[9]

However, the former group within Turkish foreign policy making succeeded. The pressure grew within Turkey as Azerbaijan began to suffer increasing defeats on the battlefield. Armenia's belief that they could have beneficial relations with Turkey exclusive of the conflict in NKR proved incorrect. The balancing act fell apart as Baku repeatedly criticized Turkey for undermining its blockade on Armenia.[10] They accused Turkey of aiding Armenia's war effort. By the end of 1992, the agreement to ship the EU wheat was falling apart as Turkey tried to use the delivery schedules as leverage upon Armenia. Shipments were supposed to be 1,000 tons daily, but in the end never exceeded more than half of that amount.[11] This was especially serious since Armenia was running out of bread and other food supplies. Turkey literally had leverage over Armenia's lifeline. The electricity deal also collapsed as Turkey reneged on the agreement.[12]

As the military situation on the ground began to change dramatically in favor of the Armenians in the end of 1992 and especially in 1993, Armenia's policy towards Turkey began to change. When Yerevan realized that their attempt at creating a policy with Turkey exclusive of the conflict in NKR was failing they made a dramatic change of course.

By April of 1993, Armenian–Turkey relations had hit a new low. When NKR forces seized the Azeri province of Kelbajar relations became hostile.

Turkey repositioned forces towards the Armenian border and Turkish President Ozal made direct threats towards Armenia.[13] These actions followed the complete closure of the Turkish border to the transshipment of all humanitarian aid to Armenia through Turkish territory.[14] Turkey's justification for its actions was that until Armenian forces withdrew from captured Azeri territory the border would remain closed.

The spring of 1993 was the second time that relations between the two states became heated but this time the chill would last far longer. The first time relations were tense was in the spring of 1992, when NKR forces captured the towns of Shusha and Lachin, the vital land corridor between Armenia and Nagorno-Karabagh. During the months leading to the fall of these two strategic towns, Armenian militias killed Azeri civilians in the village of Khodjali. What was a common occurrence amongst both sides early in the conflict became one of a number of concerns raised in Turkey by the pan-Turkists. Statements coming from Ankara following this early string of Azeri defeats prompted the Commander of CIS forces General Shapashnikov to warn "...of a third world war, if Turkey becomes involved in the Nagorno-Karabagh."[15]

The closure of Turkey's border with Armenia and Turkey's support to Azerbaijan essentially ended bilateral relations between the two countries. What remained of the Armenian–Turkish dialogue would have to come in multi-lateral forums such as the CSCE, later OSCE Minsk Group, the Black Sea Economic Cooperation (BSEC) Agreement and the United Nations. In addition, other methods were used to communicate not just between diplomats, but also the heads of state.[16]

When Turkish President Turgat Ozal died in May 1993, Armenia's President flew to Ankara to pay his respects. During his visit to Ankara, talks were held between Prime Minister Demirel, President Elchibey of Azerbaijan and Ter-Petrossyan. The opportunity presented by Ozal's death was clear: Ozal was not friendly towards Armenia and with his passing away a unique opportunity became available to lessen tension and to negotiate an end to the Nagorno-Karabagh conflict.[17]

During this same period intense negotiations were taking place on resolving the conflict in NKR. The United States, Russia and Turkey presented a plan called the Tripartite Agreement. Eventually all the parties to the conflict, including Nagorno-Karabagh, agreed to the plan. However, events in Azerbaijan led to the collapse of the Elchibey regime, which subsequently fueled chaos on the front-line. The Nagorno-Karabagh Armenians took advantage of the disorder to finally consolidate their positions and rationalize the frontlines.

With the momentary window at resolving the conflict and improving relations with Turkey closing in the spring of 1993, Armenia–Turkey relations collapsed. As Azerbaijan's military defeats mounted, Turkey increased the rhetoric. The Turkish Prime Minister Tansu Ciller went as far as to state that she would ask parliament to go to war if Armenia violated the Treaty of Kars and invaded Nakhichevan, the portion of Azerbaijan with a common border with Armenia and Turkey, but separated from Azerbaijan.[18]

The Turkish threats over Nakhichevan were in addition to growing threats from Ankara about alleged Armenian assistance to the Kurdish Workers Party (PKK). Turkey alleged that the Armenian "Special Services" had established PKK training camps throughout Armenia and occupied Azeri territories.[19] Armenia categorically denied these charges and offered Turkey the opportunity to have inspectors view the purported locations of these training camps. Armenian officials noted with interest that Turkey's claims of camps happened to be in locations of critical concern to Armenia and Karabagh; for example, the area around the Medzamor Nuclear power plant and the Lachin Corridor. The Turks went as far as accusing the leader of the PKK, Abdullah Ocalan, of being an Armenian.[20]

The war of rhetoric between the two sides continued to grow and the atmosphere between the two countries would not become remotely civil until 1995. However, in the interim Turkey supported Azerbaijan while it attempted to drive the NKR Armenians out of the territory seized within Azerbaijan. Turkish support included diplomatic support for Azerbaijan in international forums, to include the CSCE Minsk Group. By the summer and fall of 1994, proposals were floating where Turkey would send a contingent for any future peacekeeping or observer force.[21]

Armenian policy throughout this period was to look for opportunities to resolve its differences with Turkey. As stated earlier the Armenian position regarding the border closure by Turkey was that "Armenia does not place preconditions on relations with Turkey."[22] The Turkish demand that the border could not be opened without an Armenian withdrawal from Azeri territory struck Yerevan as unreasonable. Armenia had the opportunity to press claims against Turkey and in particular the issue of the Armenian Genocide, which the Ter-Petrossyan government chose not to raise. It was the issue of the Genocide which caused Armenian Foreign Minister Raffi Hovannisian to resign following comments he made while in Turkey.[23]

The fact that Hovannisian, a Diaspora Armenian from the United States, made this statement and was consequently forced out of his position is indicative of the extent to which the Ter-Petrossyan government has gone to assuage Turkish concerns over the issue of the Armenian Genocide. While it may have been naive of the Armenians to believe that with their official stance on the Genocide they could form a relationship with Turkey based on mutual economic benefits independent of the conflict in Nagorno-Karabagh. In return Turkey did not attach as much significance to Yerevan's position on the Genocide as they did to their broader political agenda of supporting Azerbaijan to exert influence in the Transcaucasus.

Turkish policy forced the Armenian leadership to seek a new security structure. It was during the heightened tensions in the summer of 1992, when Nagorno-Karabagh's military situation was desperate and Turkey continued to hamper the shipment of humanitarian assistance, that Armenia looked to Russia for recreating the security environment which existed on Armenia's border with Turkey during the Soviet Union. The reassertion of Russian power in the Transcaucasus which began in 1992, would grow to seriously hamper Turkish efforts to influence developments in the region. The growth of Armenian-Russian relations while ensuring Armenian military security, left Armenia with fewer options to exercise in the region. Armenian leaders never gave up on the option to develop relations with Turkey.

In October 1995, Armenian President Levon Ter-Petrossyan, during a speech at a gathering of Armenian-Americans in Washington hosted by the Armenian Assembly of America, stated "Nor does Armenia consider any country to be its enemy—not even Azerbaijan."[24] The nature of his speech amongst Diaspora Armenians, who are far less forgiving regarding Turkey, was indicative of Ter-Petrossyan's desire to arrive at negotiated solutions leading to the normalization of relations.

1995 did see some movement in Armenian–Turkish relations. The cause of this movement was a combination of factors. The first was the September 1994 signing of the "Contract of the Century." While Armenia was not a player at all in the negotiations leading to the contract for exploitation of Azerbaijan's oil wealth, Armenia was a silent player in terms of its potential to disrupt plans at transporting the oil and it played a role in Turkish, as well as policy in some Western capitals, for enticing Armenia from its position regarding Russia. Interestingly enough there was some convergence between the Armenian and Turkish position on the pipeline issue.

The second reason for the change in Turkish–Armenian relations was the growing sophistication of the Armenian-American lobby. Legislation in the US Congress which would have placed a ban on American aid to Turkey, held out the real possibility that the Armenian lobby would be able to pass substantive authorizing legislation which could dramatically effect US–Turkish relations. The legislation, the Humanitarian Aid Corridor Act, called for a ban on aid to nations which prevent the delivery of humanitarian aid to those in need.[25]

Turkey's response to the changes in the situation was two-fold. With the oil contract signed, the next phase of the project was to build pipelines to export the oil. Surprisingly, Turkey advocated a pipeline through Armenia. While negotiations were taking place to move Azerbaijan's flow of early oil through either Georgia or Russia, the issue of major concern was the late oil, which would involve upwards of 700,000 barrels a day. Turkey worked with Georgia as a more realistic possibility, but did not back away from advocating a late oil route through Armenia. Second, Turkey, in response to the potential for a ban in US aid to Turkey, chose to open an air corridor to Armenia. While this was more a symbolic gesture, it was an attempt by Turkey to provide some measure of gradual adjustment of policy towards Yerevan. At the most it convinced the United States that Turkey was behaving sincerely by making this gesture.[26]

However, as the spring of 1995 progressed, one event which many observers in the region missed was the trip by Istanbul district mayor Gurbuz Capan, who visited Armenia and laid a wreath at the Armenian Genocide memorial in Yerevan. This symbolic act, during the 80th anniversary of the Genocide, by an elected Turkish leader, could not have taken place without some official sanction. While it did not lead to Turkish recognition of the Genocide or even an end to Turkish attempts at revisionism, it was part of a series of incremental, low-profile steps taken by Armenia and Turkey to address troublesome issues.[27]

As time passed, the Turkish blockade of Armenia, while presenting a major impediment to the development and recovery of Armenia's economy, also began to have an effect on Turkey's eastern provinces. The people living on the Turkish side of the border wanted it reopened so that they could conduct trade with neighboring Armenia. However, both states managed to get around the blockade, by conducting low level trade through Georgia. Some of this was done without the consent of the Turkish government.[28]

By 1996, there appeared like there was going to be some major changes in Armenia–Turkey relations. Turkish Prime Minister Mesut Yilmaz stated in the spring that Turkey would reopen its border with Armenia if both Armenia and Azerbaijan could agree on a statement of principles for resolving the Nagorno-Karabagh conflict. This appeared to be a major change in Turkey's position which the Armenians were eager to see Turkey follow through on. However, pressure from Azerbaijan on Turkey, regarding potential future oil routes, forced Yilmaz to retreat from this policy.[29] Shortly thereafter the coalition in Turkey collapsed and Necmettin Erbakan's Refah party came to power in a coalition government with Ciller's True Path Party.

Since the rise of the Refah/True Path Party coalition government and the ensuing crises in Turkey's domestic governance, there has been little opportunity for a thaw in Armenian–Turkish relations.

ARMENIA'S RELATIONS WITH RUSSIA

Armenia's most important foreign relationship is with Russia. Relations with Russia have always been difficult as Armenia tries to avoid playing the role of junior partner. Concerns about Russia's role as regional hegemon have always centered on whether or not Russia can develop advantageous relations with others through its support of Armenia. This in turn has fueled concerns among Armenians that Russian support is always contingent upon how its relations develops with Azerbaijan. Armenians are concerned that they will pay a certain price if Azerbaijan–Russia relations improve.

Little differentiation is made, among Armenians, between decisions over Nagorno-Karabagh made by the Communists during the Soviet period and the current nature of Russian policy in the region. As previously state, the collapse of the Soviet Union saw a major shift in the balance of power in the Caucasus region. Russia clearly wanted to be rid of the trouble in the Caucasus and especially the growing conflict over Nagorno-Karabagh. For Yerevan this left a major power vacuum which they were concerned would be filled by Turkey or Iran.

With only two regional players left to balance, Armenia's options were limited. However, policy making in Russia towards the Transcaucasus, while in disarray at the center and focused primarily on Western Europe, was essentially left in the hands of elements of the former Soviet military stationed throughout the region. This presented all of the former Soviet States, but especially those involved in local conflicts, to bargain with the local Russian military commanders. This was the case for the 7th Army stationed in Armenia. Furthermore, the Russian Ministry of Defense took on a more active role in early negotiations over the Nagorno-Karabagh conflict. Eventually as Russia began to reorient its policy towards the former Soviet states, a convergence of interests between Russia and Armenia began to grow. During early 1992, while Armenia was still seeking to reorient itself towards the West and hoping to create a working relationship with Turkey it became clear to Armenia's leaders that Turkey was not going to be responsive so long as the war in Nagorno-Karabagh continued to go badly for Azerbaijan. By the summer and fall of 1992, when the situation on the battlefield took a turn for the worse, Armenia began to reorient its security needs towards Moscow.

How did this develop? The collapse of the Soviet Union left Armenia devoid of any security structure. While NATO is in the process of taking in three new members in 1997, in 1992 there was no talk of NATO expansion nor a Partnership for Peace (PfP). There was no security system in place other than the CSCE, which was a hollow organization, apart from its use as a forum for mediating conflict. Finally, the pressing needs of the Nagorno-Karabagh conflict would eventually call for a structure which would allow Armenia to focus its efforts east.

On May 15, 1992, Armenia signed the Tashkent agreement which created a collective security arrangement for the CIS states. While this agreement did not lead to any form of support for Armenia, it drew a line between those states in the Caucasus which were willing to participate in a reorganization of the former Soviet States under Russian direction. Neither Georgia or Azerbaijan were members. Yerevan knew that as Russia began to reassert itself in the region that Armenia would be able to benefit from the fact that it was a member of the CIS. Russia made it clear that they wanted all of the former states other than the Baltics to join the CIS and clearly sought to exploit the conflict in Nagorno-Karabagh to leverage Azerbaijan into joining the Commonwealth.[30]

Yerevan, and to a greater extent the Karabagh Armenians, wanted Russian assistance to ensure the security of Nagorno-Karabagh. The process of gaining Karabagh's security led to higher losses for Azerbaijan, which for Russia would hopefully lead to Azeri acquiescence towards membership in the CIS.

As Armenia sought to improve its position in the conflict, it needed to secure its border with Turkey. On September 30, 1992, Armenia signed an agreement with Russia in which Russian border guards would patrol the frontier with Turkey. The placing of border guards under Russian command did not mean that all of the troops were Russian. What Armenia wanted was the Russian security umbrella which would protect them from Turkey. A large percentage of the border guards were Armenian. They would be recruited locally and receive training with the Russians and remain under Russian command. This agreement was more than symbolic in that it gave the Armenians the opportunity to focus on Nagorno-Karabagh.

By the end of the first half of 1993, the Nagorno-Karabagh conflict had become one sided. The Azeris were for the most part driven out of the entire enclave, in addition to six adjoining regions which the Armenians secured. The regime in Baku had changed and Heidar Aliyev, the former KGB general and politburo member became the new President of Azerbaijan. Aliyev brought Azerbaijan into the CIS and showed himself to be more politically adept than his predecessor Elchibey.[31]

The Armenians were concerned by Aliyev's new pragmatism towards Moscow. There were also numerous signals that Aliyev was not going to direct his efforts to the negotiations process. He set out to launch a number of small scale offensives against Nagorno-Karabagh. He even brought in some 1500 Afghan Mujahideen who helped organize an offensive in November.[32] Following these events, an incident took place in which Vladimir Kazimirov, Boris Yeltsin's special negotiator for the Nagorno-Karabagh conflict, was fired upon while his vehicle was approaching Armenian territory. This led to a prompt demarche to Armenia from Russian foreign Minister Andrei Kozyrev.[33]

Clearly there was something wrong with the Russian–Armenian relationship, but there is little to explain what was taking place. What followed this incident was a large scale Azeri offensive which began in December 1993. This offensive followed an Azeri rejection of the CSCE Minsk Group's latest negotiated agreement. The Azeri attack would lead to the most intense fighting of the entire war. Azerbaijan achieved some initial success, but gained little on the ground. The casualty rates were high on both sides.[34] During this period of intense fighting the Russians pressed hard for a cease-fire. Russian Defense Minister Pavel Grachev was actively involved in the negotiations process. His role was indicative of the extent to which the Defense Ministry was actively involved in this conflict from its very origins, whether it be at the local or state level.

At the core of Russia's proposal for resolving the conflict was agreement to a cease-fire to be followed by the imposition of Russian peacekeepers along the front-line. It was during this period that Russian mediation efforts sidelined the CSCE Minsk Group. Russia's Defense Minister and Kazimirov were shuttling back and forth from Yerevan to Stepanakert to Baku.[35]

Parallel to the imposition of the cease-fire was the future status of Russia's position within the Caucasus region. All three Transcaucasian states were aware of this and each one tried to get the best bargain. Armenia, Georgia and Azerbaijan were under enormous pressure. All three states were engaged in either an active or frozen conflict and the Russians were using these problems to pressure them.

At stake for Russia was the reimposition of the former Soviet border and the emplacement of military bases throughout the region. Hard negotiations took place as the Russians wanted to patrol the border of Azerbaijan with Iran and the proposed cease-fire line in addition to reopening the radar station at Gabayla. In the case of Armenia, the Russians wanted to station a motorized rifle division and integrate Armenia into Russia's air defense network. The Russians also wanted to base troops in three sites in Georgia and patrol the Georgian ports.[36]

A cease-fire in the Nagorno-Karabagh conflict was finally arrived at on May 12, 1994. The cease-fire was formalized on July 27, when the defense ministers of Armenia, Azerbaijan, Russia and the commander of the Army of Nagorno-Karabagh signed the agreement.[37] Between the period of the cease-fire and the signing of the agreement on June 6, Armenia agreed to the basing of Russian forces on its soil near the city of Gyumri. As part of the agreement, Armenia would pay for their basing, but Armenian officers and specialists would be sent to Russian training schools at Russia's expense. The Russian forces would be based for twenty years. Once again, as with the Russian border guard units, local Armenians would be recruited to provide some 60% of the manpower. For Armenia this was a way of receiving training from the Russians on modern weapons.

The basing agreement would be the first in a long series of agreements between Armenia and Russia in which their Armed forces would cooperate on a whole host of issues ranging from technical development to training. Armenia gained from Russia by being actively tied into the Russian military establishment. In addition, the Russian military came to view the Armenian armed forces as the most competent in the region and perhaps in the former Soviet States. The Russians believed that of the Caucasian states, Armenia was the most reliable partner in the region and with a strong army they would be able to help implement Russian security policy.

During the summer of 1996, the Russian–Armenian military relationship had matured to the point where eleven protocols on military projects were signed. These protocols covered a whole host of issues. They are:

1) Protocol on bilateral military cooperation.
2) Intergovernmental protocol on equipment deliveries.
3) Protocol on radar and electronic systems.
4) Protocol on air defense cooperation.
5) Protocol on training and joint operations.
6) Protocol on organizing coalition forces in the Transcaucasus.
7) Protocol on local recruiting for combined forces.
8) Protocol on military–technical cooperation.
9) Protocol on Armenian and Russian unit interaction.
10) Protocol on military training and research.
11) Protocol on military research.[38]

From 1993 to 1995, Russia was the dominant force in the Armenia–Russia bilateral relationship. Armenia was reliant upon Russia for weapons, fuel and other necessities of war. In addition, Russia provided large amounts of economic assistance. Russia was Armenia's largest trade partner. The scale of Russia's military support would not be revealed until March 1997.

With prompting from Azerbaijan, Lev Rokhlin, the Chairman of the Duma's security committee, it was discovered for the first time the extent of arms transfers from Russia to Armenia. The numbers were significant as well as the types of weapons delivered. Armenia received tanks, armored fighting vehicles, artillery and surface-to-surface SCUD missiles. The delivery of the latter weapon system provides Armenia with the capability to strike at Azeri targets as far away as the capital, Baku. The debate that the arms transfers sparked in Moscow focused primarily on Rokhlin's assertion that the weapons were given to Armenia for free while the Russian Army is short of cash and cannot take care of its own personnel and maintain operational readiness. Rokhlin also sought to express his concern over the nature of Russia's policy in the region believing that Russian support for Armenia is done at the expense of Azerbaijan, and has shown little in the way of success.[39]

This final point is at the center of policy concern within Armenia as to the nature of Russia's vying factions. In particular, regarding the Caucasus, Russian policy is of two minds. There are those within the Russian national security bureaucracy who believe that it is in Russia's interests as a great power to reassert their control over the former Soviet borders and to prevent or limit the extent of Western penetration into the Caucasus and Central Asia. Armenia plays a major role in these security calculations. The other mindset is centered around the raw materials faction such as the Russian energy giant Gazprom and the Russian oil industry. This faction believes that as Russia becomes a market economy its best interests would be served by taking an active role in investing in Caspian oil. This group is essentially concerned with business interests. They see no conflict in working with Western oil companies in exploiting the oil wealth of Azerbaijan.

While the business faction may want to see greater Russian control over the export routes, they are in favour of the expedient resolution of the conflicts in the region so that they can all begin to derive the profits from their investments. They believe that Russia's policy in the Caucasus is too focused on pressuring Azerbaijan and therefore favors Armenia. It is for the above reasons that Yerevan is worried about the struggle within Russia which will inevitably have a major effect upon the resolution of the Nagorno-Karabagh conflict.

For Russia, Armenia's position in the Caucasus is crucial. It is the only wedge between Turkey and Azerbaijan and the rest of the Turkic world. In addition, it borders Iran, a nation which Russia has sought to create a strategic relationship. While Armenia may not have valuable raw materials, its central location in the Caucasus gives it great geopolitical value for Russia.

The Armenians understand this Russian perception of their position. However, Yerevan is concerned that it will be caught in the position of being Russia's policeman in the region. The Armenians want the Karabagh conflict solved, but do not want a solution imposed upon them as a result of great power manipulation. They want to improve relations with Turkey although they move cautiously when it comes to negotiating. Russia perceives any thaw in relations between the two states as a threat.

While Armenian–Turkish rapprochement is unlikely in the near future, for Russia this is a real concern. Armenia needs to be kept in the Russian sphere of influence because it plays such a crucial role. For Armenia, in a region where security is a luxury, Russia's role in insuring it is critical. This is why Armenia accepts the basing of Russian forces on its soil and the patrolling of its borders with Turkey and Iran. Nevertheless, Armenia wants to be integrated into the international and especially European economy.

The Armenian government does not believe that they will be able to receive requisite economic assistance needed from Russia to insure investment and eventual economic prosperity. Russia itself has a weak economy and it will be years before a recovery will take place. However, Armenia's perception of its security environment is that while the military phase of the Nagorno-Karabagh conflict is over for the time being, an even greater threat is growing.

THE ROLE OF OIL

Armenia realized from the outset of independence that at some point oil would begin to play a major role in effecting the outcome of conflicts within the region. Most importantly the development of Azerbaijan's offshore oil presented to Yerevan both a threat and the possibility of greater prosperity for the entire region. If Armenia could become a crossroads for trade and pipelines moving east-west and north-south then the benefits of oil would be obvious.

However, Armenia has yet to see any real sign that oil development and pipeline export routes will lead to any substantive gain. At the core of Armenia's concerns is that Armenia will be forced to abandon the Nagorno-Karabagh Armenians. The stakes involved in the regional oil game are high for all of the states of the Transcaucasus as well as Russia, Iran, and Turkey.

For Azerbaijan, oil brings the hope of a large influx of foreign investment, long term oil export driven growth, and possible economic domination of the

Transcaucasus. Beyond these tangible benefits it will also give Azerbaijan the opportunity to maintain its independence. Heidar Aliyev has astutely used the shares in the Azerbaijan International Operating Company (AIOC) as a means of attracting the oil companies of key European and American firms. By whetting their appetites for oil profits, Aliyev believes that he will then be able to influence the leadership of the major powers involved in the region. Oil money and the corporations which are involved in the oil business have the resultant effect of increasing foreign country interests in the region.

Whether or not this Azeri policy has been successful, it certainly led to a marked increase in the lobbying efforts on Azerbaijan's behalf in a number of capitals.[40] In the case of Great Britain, its strategic interests are primarily driven by economic interests. In the Caucasus this is even more the case as British Petroleum holds 17% share in the AIOC consortium.[41] As for the United States, its strategic interests in the Caucasus are defined by three issues of which two hold greater sway. First, initial US activity in the region was primarily driven by the prominent role of the Armenian–American lobby. They drew initial US attention to the region during the beginning of the Nagorno-Karabagh conflict in 1988. Their activity focused on the US Congress. By 1988, America's involvement with Armenia grew to the provision of continued US humanitarian assistance to the victims of the massive earthquake which struck the country. The US Agency for International Development (USAID) became actively involved in the reconstruction efforts. When the Soviet Union collapsed in 1991, US involvement in the region was primarily of a humanitarian nature, again driven by the lobbying efforts of the Armenian-American community.

Second, as the Soviet Union collapsed the US was concerned about the expansion of Iranian influence into the region. One of the pillars of American foreign policy in the Middle East is the containment of Iran which includes not only the Persian Gulf, but Central Asia and the Caucasus. In order to check any Iranian moves the US supported Turkey in its attempt at reordering the region.[42] The third issue which began to drive US policy in the region is access to export of Azerbaijan's oil to Western markets. How American policy has matured into its present concern over oil resources developed in the following way.[43]

Amoco oil corporation along with British Petroleum were the primary force in the AIOC. Negotiations between all the companies with successive Azeri governments continued for two years until they were prepared to sign an agreement in 1993. However, that agreement collapsed when internal turmoil resulting from defeats in Nagorno-Karabagh forced President Elchibey from power.[44] Heidar Aliyev called for a renegotiating of the agreement and subsequently signed the $8 billion dollar contract in September 1994. Since that time additional agreements have been signed involving US oil companies, the Russian company Lukoil and others. All together American holdings in Azerbaijan's oil industry are 29% in the AIOC, 30% in the Caspian International Petroleum Company (CIPCO), and 50.5% in the North Apsheron Operating Company (NAOC).[45] The defining moment though for active US involvement is the signing of the 1994 contract. With a deal in-hand the US oil industry began a major program of influencing US policy in the region.

This placed the Armenian government in an unusual position regarding the issue of oil and the Armenian-American lobby. While Armenia wants active US involvement in the negotiations process, the Armenian lobby advocated a more vigorous US position. In 1994, the lobby called for the appointment of an individual of Ambassadorial rank to represent the United States in the negotiating process.[46] Furthermore, in authorizing and appropriating legislation for Fiscal Years 1996 and 1997, the Armenian lobby successfully included language calling for US government plans to study pipeline routes through Armenia and Georgia.[47] This advocacy dovetailed with the American oil company advocacy for a more vigorous US policy in the Caucasus which would pressure the Republic of Armenia. In particular the oil lobby used the argument that United State's interests in the region were being hampered by US law, lobbied for by Armenians, which prevents the direct delivery of US aid to the government of Azerbaijan, Section 907.[48]

The concerns the oil companies have raised essentially state that US business interests in the region are undercut because of this discriminatory provision. Since the United is not perceived as a fair arbitrator, US oil companies will suffer and hence US interests.[49] Both former President Bush and President Clinton are opposed to Section 907, but the real impetus for lifting the provision followed the 1994 signing of the oil contract.[50]

For the Armenian government they view the interests of the oil companies as a potentially dangerous force. They have successfully lobbied their governments to pressure Armenia into making concessions in the Nagorno-Karabagh conflict. They site the skillful use by Azerbaijan in apportioning shares in each of the consortia signed since 1994. Azerbaijan has brought the Russians, French, Americans, Turks, Saudis, British, Japanese, Iranians, Italians, and Norwegians into one of a series of oil deals signed.

THE DIASPORA

Even before Armenia became independent, its Diaspora community was actively involved in the politics and future development of what remained of their ancestral homeland. There are large and active Armenian communities in the United States, Russia, Iran, France, Lebanon and even as far as the South American country of Argentina. While many of these communities were ready to provide financial assistance to Armenia in the form of humanitarian aid and in other charitable projects beginning with the 1988 earthquake, they were hesitant to provide real developmental assistance.

Many technically proficient Diaspora Armenians went to the newly independent Republic to assist in foreign aid programs which involved the distribution of humanitarian aid and technical assistance, but Armenian businessmen were hesitant to invest in the country. However, a field where politically active Armenians were able to provide a significant amount of support beyond the pocket books of the community was in the formation of lobbying organizations in the West.

In the case of Russia, we have seen that Armenia figures prominently in its security calculations, so even without the large Armenian community, it would be in Russia's interests to support Armenia. However, in the case of the West, and specifically the United States, the role of the Armenian–American lobby is crucial. Again, as described earlier, initial US involvement in the Caucasus was geared primarily toward Georgia and Armenia. In the case of Georgia, the reputation which Eduard Shevardnadze had developed in the West as the Soviet Union's Foreign Minister led to US support.

In the case of Armenia, the large Armenian Diaspora community in the US, number almost a million. This large and active population had a significant impact on US policy towards Armenia. The United States was reluctant to become too involved in the region, but because of the humanitarian situation in Armenia, combined with strong advocacy on the part of Armenian–Americans the US provided large amounts of humanitarian assistance.[51] Armenia eventually became the largest per capita recipient of US aid in the former Soviet Union and the fourth largest dollar recipient following Russia, Ukraine, and Kazakhstan.

Consistently Armenia received hard earmarks, Congressional directives appropriating funds, in fiscal years 1996 and 1997. Of the former Soviet states only Ukraine, Georgia and Armenia received hard earmarks.[52] In addition, the dollar amounts appropriated by Congress were significantly larger than the amounts sought after by the Clinton Administration. The aid provided by the United States literally kept Armenians from freezing and starving to death during the worst years of the Azeri and Turkish blockades. Equally important to the assistance, in terms of the punishing value it had on Azerbaijan, was Section 907 of the Freedom Support Act.

In 1992, when Congress passed the Freedom Support Act for the implementation of United States Assistance to the Newly Independent States of the former Soviet Union, Section 907 was placed into the law by the Armenian lobby. This law effectively prevented the direct delivery of US assistance to the government of Azerbaijan. While the law was not favored by the Bush Administration it was not a controversial issue until two years later. The United States did not have a compelling national interest in the region nor were there sufficient commercial interests until the signing of the 1994 oil contract.

For the Armenian government, the Armenian lobby was a double-edged sword. The lobby was not united. There were those whose stated position was to support the democratically elected officials of the Republic of Armenia and those who were linked to traditional Armenian political parties which continued to operate outside of Armenia after the Genocide and Sovietization of the Republic. There was tension between the differing lobbies. Yet both continued to advocate for the continued support of the Republic in terms of humanitarian and development assistance and for the maintenance of the Azerbaijan sanctions contained in Section 907.

However, following the December 1994 banning of the Armenian Revolutionary Federation (ARF) in Armenia, the divided lobby became a problem. The ARF which has offices throughout the world organized a campaign to publicize the curtailment of political activity within the Republic. This activity went as far as activating their grassroots networks in the United States to raise the human rights issues with the US Congress. The ARF through their lobbying arm, the Armenian National Committee (ANC), even brought opposition leaders to the United States to meet with Congressmen. This activity was of great concern to the Armenian government because Congress is considered to be a stronghold for the Armenian–American community. Whereas earlier the differences within the Diaspora were kept within the community, this was the first time in the US, one of Armenia's largest financial supporters, that the community very obviously was speaking with more than one voice. Armenia had largely benefited internationally because it was one of two former Soviet States whose leader was not a Communist Party member, it was relatively democratic and compared to its neighbors, Armenia enjoyed a good reputation. Armenia capitalized on the image of a struggling democracy pressured by its neighbors.

The impact of the internal situation within the Republic effected the way in which Armenia was perceived. Following the 1995 parliamentary elections which the Organization for Security and Cooperation in Europe (OSCE, formerly CSCE) declared "Free but not Fair" the criticism of Armenia and the perception that it was sliding down the path towards authoritarianism only served to mar its reputation internationally.[53] This was important for Armenia because one of its best selling points was its commitment to democracy and a market economy. Following the Parliamentary elections the government boasted about the praise they had received from the international community over their economic policies. While the results of the elections, in the short term, did not hurt Armenia's ability to receive assistance from the United States, questions were raised and elements of the Armenian lobby helped facilitate the dissemination of the story.

In comparison, Azerbaijan which held its parliamentary elections in November of the same year received minimal press coverage in the United States. This derives more so from the fact that papers which have large Armenian communities took an interest in the story of the Armenian parliamentary elections and hence in speaking to members of the community, undoubtedly those Armenians critical of the government got there views in the press. The criticism of Armenia, fueled by Armenians and primarily by the ARF presented a real problem for the government because it went from becoming an internal problem to an international one which effected Armenia's foreign relations.

The international environment became even more difficult when for the first time in post-Soviet Armenia, large scale public protest followed the September 1996, Presidential elections. Charges of governmental fraud by the opposition were widespread. The opposition parties did much to bring attention to the events taking place in Yerevan. Furthermore, the scale of the protests taking place in front of foreign Embassies and observers provided a first hand glimpse of a public relations debacle for the government.

The international effect of the electoral disturbances were the following:

1) Armenia was widely perceived as sliding towards authoritarianism and thus while there are major differences in the level of political freedom within Armenia and Azerbaijan, the international reputation of the ruling party would be viewed as equivalent to that of the party of Azerbaijan's ruling strong man, Heidar Aliyev.

2) Violence amongst Armenians in the homeland created disinterest and disgust amongst the Diaspora who would normally be willing to assist technically or financially.

3) Provide additional fuel for diasporan political parties which are opposed to the ANM and thus widen the rift amongst Diaspora Armenians.[54]

4) Damaged Armenia's reputation as the most politically stable country in the region. This could only make it more difficult to receive badly needed foreign investment.

Although the elections prompted cautious criticism from the OSCE and the United States, the net effect for the ruling party was that the international community was comfortable with the current government.[55] In particular, Ter-Petrossyan was seen as a responsible leader who kept more nationalist elements within Armenia and the Diaspora in check. While international criticism of the electoral process was restrained it was clear that the government in Yerevan had lost some of the moral authority with which it spoke about conditions inside of the country. Yet, the flow of assistance to Armenia both humanitarian and support from international financial lending institutions did not abate. While there was concern for the state of Armenian democracy there was also relief that the opposition did not succeed.

For example, the National Accord which represents the views of the opposition political parties was viewed with disapproval from the international community for the following reasons:

1) The National Accord callled for rebuilding the social safety net which existed during the Soviet period which would result in large budget deficits and higher inflation. This proposed policy ran counter to the policies established by the international finical lending institutions and the Armenian government.

2) The National Accord called for the recognition of Nagorno-Karabagh.

This second point in the oppositions platform was extremely controversial because it ran directly counter to the tactics used by the ANM in negotiating a solution to the conflict.

RELATIONS WITH IRAN

The collapse of the Soviet Union created new opportunities for both Armenia and Iran. As a Soviet Republic, Armenian relations with the Islamic Republic of Iran were largely constrained by the control of foreign affairs from Moscow with Tehran as opposed to Yerevan and Tehran.

When Armenia became independent, the prospect of a healthy relationship was initially constrained by the ever-worsening situation in Nagorno-Karabagh. Prior history made the development of normal relations with Iran difficult. While the will existed on both sides the basis did not exist. First, links between the former Soviet Union and Iran were based on the Soviet infrastructure which connected the Republic of Azerbaijan with Iran. This included railroads, roads, and ports. Furthermore, there was a large Azeri population in Northern Iran. There were more Azeris living in Iran than in the Republic of Azerbijan, and familial links existed between the two.

While there is a large Armenian population in Iran, relative to other Diaspora populations, it paled in comparison to Iran's Azeri population. The other issue which presented an initial problem for Armenia was the general concern that relations might be based on religious grounds. Armenia is a Christian country while Iran is an Islamic Republic dominated by Shiite Muslims. Azerbaijan is also a Shiite Muslim nation, which is ethnically Turkish, but has many aspects of Persian culture.

The concerns over religion and culture turned out to be overstated as the political elite in Azerbaijan, dominated by Abul faz Elchibey's, Azerbaijan Popular Front (APF) turned out to have an extremely irredentist position on Southern Azerbaijan, Northern Iran.[56] The APF called for the reunification of all Azeris and was overtly pro-Turkish and held Iran's clerics in disdain. For example, in 1989 the APF encouraged the tearing down of border outposts and fences separating Azerbaijan from Iran. This agitation directed towards Iran prior to the collapse of the Soviet Union served to alter Iran's position towards its' northern neighbors and to become involved in a balancing act.[57]

However, the conflict in Nagorno-Karabagh between Christian Armenians and Muslim Azeris created tensions between Iran and Armenia. While the Iranian leadership viewed with dismay the policies of the APF and the growing Turkish–Azeri friendship they nevertheless had to express concern over the plight of their fellow Muslims in Azerbaijan. The Islamic clerics in Tehran in order to be true to their own ideology could not easily snub Azerbaijan for geopolitical reasons.[58]

Tehran also had to be aware of the potential impact of the Karabagh conflict on its own Azeri citizens. With almost 15 million Azeris residing in northern Iran (representing almost a quarter of Iran's population), the constraints on Iranian policy in the Caucasus become obvious. Iran chose a pragmatic route in its policies in the region.[59] They sought to mediate the conflict. Iran demonstrated that it was in fact a responsible state in this region. The Iranians were able to bring Armenians and Azeris together to negotiate, however this situation would not last very long as events on the battle field and internationally sidestepped the Iranian attempts at mediation.

First, the Armenians of Nagorno-Karabagh saw their situation as desperate and did not feel that they could successfully negotiate while their very existence was precarious at best. They were concerned with security first and foremost. It was not an abstraction for the Karabagh Armenians who were virtually surrounded and under constant bombardment. During critical phases of the Iranian negotiating efforts, NKR forces seized strategic objectives, which essentially torpedoed Iranian mediation.

Second, the conflict was readily becoming internationalized and Iran's competitors in the region, most notably Turkey, viewed Iranian sponsored negotiations with growing apprehension. Iranian attempts at mediation came to an end in spring 1992. The CSCE took on the responsibility for mediating the conflict. While Iran certainly wanted to see a resolution to a potentially destabilizing conflict they were also displeased that the new forum for negotiations excluded Iran.

Armenia, which hoped that eventually it would become integrated into Europe's economic and political infrastructure, welcomed the CSCE initiatives. Yet Armenia continually sought to develop ties with Iran. Armenia's links to the outside world following the disintegration of the Soviet Union left Armenia isolated. Iran provided the possibility of another outlet.

The creation of ties between the two states literally started at ground zero. There were no major roads linking the two countries and the only connection was a pontoon bridge which spanned the Arax river separating the two states. Armenia saw in Iran a potential counterweight to both Turkey and Azerbaijan and a link for what would hopefully become a growing trade relationship with the Persian Gulf, the rest of the Middle East and Central Asia.

However, for the first few years following independence, relations would develop slowly. Yet Iran, wary of Turkish influence in the region and threatened by Azeri calls for unity with Iranian Azerbaijan took on the position that Armenia provided a useful buffer between the two Turkic states. It was in Iran's national interest to see that Armenia survived and it is an unusual case of an ideologically driven Islamic state behaving as a rational state actor with national, Persian interests, supporting a Christian state.[60]

During the period of warfare, Iran repeatedly criticized Armenian victories and complained about the plight of Azerbaijan's refugees. Yet, Iran took no substantive action against Armenia. However, the situation in the summer and fall of 1993, when Armenian forces seized all of the territory south of Nagorno-Karabagh right up to the border with Iran, created tension. Large numbers of Azeri refugees were forced to flee into Iran.

Iran did not want a repeat of the refugee crises which it had to contend with from Afghanistan and Iraq, so the Iranian Army crossed the Azeri border and set up a refugee camp in the Azeri town of Imishli. This Iranian military move in September 1993, created somewhat of a regional panic, although Iran's intentions were clear. Iran had a legitimate concern, in that every Armenian battlefield success created more refugees and hence led to greater agitation in northern Iran as word spread amongst its Azeri citizens that the Armenians were causing their brothers across the border to suffer.

There were two other periods of major tension between Armenia and Iran during the course of the conflict. The first came in October when it was reported that Azerbaijan's new leader Heidar Aliyev hired Afghan mercenaries to fight against Nagorno-Karabagh. It is reported that these Afghans attacked the NKR defense forces by crossing through Northern Iran in order to strike at the Armenians from the South. It is also reported that they were given transit from Afghanistan to Azerbaijan through Iran.

The third major crisis in Armenian-Iranian relations took place in March 1994. An Iranian C-130 used by diplomats leaving Moscow for Iran was shot down as it crossed over a portion of the Azeri-Karabagh front-line. All of the passengers died as the plane was struck by a missile. Iran demanded an apology and the Armenian government quickly moved to investigate the incident.[61]

Once the cease-fire was signed between the conflicting parties in 1994, Armenia's relations with Iran markedly improved. A new bridge was completed across the Arax river and roads and other infrastructure needed to facilitate trade between the two states were being completed. Armenian–Iran trade grew to where Iran became Armenia's largest trading partner.[62] A series of agreements were signed regarding trade issues and by 1997 Armenia was tied into Iran's electrical grid. Discussions had been underway since 1995 to construct a natural gas pipeline which would alleviate additional energy needs although where the money would come from for financing was another question.

The issue of funding economic projects between the two country's was of serious concern. Especially, since the United States was adamantly against any foreign investment in Iran's oil and gas industry. Since 1995, the United States has actively thwarted Iranian attempts at being part of the exploitation of oil and gas in Azerbaijan. The American position has to be of some concern for the Armenian government since their relations with Iran are significant.[63]

It is common knowledge in Armenia that the United States routinely pressures its European allies over their relations with Iran. The Armenians also watched as pressure from the United States in the spring of 1995 forced the government of Azerbaijan and the AIOC to push Iran out of the consortium. In the case of Armenia, the level of US assistance to Armenia is significant enough to place the US in a position to have an inordinate amount of leverage. However, given that the overwhelming majority of US aid to Armenia is of a humanitarian nature, and that Armenia is isolated geographically it would appear that the US has reluctantly accepted the growth of Armenia–Iran relations. In other words, Washington has taken a pragmatic approach towards this aspect of Armenian foreign policy.[64]

Nevertheless, Armenia still has to be careful of the extent of its cooperation especially as to how they are perceived in Washington. The Armenians are regularly described in Washington circles and especially by Azerbaijan's representation in the US as working hand in glove with the Iranians. The level of anti-Iranian rhetoric in the United States is large enough to make Armenia tread carefully as to how far their relations with Iran have developed. Azerbaijan has even leveled charges that Armenia received weapons from Iran in its fight against them.

Politically Iran has never supported the Armenian seizure of Azerbaijani territory and it has repeatedly called for the withdrawal of Armenian forces. Tehran has also been supportive of Azerbaijan's territorial integrity. However, the simple fact that Armenian-Iranian relations have developed so far is testimony to a lasting pragmatic relationship between the two states based on economic interest. Iran has essentially assisted Armenia in the period following the cease-fire to undermine the Azerbaijani blockade of their country. It has helped further Armenia's reach beyond the Caucasus through trilateral agreements between Armenia, Iran and Turkmenistan.

Through economic cooperation with Iran, Armenia circumvents the Russian transportation infrastructure and the twin blockades of Azerbaijan and Turkey. This transportation corridor through Iran is still significantly underdeveloped and the funding for modernization is still difficult to find, but it holds the prospect that in the future Armenia may be able to development a truly redundant system of links to the outside world.

THE KARABAGH CONFLICT

Since independence, Armenia sought to develop normal diplomatic relations with countries within and outside of the region. However, the Nagorno-Karabagh conflict figured deeply in the formulation of relations with its immediate neighbors and beyond. The conflict has always figured into Armenia's calculations because it is an issue in which its neighbors and competing powers have an interest whether it be for economic, geopolitical or ethnic reasons. The nature of the conflict deals with the competing principles of territorial integrity versus self-determination, which many states throughout Asia, the former Soviet Union and the Middle East are struggling to reconcile. Finally for Armenia it is an issue of national security and thus their relations are conditioned by the need to enhance their position.

In 1989, the Armenian Supreme Council (Parliament) made Nagorno-Karabagh a part of Armenia, this decision was effectively annulled when NKR declared its independence in 1991. Whether the decision to declare independence was made cooperatively with Yerevan is not yet known. Since the ANM leaders came from the Karabagh movement and used the issue to come to power in Armenia, they had to find a way to get Azerbaijan to negotiate with the Karabagh Armenians.[65] The ANM's position since independence is to call for the Azeri's to negotiate with the representatives of Nagorno-Karabagh. This has been their position since the beginning of the conflict. However, at the same time Armenia has conducted bilateral negotiations with the leadership in Azerbaijan. Whereas in multi-lateral forums they have always resorted to the former position.

Prior to the spring of 1992, a number of initiatives were made by Russia and Iran to arrange cease-fires and to try and solve the conflict. Following Iran's mediating efforts, the US, concerned with Iranian influence, and at the urging of Turkey, pushed for negotiations under the purview of the CSCE.[66] Through an arrangement of division of labor between the United Nations (UN) and CSCE, the decision was made that the CSCE, a regional security institution, would address the conflict in Nagorno-Karabagh. The Minsk group was formed in early 1992, with the objective of implementing a cease-fire and placing international observers in the conflict zone. Following this phase a peace conference would take place in Minsk where final status issues would be settled. The CSCE Minsk Group served as a forum where the warring parties could negotiate.

However, the Nagorno-Karabagh Armenians were not recognized as a party to the conflict. Instead they were allowed participation as an interested party and with the status of "elected and other representatives of Nagorno-Karabagh."[67] This presented an inherent failure of the Minsk Group, since the Chairman of the Minsk Group chose to deal indirectly with Nagorno-Karabagh representatives through Armenia's delegation. In addition, Karabagh was frequently represented through the prism of two communities: Armenian and Azerbaijani.

For Nagorno-Karabagh the method by which the Minsk Group chose to deal with them misrepresented the conflict. The CSCE, early in its process treated the conflict as intercommunal, between the Armenian and Azerbaijani inhabitants of Nagorno-Karabagh. For the Karabagh Armenians and Armenia, the real issue was between Azerbaijan and Nagorno-Karabagh. It was not until the Karabagh Armenians scored major battlefield successes with the capture of Shusha and Lachin and the formation of the State Defense Committee (which united the various Armenian militias) that the CSCE slowly began to take the Karabagh leadership in Stepanakert seriously. However, Karabagh was only allowed to participate in the third session of the Minsk Group to determine the status of their participation.[68]

Their position as a non-participant only encouraged the Karabagh Armenians to early-on resort to the battlefield. The mindset in Stepanakert was that there was no point to negotiations if you are not granted representation. While they believed that they needed to ensure the security of the enclave through military force they were given additional reasons to do so by the refusal of the CSCE Minsk group to include them as a representative to the process.

The subsequent chaos in Azerbaijan resulting from a string of battlefield defeats at the hands of the Nagorno-Karabagh Armenians, finally resulted in their participation in the talks. However, throughout this entire period of Karabagh military success, the United Nations Security Council passed resolutions condemning the seizure of Azerbaijani territory outside of the enclave of Nagorno-Karabagh. With one exception the UN never condemned the capture of Lachin, the strategic link between Armenia and Nagorno-Karabagh.

The UN passed Security Council Resolution 822, 853, 874 and 884. Each of these resolutions was passed during periods of intense fighting. The UN was careful in that they never condemned Armenia, but recognized Armenia's ability to influence the Armenians of Nagorno-Karabagh. The method with which these resolutions were drafted implied that the UN was aware of the differences of the Nagorno-Karabagh Armenians and the Republic of Armenia. Each UN resolution reiterated the international body's support for the CSCE Minsk Group process and urged that the parties to the conflict implement the Minsk Groups "timetable of urgent steps."

The CSCE process essentially came to a grinding halt as Azerbaijan changed leaders. Aliyev decided that initially the battlefield would be the place for resolving the conflict. Upon the failure of that strategy, following the long and bloody Azeri offensive which began in December 1993, and the subsequent rise of independent Russian mediation the CSCE was momentarily eclipsed.[69]

As stated earlier in this chapter, the Russian mediation process in the region was combined with intense pressure by Moscow to exert its primacy in the region on all the participants to the conflict. This pressure was also felt in Georgia where the Russians were actively involved in resolving the Abkhaz conflict. This pressure led to a renewed interest on the part of both Azerbaijan and Armenia to jump start the CSCE process in 1994. In addition, this also coincided with the signing of the $8 billion oil contract in September of that year. At the same time, the Armenian–American community lobbied extensively for the United States Congress to pressure the White House to become more actively involved in the negotiations. This culminated in a letter to President Clinton signed by 38 members of the House of Represent-atives. The letter specifically called for the appointment of a full-time negoti-ator for the karabagh conflict. The letter also mentioned the enormous economic potential of oil deposits in the region.[70]

The renewed efforts of the CSCE, supported by Armenia and Azerbaijan, stemmed from the distrust both had towards Russia. The Nagorno-Karabagh Armenians also shared this distrust especially since Russia wanted to exclu-sively place Russian peacekeepers along the cease-fire line. All sides wanted soldiers to come from other nations in addition to Russia. However, Russia wanted the bulk of the force to be Russian and under their command. Armenia wanted a peacekeeping force that had the ability to deal with viola-tions, but they also wanted CSCE observers there to keep an eye on every-one, to include the Russians. The Nagorno-Karabagh Armenians were also wary of Russian peacekeepers. In 1991, during "Operation Ring," Russian soldiers as part of the Soviet Army assisted the Azeri interior ministry to drive Armenians out of their villages in the Shahumian region of Azerbaijan.[71]

In December 1994, at the CSCE's Biennial Summit held in Budapest, attended by the heads of state of all of its constituent members, a significant breakthrough was achieved. First, the Russian mediation efforts were incor-porated into the OSCE (the status of the CSCE was elevated to an organiza-tion at this summit) and a co-chairmanship was created in which one seat was to be held by Russia. This was a recognition of the unique interests which Russia held in this region. The other and more significant breakthrough for the Armenians was that the participating countries of the Minsk Group recognized Nagorno-Karabagh as a party to the conflict.[72]

The 1994, CSCE summit raised the expectations of all parties that a solu-tion would be arrived at and that the cease-fire should be maintained. How-ever, the dynamic of the negotiations changed following the 1994 summit. While there was a heightened desire amongst the United States and Russia to find a resolution to the conflict, the growing influence of oil on the arbitra-tors of the conflict began to have a noticeable effect.

The United States took an increasingly active role in the negotiations. US efforts to resolve the conflict included behind the scenes discussions involv-ing the national security advisors of both Armenia and Azerbaijan. By the spring of 1995, the US was pushing a major effort to get Armenia and Azerbaijan to agree to a resolution of the conflict maintaining the sovereignty of Azerbaijan while at the same time guaranteeing a pipeline from Azerbaijan through Armenia.[73]

This effort failed as the dynamic between Yerevan and Stepanakert did not yield to this arrangement. Stepanakert was wary of any swap of sovereignty for oil. The issue of viable security guarantees for Nagorno-Karabagh was consistently raised, as Azerbaijan only offered heightened autonomy, which Nagorno-Karabagh perceived to be a return to the status quo ante bellum.

Yerevan was also in the difficult position of angering Russia over any possible agreement whereby they would undercut Russian ambitions to control the oil export routes. Armenia treaded carefully when it addressed this issue. Whenever the Armenian government did speak about the oil pipeline they were constrained by Russia and Stepanakert. Armenia as early as 1995, tried to separate the issue of Nagorno-Karabagh and the oil pipeline. They wanted to separate the political differences between Armenians and Azeris from economic benefits derived by oil pipelines.

This policy is reminiscent of that pursued by Yerevan towards Ankara. Armenia seeks to separate economic from political issues. This policy has failed in large part because Azerbaijan and Turkey see the two as directly linked: use economic leverage to obtain political goals.

By 1996, Armenia increasingly felt that its position within the OSCE Minsk Group was gradually weakening as the number of states engaged in the Minsk Group who had an economic stake in the exploitation of Azerbaijan's oil wealth increased. Of the eleven states engaged in the process five invested heavily in one or more of the consortiums established. Key states involved in the Minsk Group with oil companies investing in Azerbaijan are the United States, Russia, Italy, France, and Turkey. To Armenia, Azerbaijan as a member of the Minsk Group used oil as its bait to sway the positions of the Group's members.

During the summer of 1996, events in the US Congress became an additional front in the conflict. However, the importance of these events is the official US government response to what transpired in Congress and the fact that the US was becoming more proactive in the negotiating process. Since 1994, the US oil companies acting at the behest of Azerbaijan routinely try to repeal Section 907 of the Freedom Support Act. During the appropriations cycle for Fiscal Year 1997, once again they tried to repeal it, but during the early stages of this cycle the Armenian lobby was initially successful at amending the appropriations bill with the Porter Amendment which called for the delivery of United States humanitarian assistance to the people of Nagorno-Karabagh and established a ratio for disbursement of humanitarian assistance to Azerbaijan and Karabagh. This provision also addressed many

of the concerns which Non-Governmental and private voluntary organization (NGOs and PVOs.) had raised about the difficulty of assisting Azeris in
need.[74]

The US State Department responded to the legislation by issuing a statement which said "The Government of Azerbaijan has interpreted this
language as undermining its sovereignty and territorial integrity, including
over the region of Nagorno-Karabagh. The United States is committed to the
preservation of Azerbaijan's sovereignty and territorial integrity...Likewise
we support negotiated settlements to conflict in the post-Soviet space to
ensure each new nation's independence, prosperity and security."[75]

The US response to this amendment was indicative of what Yerevan perceived to be a decidedly pro-Azerbaijan shift in US policy. Even more inter-
esting was that the statement elicited a strong response from the Armenian
Foreign Ministry which accused the United States of "...encouraging Azerbaijan's rigid position in the negotiations."[76] The Armenian statement went
further by accusing the United States of predetermining the outcome of the
negotiations and siding with Azerbaijan:

> The statement also predetermines the status of Nagorno-Karabagh when, by the
> 1992 Ministerial decision of the OSCE, that status is to be negotiated, and will be
> determined at the Minsk Conference. The Foreign Ministry of Armenia considers
> siding with one of the parties to the conflict irreconcilable with the role of a media-
> tor.[77]

While the Porter Amendment did not survive the legislative process, it did
highlight the differences in opinion between Washington and Armenia over
the course of the negotiations. Armenia increasingly saw a US policy being
dominated by oil interests and having a resultant effect upon the OSCE
Minsk Group. This ascendancy of American diplomacy stems not just from
an added US interest in the region over oil. It also results from Russian weakness in the region following its debacle in Chechnya.

Russia was seen as impotent following a one-and-a-half year conflict in
which Chechen rebels defeated an unprepared, poorly trained and poorly
equipped Russian military. Russian weakness meant that Armenia did not
have a counter weight to a proactive US policy in the region which became
increasingly critical of Armenia and Nagorno-Karabakh.

In November of 1996, the self-proclaimed Republic of Nagorno-Karabagh
held Presidential elections against the will of the United States, the OSCE
and the European parliament. Key members of the Minsk Group criticized
Karabagh of jeopardizing the possibility of getting Armenia and Azerbaijan
to sign a "statement of principles" regarding the resolution of the conflict.
They worried that the elections would create a difficult atmosphere at the

December summit of the OSCE in Lisbon. The OSCE had accomplished little in the negotiations and hoped that the agreement on a statement would be one of the outcomes of the summit.[78]

Karabagh held elections on November 24, and Robert Kocharyan easily won what was determined to be a fair election.[79] The events in Karabagh stand in contrast to elections in Armenia which led to public disturbances not seen in the Republic since the collapse of Communism. Events in Karabagh and Armenia had the effect of hardening Yerevan's stand on the negotiations. The internal situation in Armenia in which the ANM's very legitimacy had come into question, combined with the image of a self-assured and confident Karabagh leadership, placed the ANM in the position of having to back Nagorno-Karabagh to the hilt. There could be no perceived concessions within Armenia on this issue in international forums.

In December the OSCE held its Lisbon Summit. For Armenia and Nagorno-Karabagh Lisbon was a retreat from the 1994 Budapest Summit. In Budapest Nagorno-Karabagh was viewed as a participant. In Lisbon the statement by the OSCE chairman-in-office issued on December 2, 1996, attempted to codify the legal status of Nagorno-Karabagh without consultation. To Armenia the OSCE accepted the formula advanced by negotiators from Azerbaijan. The statement issued by the OSCE called for the territorial integrity of Armenia and Azerbaijan, for the self determination of Nagorno-Karabagh within Azerbaijan, and for security through mutual obligations. While on the surface the statement seemed to represent basic principles, to the Armenians it addressed issues that were never in question, such as the external borders of both countries. The crux of the issue was that Nagorno-Karabagh which has struggled for independence from Azerbaijan was placed within the very state that they have been in conflict with since 1988.[80]

Armenia did not agree with the statement issued by the OSCE chairmen and issued its own statement, stating that the Lisbon document "predetermines the status of Nargorno-Karabagh, contradicting the decision of the OSCE Ministerial Council of 1992."[81]

CONCLUSION

Following the events at the close of 1996, Armenia appeared to be heading towards diplomatic isolation. It was at odds with the OSCE at its last summit. It did not have oil to entice oil companies and to sway them in their favor. The nation was still in the midst of an internal crises following the disturbances which took place during the September Presidential elections.

President Levon Ter-Petrossyan appeared to be sandwiched between the leaders of the power ministries of Interior and Defense for having saved his Presidency during the disturbances.[82]

Armenia was still under blockade by Azerbaijan and Turkey and there was no resolution to the conflict in the immediate future. How did the President react to the numerous crises?

Ter-Petrosssian began by reshuffling his ministers. Most importantly were the individuals who he chose. He brought three Ambassadors from the west to hold key positions. He chose Armen Sarkissyan the Ambassador to Great Britain to become the Prime Minister. He brought Garnik Nanagulyan from Canada (Ambassador Nanagulyan had been the number two man in Washington for three years) to become the Minister of Tourism and Investment, and he brought Alexander Arzumanyan Armenia's UN ambassador to be foreign Minister.

The choice of three men who had served in the West for at least four years or more was indicative of Armenia's attempt to reshape its image. Whether the policy was just window dressing or a real substantive shift still remains to be seen. However, the new Prime Minister went overseas and began to explain Armenia's polices on a host of issues. Most importantly his trip to the United States was used to express Armenia's position on a number of issues of political and strategic concern. While in Washington, Sarkissyan addressed Armenia's position on the OSCE Lisbon Summit and the question of oil pipelines in the region. These two issues are viewed by Armenia as being intertwined when in fact they should be exclusive of each other.

Sarkissyan reiterated that Lisbon predetermined Nagorno-Karabagh's status and that only through direct negotiations between the Karabagh Armenians and Azerbaijan, could true peace be established. He then spoke directly about the pipeline issue. He outlined three conceptual approaches to the pipeline:

1) The oil pipeline does not bring peace, but peace will help build a pipeline.
2) The oil pipeline will help establish peace in the region and will serve as a guarantee or guarantor for its consolidation and preservation.
3) The future stability of the region is very critical to the oil pipeline, in other words, oil not only fails to bring peace to the region, but might threaten it.[83]

Sarkissyan went on to state that any plans over the pipeline should take into account the following realities:

1) The Karabagh conflict has profound ethnic, historical and political legacy, and imposed solution will not resolve the conflict.

2) Pipeline routes through Armenia and other western routes are feasible due to the existing 30 months of cease-fire in the region.

3) Economic cooperation can increase the goodwill among conflicting parties, which can help to establish consensus and maintain it.

4) Armenia cannot be bypassed as a transit country, neither can it be ignored that Armenia is the most cost effective route.[84]

While the Prime Minister also spoke about the need for reconciliation within Armenia and for maintaining the course of democratization, his above comments were of greatest interest to policy makers in Washington and the capitals of other states with an interest in the region. For the first time a major political leader in Armenia openly called for a pipeline through their country. Second, in very diplomatic language Sarkissyan said that Armenia cannot be bypassed as a "transit country."

The thrust of his speech was not overlooked and unfortunately for Armenia his tenure would be short. Sarkissyan fell ill and required hospitalization. He left the country for treatment in London, where he submitted his resignation. President Ter-Petrossyan still in the midst of internal crises and with Sarkissyan's promise of achieving national reconciliation incomplete, appointed the President of Nagorno-Karabagh Robert Kocharyan as his Prime Minister. The appointment of Kocharyan in February was seen as a dramatic move by Levon Ter-Petrossyan to bolster his position domestically.

Regarding foreign relations, Kocharyan is expected to maintain a hard line on the Karabagh conflict. As the chairman of the State Defense Committee and then the President of Nagorno-Karabagh there can be no "sell out" of Nagorno-Karabagh. His appointment may give Ter-Petrossyan the opportunity to arrive at a negotiated settlement and dodge criticism, given that his Prime Minister is the ultimate patriot. With Kocharyan's approval, who can criticize any agreement?

However, Kocharyan's appointment is viewed by many outsiders as the caving in of policy to nationalists. Kocharyan in the past has intimated that any attempt by Azerbaijan to export oil via the pipeline, which is only 22 km from the front-line, will be destroyed. Prime Minister Robert Kocharyan has merely put in blunt terms what Armen Sarkissyan said diplomatically in Washington on January 10, 1997.

While many have said that Kocharyan's appointment implies a harder line it merely reiterates what Armenia has been saying for years. Azerbaijan needs to negotiate with the Karabagh Armenians and that the prospect of an oil pipeline will not change Armenia's position. Furthermore, the use by Azerbaijan of oil politics to influence the international community to pressure Armenia will not work.

As the Senior Advisor to the Armenian President, Jirair Libaridian has repeatedly said "Armenia has every reason to hope for an alternative pipeline which may pass through Armenia itself. But on no account is it prepared to compromise the rights and security of the people of Armenia and of Nagorno-Karabagh toward that end."[85] He made this statement in a letter to the editor in the *Wall Street Journal*. His letter was in response to one of a large number of articles which appeared throughout the western press regarding the transfer of Russian arms to Armenia.

For Armenia they viewed the attention given to the subject of Russian arms transfers as part of a widespread Azeri propaganda campaign to paint Armenia as an aggressive and dangerously armed state. They perceive this as part of a cover to justify future military action against Armenia and shifting the propaganda balance in Western capitals against them. The Armenians made no apologies for the arms which they acquired and believe that their military superiority has in fact helped maintain the cease-fire and provided a viable deterrence to any possible Azeri adventurism.

Yet, the response by Mr. Libaridian shows that Armenia is feeling the diplomatic isolation which Azerbaijan has successfully tailored. Libaridian's comments were expressed during a conference in Yerevan on cooperation in the Transcaucasus sponsored by the American University of Armenia.[86] Libaridian again spoke of the international community's inability to reconcile the competing principles of territorial integrity and self-determination. He said that one is not greater than the other and then proceeded to once again raise the issue of oil wealth and pipelines as a way to influence the outcome of the conflict.

Armenia is clearly feeling the pressure from the international community over Nagorno-Karabagh. It is steadily working towards building redundancy in its links to the outside world and building its military relationship with Russia. The Armenians believe that Azerbaijan is deluding itself by thinking that they will be able to change the correlation of forces and alter the situation on the ground by diplomacy or after acquired oil wealth through force.

However, Armenia has not given up on negotiations. Parallel to these negotiations Armenia continues to follow the policy of separating political issues from economic ones. They believe that at some point they may be able to develop sufficient economic links with Georgia, Iran and even Turkey in the hopes that Azerbaijan will eventually realize that their blockade has failed and that force is not an option.

1   Rouben Adalian, "Armenia's Foreign Policy: Defining Priorities and Coping with Conflict," in *The Making of Foreign Policy in Russia and the New States of Eurasia*, ed. Adeed and Karen Dawisha (Armonk, NY, 1995), pp. 310–311.

2   Bruno Coppieters, "Conclusions: The Caucasus as a Security Complex," in *Contested Borders in the Caucasus*, ed. Bruno Coppieters (Brussels, 1996), pp. 194–195.

3   Richard Hovannisian, "Historical Memory and Foreign Relations: The Armenian Perspective," in *The Legacy of History in Russia and the New States of Eurasia*, ed. S. Frederick Starr (Armonk, NY, 1994), p. 252.

4   Ibid, p. 253.

5   Ibid.

6   Fiona Hill and Pamela Jewett, *Report on Ethnic Conflict in the Russian Federation and Transcaucasia*, Strengthening Democratic Institutions Project (Cambridge, MA: Harvard University, John F. Kennedy School of Government, July 1993), p. 78.

7   Suha Bolukbasi, "Ankara's Baku-Centered Transcaucasia Policy: Has It Failed?," *Middle East Journal*, vol. 51, no. 1 (1997), p. 84.

8   Shireen T. Hunter, *The Transcaucasus in Transition: Nation-Building and Conflict* (Washington, D.C.: The Center for Strategic & International Studies, 1994), pp. 163–164.

9   Bolukbasi, p. 85.

10 Ibid.

11 Fred Woods, Yerevan, to the Honorable Joseph Kennedy, Washington, D.C., February 1992, background and current need for Turkish wheat, in hand of Joseph Masih, Washington, D.C.

12 *Armenian Assembly of America Daily Report*, February 25, 1993, p. 1.

13 Simon Payaslian, "Ozal's Last Stand," *Armenian International Magazine*, April/May 1993,

14 "Armenia and Azerbaijan Retreating," *The Economist*, April 10, 1993, p. 58.

15 Dmitri Trenin, "Russia's Security Interests and Policies in the Caucasus Region," in *Contested Borders in the Caucasus*, ed. Bruno Coppieters (Brussels, 1996), p. 97.

16 Adalian, p. 318.

17 "Armenian President Leaves for Turkey: Four Sided Negotiations Are Probable," *AZG*, April 21, 1993, in *Monthly Digest of News From Armenia* (June 1993), p. 25.

18 "Turkish Government Ready to Provide Military Assistance to Azerbaijan," *Yerkir*, September 7, 1993, in *Monthly Digest of News From Armenia* (October 1993), p. 20; Paul Quinn, "Turkey Warns of War Over Armenian Advance," *Boston Globe*, September 8, 1993, LEXIS/NEXIS; Hugh Pope, "Turkey Puts its Caucasus Troops on Border Alert," *The Independent*, September 4, 1993, LEXIS/NEXIS.

19 "Government Names Iraq, Syria, and Armenia as 'Sources of Terrorism,?" *Mideast Mirror*, September 27, 1993, LEXIS/NEXIS.

20 Sinan Onus, "Intelligence Report Details Armenia-PKK Ties," *Aydinlik*, January 29, 1994 in *FBIS Daily Report: West Europe*, February 3, 1994, p. 36; "Turkish Aggression," *Yerkir*, September 4, 1993, in *Monthly Digest of News From Armenia* (October 1993), pp. 20–21.

21 Ross Vartian, "Turkey is the Villain in Azerbaijan War," *The Wall Street Journal*, December 21, 1994, LEXIS/NEXIS.

22 Jirair Libaridian, Speech at Carnegie Endowment, Washington, D.C., July 24, 1996.

23 Hovannisian, p. 251; Hunter, p. 47.

24 Levon Ter-Petrossian, Speech before the Armenian Assembly of America Tribute Banquet, Washington, D.C., October 25, 1995.

25 *Foreign Operations, Export Financing, and Related Programs Appropriations Act*, Public Law 104–107, sec. 562, February 12, 1996.

26 Statement of the President, *White House Press Release*, April 23, 1995.

27 Ross Vartian, "Armenian Genocide Denial," *The Wall Street Journal*, September 11, 1995, p. A21.

28 Congress, House of Representatives, Committee on International Relations, *U.S. Interests in the Caucasus Region*, 104th Cong., 2nd Sess., 30 July 1996, p. 70.

29 Ibid, p. 48.

30 Oles M. Smolansky, "Russia and Transcaucasia: The Case of Nagorno-Karabagh," in *Regional Power Rivalries in the New Eurasia: Russia, Turkey and Iran*, ed. Alvin Rubenstein and Oles Smolansky (Armonk, NY, 1995) p. 212.

31 "Azerbaijan to Join CIS," *AZG*, September 7, 1993, in *Monthly Digest of News From Armenia* (October 1993), p. 16.

32 Daniel Sneider, "Afghan Fighters Join Azeris-Armenian War," *The Christian Science Monitor*, November 16, 1993, p. 7.

33 "Guilty Parties will be Punished," *Yerkir*, November 27, 1993, in *Monthly Digest of News From Armenia* (February 1994), p. 27.

34 "NKR Fighters Obliged to Bury Dead Azeri Soldiers," *Hayastani Hanrapetutyun*, January 13, 1994, in *Monthly Digest of News From Armenia* (February 1994), p. 51.

35 "Russian Foreign Ministry Satisfied with Agreement on Karabagh," *AZG*, February 24, 1994, in *Monthly Digest of News From Armenia* (April 1994), p. 24.

36 "Grachev Discusses Russian Military Bases in Armenia and Georgia," *Lragir*, June 10, 1994, in *Monthly Digest of News From Armenia* (June/July 1994), p. 25; "Russia to have a Military Base in Armenia," *Lragir*, June 11, 1994, in *Monthly Digest of News From Armenia* (June/July 1994), p. 25.

37 "Karabagh Armistice," July 27, 1994, in *Monthly Digest of News From Armenia* (August 1994), pp. 34–35.

38 Rouben Adalian and Joseph Masih, ed., *Armenia and Karabagh Factbook*, (Washington, DC: Armenian Assembly of America, July 1996), p. 19.

39 "Armenia, Russia: Rokhlin Details Arms Supplied to Armenia," *FBIS-SOV-97067*, April 3, 1997.

40 David Ottaway and Dan Morgan, "Former Top U.S. Aides Seek Caspian Gusher; Scowcroft, Sununu, Baker, Benson Help Lobby for Oil Policy Change," *The Washington Post*, July 6, 1997, p. A1.

41 "Long in Coming: Azeri Pact is Signed," *Platt's Oilgram News*, September 21, 1994, p. 1.

42 Rosemarie Forsythe, *The Politics of Oil in the Caucasus and Central Asia*, Adelphi Paper 300, (London: International Institute of Strategic Studies, 1996), p. 20.

43 Ibid, pp. 17–18.

44 Ibid, p. 39.

45 *Caspian Region Energy Development Report*, U.S. Department of State, 1997, pp. 21–22.

46 Frank Wolf, et al, Washington, D.C., to President Clinton, Washington, D.C., September 29, 1994, letter to President Clinton requesting greater involvement in negotiations.

47 Making Appropriations for the Department of Defense for Fiscal Year 1997, Conference Report to Accompany HR 3610, 104th Cong., 2nd Session, September 28, 1996, p. 969; Department of State Authorization Bill, S. 908, 104th Cong., 1st Session, June 9, 1995, p. 121; Foreign Aid Authorization Bill, S. 961, 104th Cong., 1st Session, June 23, 1995, p. 106.

48 Freedom for Russian and Emerging Eurasian Democracies and Open Markets Support Act of 1992, Public Law 102–511, sec. 907, October 24, 1992.

49 *Caspian Region Energy Development Report*, pp. 17–18.

50 Ibid, p. 7.

51 Dick Kirschten, "Ethnics Resurging," *National Journal*, February 25, 1995, p. 487; Frank Greve, "Ethnic Lobby Powers Up," *Akron Beacon Journal*, September 3, 1995, p. G1.

52 Making Omnibus Consolidated Appropriations, Public Law 104–208, September 30, 1996, p. 131; Public Law 104–107, February 12, 1996, p. 713.

53 Parliamentary Elections in Armenia, *OSCE Parliamentary Assembly, Press Release*, June 7, 1995.

54 "U.S. Voice Deep Concern About Irregularities in Balloting and Vote Tabulation in Armenian Election," *Armenian National Committee of America, Press Release*, October 22, 1996.

55 "Armenian Presidential Election," Statement by Nicholas Burns, Spokesman, U.S. Department of State, October 22, 1996; "Armenian Presidential Election Final Report," OSCE/Office for Democratic Institutions and Human Rights, September 22, 1996

56 Hunter, p. 79.

57 Abdollah Ramezanzadeh, "Iran's Role as Mediator in the Nagorno-Karabagh Crisis," in *Contested Borders in the Caucasus*, ed. Bruno Coppieters (Brussels, 1996), pp. 166–167.

58 Ibid, p. 168.

59 Hovannisian, p. 261.

60 Ramezanzadeh, pp. 169–170.

61 "Committee on Armenian–Iranian Relations Meets," *Hayastani Hanrapetutyun*, April 1, 1994, in *Monthly Digest of News From Armenia* (May 1994), pp.20.

62 "Armenia: Ter-Petrosyan on Foreign Relations with Turkey, Iran," *FBIS–SOV–96–179*, September 13, 1996.

63 Margaret McQuaile, "Iran Role in Caspian Rejected by Firms: Possible Impact from Clinton's Conoco Action," *Platt's Oilgram News*, March 24, 1995, p. 1.

64 Congress, House of Representatives, Committee on International Relations, *U.S. Interests in the Caucasus Region*, 104th Cong., 2nd Sess., 30 July 1996, pp. 78–79.

65 Adalian, p. 327.

66 Olivier Paye and Eric Remacle, "UN and CSCE Policies in Transcaucasia," in *Contested Borders in the Caucasus*, ed. Bruno Coppieters (Brussels, 1996), p. 115.

67 Ibid, p. 117; The Armenian Center for National and International Studies, *Nagorno-Karabagh: A White Paper*, (Washington, DC: Sponsored by the Armenian Assembly of America, March 1997), p. 10.

68 Ibid.

69 Paye and Remacle, pp. 120–122.

70 Frank Wolf, et al, Washington, D.C., to President Clinton, Washington, D.C., September 29, 1994, letter to President Clinton requesting greater involvement in negotiations.

71 David Murphy, "Operation 'Ring' the Black Berets in Azerbaijan," *Journal of Soviet Military Studies*, vol. 5, no. 1, March 1992, p. 80.

72 "Towards a Genuine Partnership in a New Era," CSCE, Budapest Document, December 1994, pp. 11–12; Nagorno-Karabagh White Paper, p. 12.

73 "U.S. Touts Line's Benefits in Caucasus," *Platt's Oilgram News*, April 21, 1995, p. 1; "Azeris Resist Pipeline Through Armenia," *Platt's Oilgram News*, May 4, 1995, p. 1.

74 Foreign Aid Appropriations Bill, HR 3540, 104th Cong., 2nd Session, June 12, 1996, p. 21–22.

75 "Administration Position on Aide to Azerbaijan," Statement by Nicholas Burns, Spokesman, U.S. Department of State, June 12, 1996.

76 Statement by Ministry of Foreign Affairs of the Republic of Armenia, June 15, 1996.

77 Ibid.

78 Liz Fuller, "When Should Unrecognized States Hold Elections?" *Open Media Research Institute (OMRI) Analytical Brief*, November 27, 1996, p. 2.

79 Ibid.

80 OSCE Lisbon Document, 1996, 3 December 1996, p. 8.

81 Ibid.

82 Emil Danielian, "Resignation of the Armenian Prime Minister: Reasons and Implications," *OMRI Analytical Brief*, November 6, 1996, vol. 1, no. 439, p. 1.

83 Armenian Prime Minister Armen Sarkissian's Center for Strategic International Studies (CSIS) Speech, Washington, D.C., January 10, 1997, p. 4.

84 Ibid.

85 Jirair Libaridian, "Armenia's Antagonists," *The Wall Street Journal*, May 2, 1997, LEXIS/NEXIS.

86 Jirair Libaridian, "The Politics of Promises," Speech at American University of Armenia Conference on Transcaucasus Today: Prospects for Regional's Integration, June 23, 1997.

Bibliography

Adalian, Rouben. "Armenia's Foreign Policy: Defining Priorities and Coping with Conflict." In *The Making of Foreign Policy in Russia and the New States of Eurasia,* edited by Adeed Dawisha and Karen Dawisha & Armonk, NY: M.E. Sharpe, 1995.

Alexeyeva, Ludmilla. *Soviet Dissent: Contemporary Movements for National, Religious, and Human Rights.* Middletown, CT: Wesleyan University Press, 1987.

Allison, Roy, ed. *Challenges for the Former Soviet South.* London: Royal Institute of International Affairs, 1996.

Alstadt, Audrey L. *The Azerbaijani Turks: Power and Identity under Russian Rule.* Stanford, CA: Hoover Press, 1992.

Altstadt-Mirhadi, Audrey. "Baku: Transformation of a Muslim Town." In *A City in Late Imperial Russia,* edited by Michael Hamm. Bloomington, IN: Indiana University Press, 1986.

Anderson, Benedict. *Imagined Communities: Reflections on the Origin and Spread of Nationalism.* London: Verso Editions, 1991.

Anlian, Steven, and Irina Vanian. "Armenia: Reform Amid Crisis." In *Economic Restructuring of the Former Soviet Bloc: The Case of Housing,* edited by Raymond Struyk. Washington, DC: Urban Institute Press, 1996.

Armenian Assembly of America. *Armenia Factbook.* Washington, DC: Armenian Assembly of America, 1994.

Armenian Assembly of America. *Armenia and Karabagh Factbook.* Washington, DC: Armenian Assembly of America, 1996.

Armenian Assembly of America. *President Levon Ter-Petrossian on the Armenian Constitution.* Washington, DC: Armenian Assembly of America, 1994.

Armenian Assembly of America. *The State of the Republic of Armenia: Levon Ter-Petrossian and Babken Ararktsian.* Washington, DC: Armenian Assembly of America, 1994.

Atamian, Sarkis. *The Armenian Community: The Historical Development of a Social and Ideological Conflict.* New York: Philosophical Library, 1955.

Aves, Jonathan. "National Security and Military Issues in the Transcaucasus. The Cases of Georgia, Azerbaijan, and Armenia." In *State Building and Military Power in Russia and the New States of Eurasia,* edited by Bruce Parrott. Armonk, NY: M.E. Sharpe, 1995.

Baddeley, John F. *The Russian Conquest of the Caucasus.* New York: Russell & Russell, 1969.

Barylski, Robert V. "The Caucasus, Central Asia and the Near-Abroad Syndrome," *Central Asian Monitor,* Nos. 4 & 5, 1993.

Barros, James. *The Aland Islands Question: Its Settlement by the League of Nations.* New Haven, CT: Yale, 1968.

Barseghov, Yu. *Inknoroshman Iravoonkuh Azgamijyan Problemneri Demokratakan Ludzman Himkn Eh.* Erevan: "Haiastan," 1990.

Bonnell, Victoria, Ann Cooper and Gregory Freidin, eds. *Russia at the Barricades: Eyewitness Accounts of the August 1991 Coup.* Armonk, NY: M.E. Sharpe, 1994.

Bournoutian, George. *A History of the Armenian People. Vol. I: Pre-History to 1500 A.D.* Costa Mesa, CA: Mazda Publishers, 1993.

Bournoutian, George. *A History of the Armenian People. Vol. II: 1500 A.D. to the Present.* Costa Mesa, CA: Mazda Publishers, 1994.

Bournoutian, George A. *A History of Qarabagh: An Annotated Translation of Mirza Jamal Javanshir Qarabaghi's Tarikh-e Qarabagh.* Costa Mesa, CA: Mazda Publishers, 1994.

Brook, Stephen. *Claws of the Crab: Georgia and Armenia in Crisis.* London: Sinclair-Stevenson, 1992.

Center for Democracy in the U.S.S.R. *Soviet Events of 1989 and 1990 as Reported by the Express Chronicle.* NY, 1991.

Chorbajian, Levon, Patrick Donabedian and Claude Mutafian. *The Caucasian Knot—The History and Geo-Politics of Nagorno-Karabagh.* London: Zed Books, 1994.

Commission on Security and Cooperation in Europe. *Report on Armenia's Parliamentary Election and Constitutional Referendum.* Washington, DC. August 1995.

Connor, Walker. *The National Question in Marxist-Leninist Theory and Strategy.* Princeton, NJ: Princeton University Press, 1984.

Constitution (Fundamental Law) of the Union of Soviet Socialist Republics. Moscow: Novosti, 1988.

Coppieters, Bruno, ed. *Contested Borders in file Caucasus.* Brussels: VUB University Press, 1996.

Corley, Felix. *Religion in the Soviet Union: An Archival Reader.* NY: New York University Press, 1996.

Corley, Felix. *"The Armenian (Church Under the Soviet Regime, Part I: The Leadership of Kevork. "* Religion, State, and Society, Vol. 24, No. 1 (1990).

Crow, Suzanne. "Russia Seeks Leadership in Regional Peacekeeping," *RFE/RL Research Report,* Vol. 2, No. 15, 9 April 1993.

Curtis, Glenn, ed. *Armenia, Azerbaijan, and Georgia: Country Studies.* Washington, DC: Federal Research Division, Library of Congress, 1995.

Dadrian, Vahakn. *The History of the Armenian Genocide: Ethnic Conflict from the Balkans to the Caucasus.* Providence, RI: Berghahn Books, 1995.

Davis, Leslie. *The Slaughterhouse Province: An American Diplomat's Report on the Armenian Genocide, 1915–1917.* New Rochelle, NY: Aristide Caratzas Publisher, 1989.

Dawson, Jane. *Eco-Nationalism: Anti-Nuclear Activism and National Identity in Russia, Lithuania, and Ukraine.* Durham, NC: Duke University Press, 1996.

Denber, Rachel. ed. *The Soviet Nationality Reader. The Disintegration in Context.* Boulder, CO: Westview Press, 1992.

Dudwick, Nora. "Armenia: Paradise Lost?" In *New States, New Politics: Building the Post-Soviet Nations,* edited by Ian Bremmer and Ray Taras. Cambridge: Cambridge University Press, 1997.

Dudwick, Nora. "A Qualitative Assessment of the Living Standards of the Armenian Population October 1994–March 1995." Draft. *Armenia Poverty Assessment Working Paper* No. 1, World Bank, June 1995.

Embassy of the Republic of Armenia. *Armenia: An Emerging Democracy.* Washington, DC. 1994.

Feshbach, Murray. *Ecological Disaster Cleaning Up the Hidden Legacy of the Soviet Regime.* NY: The Twentieth Century Fund Press, 1995.

Feshbach, Murray and Alfred Friendly. *Ecocide in the USSR: Health and Nature Under Siege.* NY: Basic Books, 1992.

Fischer, Michael, and Stella Grigorian. "Six to Eight Characters in Search of Armenian Civil Society amidst the Carnivalization of History." In *Perilous States: Conversations on Culture, Politics, and Nation,* edited by Marcus Garvey. Chicago: University of Chicago Press, 1993.

Fuller, Elizabeth. "No Confederation on the Horizon," *Transition.* Vol. 1, No. 12, 14 July 1995.

Fuller, Elizabeth. "Ruling Party Strengthens Its Hold on Power," *Transition,* Vol. 1, No. 19, 20 October 1995.

Fuller, Elizabeth. "Paramilitary Forces Dominate Fighting in Transcaucasus," *RFE/RL Research Report,* Vol. 2, No. 25, 18 June 1993.

Fuller, Elizabeth. "Russia's Diplomatic Offensive in the Transcaucasus," RFE/RL Research Report, Vol. 2, No. 39, 1 October 1993.

Fuller, Elizabeth. 'The Transcaucasus: War, Turmoil, Economic Collapse,' RFE/RL Research Report, Vol. 3, No. 1, 7 January 1994.

Furtado, Charles and Andrea Chandler, eds. *Perestroika in the Soviet Republics: Documents on the National Question.* Boulder, CO: Westview Press, 1992.

Gellner, Ernest. *Nations and Nationalism.* Ithaca, NY: Cornell University Press, 1983.

Gleason, Gregory. *Federalism and Nationalism: The Struggle for Republican Rights in the USSR.* Boulder, CO: Westview Press, 1990.

Goltz, Thomas. "Letter from Eurasia: The Hidden Russian Hand," *Foreign Policy,* Fall 1993, pp. 92–116.

Gottlieb, Gidon. *Nation Against State: A New Approach to Ethnic Conflict and the Decline of Sovereignty.* New York: Council on Foreign Relations, 1993.

Gunter, Michael. *"Pursuing the Just Cause of their People": A Study of Contemporary Armenian Terrorism.* New York: Greenwood Press, 1986.

Haik Research Institute. *Lernayeen Gharabaghi Hemnakhntri Vorosh Iravakaghakakan Hartser.* Erevan, 1994.

Helsinki Watch. *Bloodshed in the Caucasus: Escalation of the Armed Conflict in Nagorno Karabakh,* September, 1992.

Hill, Fiona. *Report on Ethnic Conflict in the Russian Federation and Transcaucasia, July* 1993. Cambridge, MA: Harvard University, 1993.

Hovannisian, Richard. "Historical Memory and Foreign Relations: The Armenian Perspective." In *The Legacy of History in Russia and the New States of Eurasia,* edited by S. Frederick Starr. Armonk, NY: M.E. Sharpe, 1994.

Hovannisian, Richard. ed. *The Armenian Genocide: History, Politics, Ethics.* NY: St. Martin's Press, 1992.

Hunter, Shireen. *The Transcaucasus in Transition: Nation-Building and Conflict.* Washington, DC: Center for Strategic and International Studies, 1994.

Huttenbach, Henry. "Crisis in Caucasia. *The Search for Regional Stability and Security: A Study of Post-Soviet Disorder in Transcaucasia."* Paper presented at the Russian Littoral Project, University of Maryland, October–November 1994.

Jones, S.F. "Religion and Nationalism in Soviet Georgia and Armenia." In *Religion and Nationalism in Soviet and East European Politics,* edited by Pedro Ramet. Durham, NC: Duke University Press, 1989.

Karklins, Rasma. *Ethnic Relations in the USSR: The Perspective From Below.* Boston: Allen and Unwin, 1986.

Kohl, Philip and Gocha Tsetskhladze. "Nationalism, politics and the practice of archeology in the Caucasus." In *Nationalism, Politics and the Practice of Archeology,* edited by Philip Kohl and Clare Fawcett. Cambridge: Cambridge University Press, 1995.

Lapidus, Gail. "Gorbachev and the 'National Question': Restructuring the Soviet Federation." *Soviet Economy, Vol. 5,* No. 3, July–September 1989, pp. 201–250.

Leitzinger, Antero. ed. *Caucasus and an Unholy Alliance.* Helsinki: Kirja-Leitzinger Books, 1997.

Lenin, V. I. *The Right of Nations to Self-Determination.* Moscow: Progress Publishers, 1976.

Libaridian, Gerard. ed. *The Karabagh File: Documents and Facts on the Question of Mountainous Karabagh 1918–1988.* Cambridge, MA: Zoryan Institute, 1988.

Libaridian, Gerard. ed. *Armenia at the Crossroads: Democracy and Nationhood in the Post-Soviet Era.* Watertown, MA: Blue Crane Books, 1991.

Linz, Juan and Alfred Stepan. *Problems of Democratic Transition and Consolidation: Southern Europe, South America, and Post-Communist Europe.* Baltimore, MD: The Johns Hopkins University Press, 1996.

Lough, John. "Defining Russia's Relations with Neighboring States," *RFE/RL Research Report,* Vol. 2, No. 20, 14 May 1993.

Luchterhandt, Otto. *Nagorny Karabakh's Right to State Independence According to International Law.* Boston: Baikar Association, 1993.

Maksoudian, Krikor. "Religion in Armenia Today," paper delivered at the Annual Vardanants Lecture, Library of Congress, May 1997.

Malkasian, Mark. *"Gha-ra-bagh!" The Emergence of the National Democratic Movement in Armenia.* Detroit, MI: Wayne State University Press, 1996.

Marsden, Philip. *The Crossing Place: A Journey Among the Armenians.* New York: Kodansha International, 1995.

Masih, Joseph." *Military Strategy in Nagorno-Karabakh. "* Jane's Intelligence Review, April 1994.

Melson, Robert. *Revolution and Genocide: On the Origins of the Armenian Genocide and the Holocaust.* Chicago: University of Chicago Press, 1992.

Mesbahi, Mohiaddin. "Russian Foreign Policy and Security in Central Asia and the Caucasus," *Central Asian Survey (I 993),* 12(2), pp. 181–215.

Miller, Donald and Lorna Touryan Miller. *Survivors: An Oral History of the Armenian Genocide.* Berkeley, CA: University of California Press, 1993.

Mouradian, Claire. *L'Armenie.* Paris: Presses Universitaires de France, 1995.

Murphy, David. "Operation 'Ring' The Black Berets in Azerbaijan," *Journal of Soviet Military Studies,* Vol. 5, No. I (March 1992),

Nichol, James. *Diplomacy in the Former Soviet Republics.* Westport, CT: Praeger Publishers, 1995.

Nolyain, Igor. "Moscow's Initiation of the Azeri-Armenian Conflict." *Central Asian Survey ,* Vol. 13, No. 4 (1994).

Richard, Giragosian. *Transcaucasus: A Chronology.* ed. Washington: Armenian National Committee of America, 1992–1997.

Riggs, Henry. *Days of Tragedy in Armenia: Personal Experiences in Harpoot, 1915–1917.* Ann Arbor, MI: Gomidas Institute Books, 1997.

Roniger, Luis and Ayse Gunes-Ayata. eds. *Democracy, Clientelism, and Civil Society.* Boulder, CO: Lynne Rienner Publishers, 1994.

Rosenau, James. *Turbulence in World Politics.* Princeton, NJ: Princeton, 1990.

Rubinstein, Alvin and Oles Smolansky. eds, *Regional Power Rivalries in the New Eurasia: Russia, Turkey, and Iran.* Armonk, NY: M.E. Sharpe, 1995.

Samuelian, Thomas. "Cultural Ecology and Gorbachev's Restructured Union." *Harvard International Law Journal,* Vol. 32, No. 1, Winter 1991.

Schwartz, Donald and Razmik Panossian. eds. *Nationalism and History: The Politics of Nation-Building in Post-Soviet Armenia, Azerbaijan and Georgia,* Toronto: University of Toronto Centre for Russian and East European Studies, 1994.

Shahmuratian, Samvel. ed. *The Sumgait Tragedy. Volume I.– Eyewitness Accounts. New* Rochelle, NY and Cambridge, MA: Aristide Caratzas Publisher and Zoryan Institute, 1990.

Simon, Gerhard. *Nationalism and Policy Toward the Nationalities in the Soviet Union: From Totalitarian* Dictatorship *to* Post-Stalinist Society. Boulder, CO: Westview Press, 1991.

Somakian, Manoug. *Empires* in *Conflict: Armenia and the Great Powers 1895–1920.* London: I. B. Tauris Publishers, 1995.

Suny, Ronald Grigor. *Looking Toward* Ararat: *Armenia in Modern History.* Bloomington, IN: Indiana University Press, 1993.

Suny, Ronald Grigor. ed. *Transcaucasia: Nationalism and Social Change.* Ann Arbor, MI: University of Michigan Press, 1997.

Suny, Ronald Grigor. *The Revenge of the Past–Nationalism, Revolution, and the Collapse of the Soviet Union.* Stanford: Stanford University Press, 1993.

Suny, Ronald Grigor. "Tiflis: Crucible of Ethnic Politics, 1860–1905." In *The City in Late Imperial Russia,* edited by Michael Hamm. Bloomington, IN: Indiana University Press, 1986.

Swietochowski, Tadeusz. *Russia and Azerbaijan: A Borderland in Transition.* New York: Columbia University Press, 1995.

Pipes, Richard. *The Formation of the Soviet Union: Communism and Nationalism, 19171923.* (Cambridge: Harvard University Press, 1954).

Tatevosyan, Ara. "Nagorno-Karabakh's New Army of 'Iron Will and Discipline'." *Transition,* 9 August 1996.

Touryantz, Hagop. *Search for a Homeland.* NY: H.J. Touryantz, 1987.

Valesyan, Armen. "Armenia." In *Environmental Resources and Constraints in the Former Soviet Republics,* edited by Philip Pryde. Boulder, CO: Westview Press, 1995.

Verluise, Pierre. *Armenia in Crisis: The 1988 Earthquake.* Detroit, MI: Wayne State University Press, 1995.

Walker, Christopher. *Armenia: The Survival of a Nation,* New York: St. Martin's Press, 1990.

Walker, Christopher. ed. *Armenia and Karabagh: The Struggle for Unity.* London: Minority Rights Publications, 1991.

Wixman, Ronald. *The Peoples of the USSR: An Ethnographic Handbook.* (Armonk, NY: Sharpe, 1984).

Index

Aghalovyan, Lenser, 56
agriculture, 66–67, 69, 75, 81
AIOC, Azerbaijan International
Operating Company,
110–111, 118
Aliyev, Heidar, 4, 105–106, 110,
114, 118, 121
Amoco, 110
ANA, Armenian National Army,
23, 28
ANC, Armenian National
Committee, 113
ANM, Armenian National Movement,
16, 19, 23–24, 38, 35, 41,
43, 45, 48–52, 54, 58–60,
65, 68, 87–89, 95, 97,
114–115, 120, 125
APF, Azerbaijan Popular Front,
16, 19, 116
Araksyan, Babken, 46
Armenian Apostolic Church, 38,
42, 53
Armenian armed forces, 43, 107
Armenian Assembly of America, 102
Armenian Communist Party,
4, 10–12, 19, 29–31,
36–37, 56
Armenian Diaspora, 70, 80, 83,
111–112
Armenian language, 3, 8
Armenian lobby, 102, 111,
113–114, 123
Armenian Parliament, 28, 75, 114
Armenian Republic, 10, 24–25,
43, 53
Armenian Revolutionary
Federation, 12, 31, 35, 45,
47, 52, 55–56, 113

Armenian Supreme Soviet,
10–11, 13, 17, 27
Armenian Writers' Union, 32, 50
ArmenTel, 83–84
Arzumanyan, Alexander, 58, 126
ASALA, Armenian Secret
Army for the Liberation of
Armenia, 44
ASALA-RM, Armenian Secret
Army for the Liberation of
Armenia-Revolutionary
Movement, 44
Asatryan, Bagrat, 74
Avakyan, Vahan 50
Azerbaijan, Sumgait, 7, Escalation
of NK conflict in 1988, 10–11,
Black January, 17–19, Turkey's
support for and position toward,
97–104, Russian involvement in
Azerbaijan and Armenia, 104–109,
oil politics 109–111, Section 907
and Armenian Diaspora, 111–115,
negotiations in Karabagh conflict,
119–125
Azerbaijani Communist Party, 4,
10, 16–17, 33
Azerbaijani Supreme Soviet,
10–11, 16, 18

Badalyan, Sergei, 56
Bagirov, Kyamran, 7, 10
Bagratyan, Hrant, 57–59, 76
Baku, 3, 4, 5, 13, 16–19, 29,
60–61, 97, 99, 105–106, 108
Balayan, Zori, 35, 45
Baltic Council, 19
Batumi, 67, 71, 95
Black January, 18

For Product Safety Concerns and Information please contact our EU
representative GPSR@taylorandfrancis.com
Taylor & Francis Verlag GmbH, Kaufingerstraße 24, 80331 München, Germany

www.ingramcontent.com/pod-product-compliance
Ingram Content Group UK Ltd.
Pitfield, Milton Keynes, MK11 3LW, UK
UKHW021610240425
457818UK00018B/481